14.50

1347 113 210 Sept 21, 1971

TUTANKHAMEN

ARTHUR WEIGALL

THE AUTHOR, WITH THE EGYPTIAN GOVERNOR OF THE PRO-
VINCE, STANDING IN FRONT OF THE TOMB OF TUTANKHAMEN

TUTANKHAMEN
And Other Essays

BY

ARTHUR WEIGALL

ILLUSTRATED

KENNIKAT PRESS
Port Washington, N. Y./London

TUTANKHAMEN

First published in 1924
Reissued in 1970 by Kennikat Press
Library of Congress Catalog Card No: 73-115210
ISBN 0-8046-1103-3

Manufactured by Taylor Publishing Company   Dallas, Texas

PREFACE

IT is not many months since a volume of my essays and papers on Egyptological matters was published, under the title of "The Glory of the Pharaohs"; but the interest aroused in the whole subject of Egyptian research by the discovery of the tomb of Tutankhamen has created a definite call for another volume of the same kind. In the previous collection there were, amongst some miscellaneous articles, three or four papers which had a close bearing on the excavations in the Valley of the Tombs of the Kings; and I there gave some account of the work conducted under my supervision in that royal necropolis. In this new volume there is again a varied collection of papers dealing with different aspects of Egyptian research, but the first few chapters are directly concerned with the new tomb.

Never before has the public been so widely stirred by an archæological discovery as it has been by the opening of the sepulchre of Tutankhamen, and on all sides one may observe an eager desire to learn something about the past ages of man both in Egypt and in other countries. The cynic has already been aroused by it to scoff at what he terms the pursuit of a new nine-days' wonder; but I am inclined to believe that the finding of this ancient Pharaoh's tomb has revealed an almost universal love of ancient things, until now largely suppressed by the clamour of the concerns of the present day, and I think that the world at large is at last about

v

to claim that inheritance in the regions of the Past to which the archæologist has opened the road. The estate of Egyptology has been long enough the exclusive domain of the scholar. His pioneer work is hardly begun, it is true; but from now onwards, I believe, he will have to labour under the eyes of an ever-increasing public who will follow him into those regions, and will continuously demand to know what he has found.

This is all to the good. Upon the Egyptologist it will have a humanising effect which is badly needed; and upon the public a knowledge of the Past cannot fail to exert a broadening influence. In this life of ours which, under modern conditions, is lived at so great a speed, there is a growing need for a periodical pause wherein the mind may adjust the relationship of the things that have been to those that are. So rapidly are our impressions received and assimilated, so individually are they shaped and adapted, that, in whatever direction our brains lead us, we are speedily carried away from that broad province of thought which is our common heritage. But, a man who travels alone finds himself, in a few months, out of touch with the thought of his fellows; and, similarly, a man who journeys continuously along the narrow road of his own modern experience finds himself grown impatient of the larger outlook of the world's continuity, and just as the solitary man must needs come into the company of his fellows if he would retain a healthy mind, so the man who lives in his own confined present must allow himself an occasional visit to the realm of the past if he would keep his balance.

Heraclitus, in a quotation preserved by Sextus Empiricus,* writes: "It behooves us to follow the common

* Bywater: *Heracliti Ephesii Reliquiae*, p. 38.

reason of the world; yet, though there is a common reason in the world, the majority live as though they possessed a wisdom peculiar each unto himself alone." Every one of us who considers his mentality an important part of his constitution should endeavour to give himself ample opportunities of breathing the breath of this "common reason," which comes like a cool breeze from the regions of the Past. We should remember the yesterdays, that we may know what all the bother of to-day is about; and we should foretell to-morrow not by to-day but by every day that has been.

Forgetfulness is so common a human failing. In our rapid transit along the individual pathway of our life we are so inclined to forget the past stages of the journey. All things pass by and are swallowed up in a moment of time. Experiences crowd upon us; the events of our life occur, are recorded by our busy brains, are digested, and are forgotten before the substance of which they were made has resolved into its elements. We race through the years, and our progress is headlong through the days.

Everything we have used, as it is done with is swept up into the basket of the Past, and the busy scavengers, unless we check them, toss the contents, good and bad, on to the great rubbish heap of the world's waste. Loves, hates, gains, losses, all things upon which we do not lay fierce and strong hands, are gathered into nothingness, and, with a few exceptions, are utterly forgotten.

And we, too, will soon have passed, and our little brains which have forgotten so much will be forgotten. We shall be throttled out of the world and pressed by

the clumsy hands of death into the mould of that same
rubbish-hill of oblivion,

> . . . where lie
> Days past like dreams, and waning moons slid by,
> And mixed heaps of lost mortality,

unless there be a stronger hand to save us. There is
only one human force stronger than death, and that force
is History, for by it the dead are made to live again.

Sometimes, then, in our little race from day to day
it is necessary to stop the headlong progress of our individual experience, and, for an hour, to look back upon
the broad fields of the Past. "There is," says Emerson,
"a relationship between the hours of our life and the
centuries of time." Let us give history, and archæology its due attention; for thus not only shall we be
rendering a service to all the dead, not only shall we be
giving a reason and a usefulness to their lives, but we
shall also bring to our own brains a balance which cannot
easily otherwise be obtained; we shall adjust our
thoughts to the big movement of the world; and, above
all, we shall learn how best to do our duty in this wonderful age to which it is our inestimable privilege to belong.

CONTENTS

ILLUSTRATIONS

TUTANKHAMEN

TUTANKHAMEN

CHAPTER I

THE FUTURE OF EXCAVATION IN EGYPT

DURING the last two or three years a great and astonishing change has taken place in the attitude and bearing of educated Egyptians. In 1882 the nation was bankrupt, and the native government had, by frenzied taxation, reduced the country to such complete chaos, that European intervention was necessary; and this had led to an anti-foreign movement which had to be suppressed by force. The British Occupation resulted; and from that time until the outbreak of the great war, Egypt remained under British supervision and guidance, having little more than a nominal control over its own affairs. The British Government, however, had always said that this Occupation was only a temporary measure, which would be terminated as soon as the Egyptians showed clear signs of being able to govern themselves; and now the time is fast approaching when we shall honour that promise, and shall leave this interesting people more or less to its own devices.

Already the first steps in evacuation have been taken, and great numbers of British officials have retired from service under the Egyptian Government. At the same time, native officials have been given much wider con-

trol; and now it may be said that British management
of the country's affairs has been reduced to a condition
almost as nominal as was native management twenty
or thirty years ago. This has led to the change to which
I have referred. No longer do the upper-class Egyptians remain in the background like good children who
should "be seen but not heard"; no longer do they go
about their unobtrusive business, leaving the activities
and labours of government in the hands of their pur-
poseful, high-minded, and energetic British guardians.
No longer is Egypt a sort of exhibition to which crowds
of European and American sight-seers flock, so that
they may enjoy themselves, and smile at the quaint natives, under the kindly eye of the British policemen.

To-day, thanks to England, Egypt is an independent
nation, and Egyptians are becoming increasingly conscious of the fact that the land is theirs, and that foreign
visitors are their guests, any privileges which the latter
enjoy being given to them by their native hosts, and
these hosts asking in return a degree of consideration
and politeness which in earlier years they had neither
the power nor the wish to exact. There is a new attitude
of self-assertion to be observed, which, while it may
somewhat startle a few of the old-fashioned British
officials, is received by the majority with gladness, as
being a sign of the recovery of this most engaging people
from its long sickness.

But amongst those who have not yet adjusted their
minds to the new order, many of the European and
American excavators and Egyptologists are, unfortunately, to be classed; and in this chapter I want to
warn them that unless they speedily correct their attitude, and recognise the great obligation which they owe

to their hosts, they may cause the stopping of all foreign excavation in Egypt. It is a subject which should be of interest to the general public at this time, when the whole world has been stirred by the discovery of the tomb of Tutankhamen; and I do not hesitate, therefore, to discuss it in a book of this kind. For several years I served the Egyptian Government in the capacity of Inspector-General of Antiquities; and it was then my duty both to assist these excavators in their work, and, at the same time, to maintain what may be called the proprietorship of the Egyptian nation in the sites conceded to foreign archæologists. I thus became accustomed to view the matter from the two standpoints; and now that the balance of authority is swinging over, so that soon the Egyptian and not the foreign attitude towards excavation will first have to be reckoned with, I feel able to give my warning with knowledge and experience.

For many years now excavating concessions in Egypt have been granted to foreigners on very generous terms by the Egyptian Government. Each application for such a concession came before the Archæological Committee, which consisted of the Director-General of the Department of Antiquities, various native and English high officials, and a few interested antiquarians of different nationalities; and if the credentials of the applicant were satisfactory, the concession was granted on the understanding that proper scientific records would be made and published, that the Department of Antiquities had the right to intervene and stop or rearrange the work at any time, that everything found belonged to the Egyptian nation, but that half the antiquities would be given to the excavator whenever such a gift was consistent with the interests of the national museum in Cairo.

In theory this meant that the unique pieces were to be retained in Egypt, but in practice it came to be understood that if several objects of first-rate importance were found they would be divided equally between the excavator and the Cairo Museum. In certain cases, owing to the kindness or the weakness of the authorities, the excavator got the best of the bargain, the two most important instances of this being the removal to the United States of the statues of the Pharaoh Mykerinos and his queen, and the retention by German excavators of the marvellous works of art discovered by them at Tell-el-Amârna.

Every now and then the archæological world was disturbed by some instance of an excavator having taken advantage of these generous terms to enrich himself; but on the whole the granting of concessions under this arrangement led only to the enrichment of the world's museums, and to the advancement of knowledge. Constant care had to be exercised, however, to prevent concessions being granted to the wrong kind of excavators, that is to say, to men who wished to make money out of their "finds"; for it is the first principle of scientific work that the sites which are unproductive of portable objects and which are therefore but a waste of time to the loot-hunter, must be excavated with as much care as those which yield plenty of antiquities, and that as much attention must be given to the recording of the position and measurements of bare walls and other dull material as to that of rich deposits of objects, the increase of archæological information of all kinds being the true aim rather than the acquisition of museum specimens.

The Egyptian Government, whenever it had the money to spare, also conducted excavations; and there were certain sites which it reserved for itself. Amongst these was the Valley of the Tombs of the Kings at Thebes; and here, in the last years of the nineteenth century, important excavations were conducted by the then Director-General of Antiquities, which led to the discovery of the tombs of the Pharaohs Thutmose I, Thutmose III, Amenhotep II, and others.

Shortly after these discoveries were made there came up the Nile a certain elderly American gentleman, Mr. Theodore Davis, who was so attracted by the beautiful climate of Upper Egypt, that he bought a house-boat, or *dahabiyeh,* and decided to spend each winter in the neighbourhood of Thebes. In 1902 he generously offered to give a sum of money to Mr. Howard Carter, then Inspector-General of Antiquities, in order to enable him to conduct further excavations in the royal valley, the funds of the Department being at the time somewhat low and work being suspended. The offer was accepted by the authorities on the understanding that Mr. Davis was simply identifying himself with the Cairo Museum, and was not regarding himself as having any concessionary rights; and in 1903 the tomb of Thutmose IV was discovered during the work carried out with his money. In the same year the tomb of Queen Hatshepsut was dug out by Mr. Carter, on behalf of the Government, again at Mr. Davis's expense; and thus this keenly interested American gentleman came to be regarded, so to speak, as the banker behind the Cairo Museum excavations in this Government reserve.

In 1904 Mr. J. E. Quibell took Mr. Carter's place at Luxor, and continued the work on the same terms;

and in 1905 I was appointed Inspector-General, and for some weeks Mr. Quibell and I were working together at Thebes. During this time the tomb of Yuaa and Tuau, the father and mother of Queen Tiy, was discovered; and at the close of the work Mr. Quibell left Thebes. I did not feel able, however, both to conduct these excavations and to administer the inspectorate; and I therefore insisted that if the work were to continue, Mr. Davis and the Department must employ an archæologist to direct it under my supervision.

This was done, Mr. E. R. Ayrton being appointed; and in the following years the tombs of Queen Tiy and Akhnaton, Horemheb, Septah, and others, were discovered, Mr. Davis financing the Government, and the work being conducted under my inspection on behalf of the Cairo Museum, to which all the antiquities were taken, with the exception of a few objects given to Mr. Davis as souvenirs. As soon as a tomb was found I took charge of the work, and the expenses of packing the objects, etc., were defrayed by the Government, Mr. Davis only paying for the actual excavation.

The position was not altogether an easy one for me; for, naturally, Mr. Davis year by year identified himself more closely with the work, and was inclined at length, very understandably, to resent government supervision. On the other hand, it was my business to maintain the authority of the Department I served, and to uphold the proprietorship of the Egyptian nation in this royal necropolis, against an increasing tendency on the part of visitors to regard the Valley as Mr. Davis's own property, and the objects he found as his gift to the Cairo Museum. However, thanks to his good nature, the serenity of our work was ruffled by but few breezes, and

I was able to uphold the two main principles for which
I stood, namely, that the Egyptian Government ought
to be master in its own house, and that excavation by
amateurs was only permissible when trained archæologists were in charge. It must clearly be understood that
Mr. Davis never was, and never regarded himself as, a
benefactor of mankind or anything of that sort. He
generously contributed a certain sum of money each year
to these excavations—a sum which the Egyptian Government might easily itself have paid; and in return he
had the great pleasure and the many thrills of treasure-
hunting under the most ideal conditions. From the
European or American point of view he was to be
thanked for his fine patronage of Egyptology, and from
the Egyptian standpoint he was under a debt to the
native government for permitting him to excavate in
this royal necropolis.

Mr. Davis was by no means the only wealthy
amateur who was attracted by this most enjoyable
method of spending the winter. Thebes is a popular
winter resort, where visitors live an extremely comfortable existence in magnificent hotels or luxurious
dahabiyehs or steamers; and in this perfect climate nothing can pass the time so pleasantly as a little leisurely
excavation, provided that the actual work is done by
others. One employs an archæologist to make the
records, and a handful of natives to do the digging; and
the whole thing costs but a few hundred pounds, in return for which one has a goal for the daily ride or walk,
a pleasant picnic luncheon each day, and the continuous
expectation of a romantic haul of treasures.

Lord Northampton excavated thus in another part
of the Theban necropolis; Lady William Cecil spent a

happy winter in this manner amongst the tombs at
Aswân; Mr. Robb Tytus, a rich young American, dug
out part of the palace of Amenhotep III, at Thebes;
two ladies, Miss Benson and Miss Gourlay, excavated
part of the temple of Mut at Karnak; and so forth.
In each case an archæologist was employed to do the
actual work, and there was no objection to be raised on
scientific grounds.

In this manner Lord Carnarvon also began his career
as an excavator, being attracted to Thebes by the
climate, and desiring an easy occupation to pass the
time, but in his case he commenced operations without
the aid of any trained archæologist other than myself,
and as I was generally very busy, the hard work had to
be undertaken by himself. In the second season, however, and thence onwards, he employed Mr. Carter, who
had retired from Government service, to look after the
work for him; and admirable excavations were carried
out in various parts of the Theban necropolis. The sites
chosen were not government reserves, and therefore he
was allowed to take half the antiquities found, whereas
Mr. Davis, working in the Valley, could take nothing.
The objects thus acquired were supplemented by shrewd
and tasteful purchases, and soon the "Carnarvon collection" came to be one of the most important in England.
I do not know how many thousands of pounds Lord
Carnarvon spent on the excavations or in the shops, but
it may safely be said that the antiquities which were thus
obtained had a market value greatly in excess of the
sum laid out. I do not think, however, that he regarded
the matter from a financial point of view, for he had
gradually become very much interested in Egyptology,
and thoroughly enjoyed the work; but the oft-repeated

statement—never, I think, made by himself—that his self-sacrificing expenditure in the cause of science had left him very greatly out of pocket is quite incorrect. He always knew that his collection would one day be sold, and thus while he was spending money on this fascinating and useful hobby he was able to feel, if he thought about it at all, that it was actually a very profitable investment.* The point I wish to make is that in his case, native opinion was justified in thinking that his thanks were due to the Egyptian Government for a great privilege conferred, just as foreign opinion was justified in regarding his work as of great benefit to Egypt. If we in England were to allow an Egyptian to dig up our kings in Westminster Abbey the excavator would obviously be under as great an obligation to us as we were to him.

In 1912 I left Upper Egypt, and shortly afterwards Mr. Davis died at a ripe old age. Then came the war, and excavation was suspended. Two or three years later Mr. Carter persuaded Lord Carnarvon to ask the Egyptian Government to let him take up Mr. Davis's work in the Valley of the Kings; but this being a government reserve the excavating-contract stipulated, I understand, that everything found in any untouched tomb which might be discovered should go to the Cairo Museum, but that any antiquities found loose in the rubbish or in disturbed deposits should be subject to the usual half-and-half division. Like Mr. Davis, therefore, Lord Carnarvon thus became a privileged worker for the Cairo Museum, directly under the formal supervision of the Government in the person of Mr. R. Engel-

* In his Will, made upon his deathbed, Lord Carnarvon generously suggested that his widow might offer the collection to the British Museum for £20,000, a figure, as he stated, far below its value.

bach, who had taken my place as Inspector-General of Antiquities; but he had this advantage over Mr. Davis, that he had always a chance of obtaining for himself a share of some of the "finds," to add to his collection.

The work, however, though not very expensive, proved to be unproductive of antiquities. In my time, we had cleared a large part of the Valley, and we knew that the tomb of Tutankhamen, and perhaps those of one or two minor personages, alone remained to be found. Lord Carnarvon at length desired to abandon the site, but Mr. Carter persuaded him to hold on until it could be said that the Valley had been completely examined. Then, suddenly, came the great discovery. Lord Carnarvon, who, at the time, was in England, immediately went out to Egypt, and, having seen the amazing contents of the first chamber of the new tomb, returned to England to make arrangements to meet the situation.

Meanwhile, the director of some neighbouring excavations which were being conducted by the Metropolitan Museum of New York, seeing that Mr. Carter was wholly unprepared to handle so great a quantity of antiquities, very generously placed his staff at Lord Carnarvon's disposal; and thus the long and difficult work of preserving and removing the objects was begun.

Public interest in the discovery was widespread, and in England Lord Carnarvon, somewhat bewildered, found himself a famous man. Moreover, to his surprise, he was told that there was a fortune in his discovery. There were the photographic rights to be disposed of to some enterprising journal; there were the kinematograph rights to be negotiated for; there were the usual rights in his anticipated book on the subject; and, above all, there were the newspaper rights in his daily service of news as the work developed. The money expended during the past years of unproductive work in the Valley would thus be repaid with interest; and though the antiquities themselves belonged to the Cairo Museum, he had the satisfaction of finding—by chance and not by design—that his happy days at Thebes in the indulging of his delightful hobby seemed likely to turn out to be most profitably spent.

Then came his natural and understandable, but, to my mind, unfortunate mistake. In the excitement of the moment, and in the flurry caused by a descent of eager journalists upon him, he sold to the London *Times* the absolutely exclusive rights to all information in regard to his discovery; and that newspaper announced in its columns that "neither Lord Carnarvon nor any member of his party will supply news, articles, or photographs to any other individual, newspaper, or agency," and it was further stated that this promise to give no information to anybody whatsoever, other than the *Times* journalists, was to hold good until "the completion of the excavation of all the chambers of the tomb." Immediately, of course, a storm of protest from the Egyptians themselves broke about his devoted head. No one, of course, blamed the *Times,* which was quite within its rights. But Lord Carnarvon was reminded that the tomb was in no sense his property, since it belonged to the Egyptian nation; and it was pointed out to him that in thus accepting money for his exclusive news in regard to discoveries which he had made only by courtesy and under the nominal supervision of the Egyptian Government, he had committed a grave breach of etiquette. "It is an unheard-of thing,"

said the native Minister of Public Works, "that we
Egyptians should have to go to a London newspaper
for all information regarding a tomb of one of our own
Kings."

Thus, when he returned to Egypt he found himself
harassed and perplexed by a most awkward situation;
but in loyalty to his agreement with the *Times* he faced
the storm with as much indifference as he could command, and went about his business encouraged by a little
group of rather thoughtless friends, who had been accustomed for years to regard the Egyptians as quietly
acquiescing in the right of the excavator to do as he
chose, in the cause of science.

The position of the Egyptian Department of Antiquities was most difficult. They had a perfect right at
this point to take charge of the proceedings, but Mr.
Carter and his staff were doing the work admirably, and
it would have been very unkind to dismiss them. On
the other hand, Lord Carnarvon and Mr. Carter, with
the help of the Metropolitan Museum of New York,
knew well enough that the work was in the best possible
hands, and very naturally they showed some objection to
the inspections made by Mr. Engelbach, the Inspector-
General of Antiquities, just as Mr. Davis had resented
my own official supervision of his work. The situation
was most uncomfortable for Mr. Engelbach, but with
great tact he did his best to uphold Egyptian rights and
to do his duty to the nation which employed him, without in the process diminishing the authority of the
excavators, whose point of view he could so well understand.

The chief troubles caused by Lord Carnarvon's action may be classed in five groups. Firstly, the arrange-

ment with the *Times* called Egyptian public attention
to the whole question of the rights and status of the
foreign excavator in Egypt. Is the excavator, it was
asked, a sort of owner of the area of his work, and are
his discoveries his own secret, to be hidden from the
Egyptians and the world until he choose to disclose it?
Or is he Egypt's guest, and under a great obligation to
that country for allowing him to excavate? At the time
of Lord Carnarvon's discovery the Director General of
Antiquities was endeavouring, as he still is, to introduce
a law which shall prohibit foreign excavators from taking
any of their "finds" out of the country. According to
this proposed law all antiquities discovered will have to
go the Cairo Museum; and this will put a stop to those
excavations which are financed by European or American museums rather for the purpose of obtaining antiquities to fill their show-cases, than for the unrewarded
gathering of archæological information. And this law
being under consideration, it was felt to be most unfortunate that Lord Carnarvon should, by his quite
innocent action have asserted a sort of proprietorship of
the tomb he had discovered, thereby causing many
Egyptians to wish to send him about his business.

Secondly, various London newspapers refused to
take the service of news offered for sale by the *Times;*
and they therefore sent their correspondents to Thebes
to obtain what news they could in the teeth of all opposition. Thus a journalistic battle was at once entered into; and important native journals, such as *Al-
Ahram,* joined the fray with zest, demanding to know
what right an excavator had to sell exclusive information in regard to Egypt's own sacred dead, and, indeed,

what right he had to excavate at all, especially in a government reserve.

Thirdly, the contract with the *Times* imposed a bond of silence upon the hard-working and most high-principled excavators, obliging them to act in a rather ludicrous manner which to their friends and colleagues seemed reminiscent of the simplicity of childhood, and to the Egyptians appeared indicative of the knavery of bad men. They had to slink about with shut mouths, in a manner of brigands; and they gave the impression throughout native Egypt that they were trying to obtain some of the objects for sale abroad. Wild stories were circulated as to the removal by aeroplane of millions of pounds' worth of gold; and the ladies of the party were said to have left the tomb with wonderful jewels hidden under their skirts.

The tomb was discovered at a time when the political situation was so delicate that the utmost tact was required to avoid trouble with the Egyptians. Yet, at the opening of the first chamber no representation of the Egyptian Department of Antiquities had been present; and native gossip said that not only had Lord Carnarvon deliberately slighted and insulted the Egyptian nation, but that he had purposely so arranged matters in order to obtain possession of the treasures. The fact that he was an honourable man, incapable of such actions, had no weight with the unreasoning gossips.

Fourthly, the contract with the *Times* obliged the excavators sometimes to attempt to refuse free access to the tomb to Egyptologists who had some connection with a newspaper, as all Egyptologists must have from time to time in the interests of that publicity which is needed to obtain support for scientific work. Thus the excavators cut themselves off from possible advice and help, and unconsciously established a precedent of a rather startling nature. The Egyptologists and others thus shut out at once applied direct to the Egyptian Government for permission to enter the tomb, which was readily granted; and in this manner a definite trial of strength between the Government and the excavators took place, which is bound to re-act upon the future relations of the two.

Fifthly, the accidental turning of the discovery to such lucrative account was likely to encourage all kinds of commercial enterprises, and to let loose on Egypt a horde of undesirable diggers anxious simply to obtain loot or to make a discovery which could be exploited by a newspaper. Egyptians themselves, untrained in scientific methods, would demand excavating concessions, and they could only be checked by the passage of the proposed law mentioned above.

These five points will make it sufficiently clear, I think, that on the grounds of archæological principle as well as on those of expediency there should have been no course open to an earnest Egyptologist other than that of resisting the innovation. Yet, as a matter of fact, most Egyptologists sided with the hard-working and most competent excavators, who themselves may be credited with the best of intentions. I may mention that in the sequel the monopoly of the news was quite unable to be maintained, and when the inner chamber of the tomb was opened the main facts were announced to the world through all the important newspapers simultaneously. That, however, is not my present point: I wish only to show that the attitude of an excavator in laying claim to this sort of proprietorship of the area he has been allowed to excavate can only lead to situations dangerous to the interests of Egyptology at this present time when native opinion has to be considered so carefully.

I believe that unless foreign excavators in Egypt adjust themselves speedily to the new conditions in that country, they will cease to be given digging-concessions. Egypt, as I have said, is now fast assuming charge of its own affairs, and we English are retiring from its councils. A new interest in their history and archæology is developing amongst better-class Egyptians; and not long will they permit foreign Egyptologists to work as they have worked before, with greater regard for their own museums and their own public than for the interests of Egypt itself.

I will give an instance of what I mean. In the old days the excavator conducted his season's work in privacy, regarding visitors as intruders who interrupted him. I have heard Lord Carnarvon and the excavators of the Metropolitan Museum of New York declare, understandably enough, that it was intolerable that their work should be held up by the arrival of some party wishing to be shown over the excavations; and though the ever-increasing interest in the great discovery obliged them at length to allow several Egyptian notables to visit the work, they much objected, sometimes, to this necessity. Excavators must try to remember, however, that they are the guests of the Egyptian nation; and in future they must so adjust their plans that from time to time native visitors may be taken over the works. They must show a real desire to educate these people in their history, and they must regard it as one of the duties imposed upon them by the terms of their concession, and not as a waste of time. In the case of the tomb of Tutankhamen a number of native pressmen, at the special invitation of the Egyptian Government, came all the way from Cairo to Luxor to see the sepulchre, but the excavators, not having been properly notified of the visit, at first wished to refuse them admission, and finally allowed them to see the first chamber from behind a barrier across the entrance passage, yet did not permit them to look at the antiquities which had already been removed to a neighbouring workshop. This sort of clash on a point of etiquette ought never to have taken place.

There should be no secrecy on the part of excavators in regard to their "finds," nor any thought that information concerning any particular discovery belongs to them alone and not to the public. When the Germans discovered the now famous head of Queen Nefertiti at Tell-el-Amârna in 1913, and, for some unaccountable reason, were allowed to take it to Berlin, they kept the matter as dark as night; and it is only now, ten years later, that photographs of it are beginning to circulate. Less than a year ago an English Egyptologist showed me these pictures in profound secrecy, telling me that on no account must they be made public, lest a breach of etiquette be committed.

Breach of fiddlesticks! All information regarding "finds" made in excavations in Egypt should, if only for the sake of politeness, be at the disposal of the Egyptian nation as rapidly as possible, and thence should be passed on to the world at large. This was done, for example, by Professor Petrie's party, who, having made a discovery of importance during the same season which saw the opening of the tomb of Tutankhamen, announced it in a free bulletin to the Press at large. The only serious question of etiquette which arises is that in regard to Egypt: in what manner can the excavator best show his appreciation of the privilege conferred on him by the Egyptian Government in allowing him to excavate at all?

It is to be argued that Lord Carnarvon's discovery put Egypt under a great obligation to him; and, though we consider this true, thoughtful Egyptians have expressed an opposite view. The tomb, they say, was so safely buried beneath tons of rock that it was in no danger, and its treasures might well have been left to the better handling of a future generation. As it is, a mass of material has been discovered at a time when there is no proper place to house it, and when our knowledge of how to preserve it is very limited. "Is the world fit to assume responsibility for all these treasures of the past?"—asks Professor Petrie—"to ensure that fanaticism, violence, or greed will not extinguish them?—to guarantee them for some more thousands of years of existence? Or is all this exposure the last stage?" Have these wonderful objects survived the siege of nearly thirty-three centuries, only to be shown to us of this one generation and then to fall to pieces because conditions are not ready for their preservation?

This line of thought is not fanciful, and it must be considered seriously. When Mr. Davis found the tomb of Queen Tiy and Akhnaton we came upon a funeral-shrine made of wood, covered with plaster on which figures were modelled. The shrine had been taken to pieces in ancient times and these modelled surfaces were lying against the walls at various angles. We were able to photograph them and to copy the inscriptions; but a few hours after the introduction of the outside air the plaster-work had cracked and crumbled and fallen off the wood beneath. If objects in such a condition had been found in the tomb of Tutankhamen, they, too, would have perished before means of preserving them could have been procured.

It may perhaps be said with truth that we are not yet ready to conduct excavations of this kind; and I do not suppose that Mr. Lucas, the extremely able chemist who was employed by Lord Carnarvon, will deny that, with all his skill, the work might have been done better by a future generation. And as to the housing of these objects, all those who know the Cairo Museum, built, as it is, beside the Nile in a climate having a humidity which rises to 80 per cent, with an annual mean of about 70 per cent, will admit that that building is entirely unfit to receive them; whereas, in another thirty or forty years there may be a safe museum and some proper show-cases ready to preserve them.

The staff at Cairo is too small and too hard-worked to deal with the rapidly increasing mass of antiquities, and ruinous confusion grows ever more confused. The building, though fairly new, is dilapidated, and part of the roof fell in a short time ago, destroying many fine objects. If antiquities removed from a tomb where they were perfectly safe are thrown pell-mell into an under-staffed museum in a damp climate and left there to rot, excavation becomes utterly immoral; and in fact the act of excavation should involve both the immediate safe-guarding of the objects found and complete arrange-ments for their perpetual preservation. Lord Carnarvon's excavations have suddenly sprung this mass of glorious relics of the past upon an unprepared present, and the grave question of how to hand them on intact to the future is one which, perhaps, has not been properly considered.

The search for, and the finding of, a royal tomb, however, is "a gorgeous experience," to employ a phrase used by Professor Petrie in congratulating the discoverers of this particular sepulchre; and we may well understand their desire to dig in the Valley of the Kings. But let us face the truth and realise that Lord Carnarvon's splendid find, while it has given such a great "lift" to Egyptology, is thought by many persons to be a doubtful benefit to posterity. When the discovery had been made, Mr. Carter and the staff lent to him by New York did the best that this generation can do to meet their obligations and to shoulder their responsibilities; but the risks were great, and one cannot say whether there is any hope of a long lease of life for the objects which have been brought to light, or whether future generations will be able to thank the excavators for opening this tomb.

So much for this the greatest archæological find of modern times; and I do not at all willingly criticise one whose curious, interesting, and charming personality so tragically passed from this world at a time when his name was on millions of lips. But the case is typical, and shows so clearly the point of view of the foreign excavator as opposed to that of the native. The excavation of sites which are in danger from some cause is another matter, and in such cases the Egyptians should be grateful; though it may be said that, under existing conditions, the benefit is generally mutual as between the foreign excavator and the Egyptian Government. The latter is relieved of expense, and the former usually gains in objects the value of what he has spent upon the work. Be this as it may, however, the Egyptians are of opinion that thanks are due to them for allowing foreigners to dig; and my object in this chapter is to warn excavators and those interested in their work that they must accept that point of view, right or wrong. They must endeavour to be more simple, more obliging, more gracious, more considerate of Egyptian feeling. In vulgar language, they must get off their high horse.

In protesting against the proposed law which is designed to prevent antiquities leaving Egypt, and which is to be similar to the law now existing in Italy and Greece, they must not arrogantly demand their rights: they have none. Rather, they should marshal the arguments on both sides, and draw their correct conclusions in a diplomatic manner. The two sides of the case may be stated as follows:

On the Egyptian side it may be said that Egypt is the natural home for Egyptian antiquities, and that the modern Egyptians are the rightful stewards of the relics of their ancestors. On the excavators' side the reply may be made that antiquities are the property of all mankind, not of one nation, and that Europeans and Americans are at present far more able to appreciate these relics of early man than are the Egyptians.

Those in favour of retaining all Egyptian antiquities in Egypt can argue that the Cairo Museum will always have a certain number of European scholars in its employ, and these, with the natives now being trained, will be able to take care of the collection; whereas objects which leave the country often pass into unskilled hands. In reply it may be said that, as a whole, the excavators of foreign museums are more skilled than those likely to be employed at Cairo, and that the services of larger numbers of trained men can be engaged than can be afforded by the Cairo Museum, which now, at any rate, is so badly understaffed.

Again, the Cairo Museum, it is to be said on the one hand, can easily be converted into a satisfactory storehouse, and proper air-tight show-cases can be obtained. Moreover, the climate is more fitted for the preservation of the fragile objects than is that of certain European or American cities. On the other hand, it is to be said that at present the Cairo Museum is a wretchedly unsafe building, and that there is no guarantee that it will be improved. Cairo, too, has a humid atmosphere, as I have said above, no better in this respect than that of many foreign capitals.

On the Egyptian side it is to be argued that if Egyptian antiquities continue to be distributed over the world, Egyptologists will have to spend their time in wandering over the face of the earth when they wish to study the objects themselves; whereas if the objects are massed in one place their labours will be greatly lessened. On the side of the excavators, the answer is that Egypt is very far away from the world's chief seats of learning, and that widely-spread collections mean widely-spread interest.

Cairo, it will be said, is as safe a capital as any other; for the Egyptians will always be under the eye of the great Powers. European capitals, and perhaps American, are open to riots and disturbances more grave than any to be expected in Egypt. The reply is that, in the troubled state of the world, it is bad policy to place all our eggs in one basket. The wider the distribution of the collections the less will be the fear of a great disaster to them.

Those in favour of the new law can argue that excavations by foreigners will still be permitted and that the results in increased knowledge will be sufficient reward for the workers. The excavators can reply with the unfortunate truth that foreign excavations will very largely cease for want of subscriptions, if there is to be no return in actual objects.

Such is a bare outline of the arguments on either side; and the point I wish to make is that the foreign excavators have no cause for complaint. They have freely filled their museums during the past years with antiquities obtained from Egypt, and their attitude now must be one not of outraged dignity but of gratitude for past favours and hope for continued indulgence. If they will show a real interest in the archæological education of the Egyptian people, and will always recognise the right of the Egyptian Government to maintain its nominal proprietorship, they will go far to ease a situation which is very unpromising for the future of excavation in Egypt.

CHAPTER II

THE VALLEY OF THE TOMBS OF
THE KINGS

THE famous Valley of the Tombs of the Kings, or *Bibân-el-Malûk* as the natives call it, in which the tomb of Tutankhamen has recently been found, was first used as a burial-place for the Pharaohs of Egypt during the sixteenth century B.C. Previous to this the kings were buried in various parts of the country, according to the position of their capital; and sometimes a Pharaoh had two tombs prepared for him, though it is not known whether, in such cases, it was intended that the body should lie for a time in each of the sepulchres, or whether one of the two was simply a sort of extra residence for the royal *Ka,* or spirit. At any rate, we must understand that an ancient Egyptian burial was not, as with us, a means of disposing of a dead body, but was a method of preserving it and providing a comfortable home for it and the spirit which still dwelt in it.

The kings of the earliest dynasties (B.C. 3600 to 3100) were buried in large brick tombs in the western desert behind the city of Abydos in Upper Egypt. Mena, the first Pharaoh of a united Egypt (B.C. 3520) seems to have had two tombs, one at Abydos and one at Nakâdeh. King Zeser (B.C. 3100) built for himself the great Step-Pyramid at Sakkâra, near Memphis, his capital; but he seems also to have had a sepulchre at Bêt

38

Khallâf, near Abydos. Sneferu, who reigned shortly
after this, was buried in a pyramid-like tomb at Meidûm,
some miles above Memphis; but he also appears to have
erected another pyramid-tomb for himself at Dahshûr,
near Sakkâra.

Then came Khufu (Cheops) (B.C. 3020-2997) who
built the Great Pyramid at Gizeh as his sepulchre. His
successor, Dedefra, made his tomb at Abu Roash, a few
miles to the north of this; but the next king, Khafra
(Khephren) (B.C. 2989-2923) returned to Gizeh and
erected the Second Pyramid there, his successor, Men-
kaura (Mykerinos), building the Third Pyramid, close
to it. The Pharaohs Sahura, Neferarkara, and Nuserra
of the Fifth Dynasty (B.C. 2863-2811) were buried in
pyramids at Abusîr, between Gizeh and Sakkâra; but
King Unas (B.C. 2775-2745) was buried at Sakkâra, as
were also the kings of the succeeding dynasty, down to
B.C. 2595.

Then followed the first of Egypt's two "dark ages,"
and when the light returns, in B.C. 2280, we find the
reigning house—the Eleventh Dynasty—living at
Thebes, and burying its kings in the western desert opposite that city, an area which was to become the famous
Theban Necropolis. The Pharaoh Nebhapetra Menthuhotep of this dynasty caused himself to be buried at
Dêr el-Bahri, in a pyramid surrounded by temple-like
buildings, at the foot of the great cliffs which faced the
city of Thebes; and not far away he caused a rock-cut
tomb to be made for him as a second sepulchre. Other
Pharaohs of this period erected brick pyramids for
themselves in another part of this necropolis.

King Amenemhet II (B.C. 2058-2023) of the Twelfth
Dynasty was buried in a pyramid at Dahshûr, near Sak-

kâra; and his successor, Senusert II, chose to build his
pyramid at Illahûn, at the entrance of the Fayûm. The
great Senusert III (B.C. 2007-1969) had two tombs, the
one a pyramid at Dahshûr, and the other a rock-cut
sepulchre, discovered by Professor Petrie and myself in
the desert behind Abydos, not far from the tombs of the
earliest kings. The site chosen for this latter tomb was
a stretch of open desert near the foot of the western hills.
A pit was excavated in the sand, and when bed-rock
was reached a tunnel was made sloping down for some
650 feet into the rock. The sides of the internal chambers were cased with quartzite, sandstone, granite, and
limestone; and there was a magnificent sarcophagus of
red granite. It was the first of the great tunnel-tombs
of the Pharaohs, and served as the prototype for the
royal sepulchres of the Eighteenth Dynasty. Amenemhet III (B.C. 1969-1921) also had two burial-places, both
pyramids, one at Dahshûr, and the other at Hawâra,
near Illahûn. The second "dark age" followed, and
when the story of the Pharaohs is able to be resumed
the city of Thebes is once more the capital and the
Pharaoh Ahmose I (B.C. 1580-1557) the founder of the
Eighteenth Dynasty, is on the throne.

Thebes, it should be mentioned, was situated on the
east bank of the Nile, some 450 miles above Memphis
and the later Cairo; and on the west bank stood the
pyramids of some of the earlier Kings, grouped at the
foot of the desert hills which here come forward in a
magnificent range to within a mile or two of the river.

Now, it was the Egyptian custom to bury a large
amount of rich funeral-furniture and jewellery with
their illustrious dead, in order that the spirit might have
at hand those comforts and luxuries which the body had

A GENERAL VIEW OF THE VALLEY OF THE TOMBS OF THE KINGS

enjoyed in life; and the mummies themselves were adorned with valuable necklaces and other personal ornaments, while the coffins were often decorated with gold. There was thus always a great temptation to rob these tombs, and in the chaotic period previous to the foundation of the Eighteenth Dynasty, some of the Pharaonic pyramids had been plundered and the objects of value stolen. It became necessary, therefore, for the kings to consider a new method of burial which would secure some measure of safety for their bodies in the years to come. If the mummy and its resting-place were destroyed the spirit would be rendered homeless, and if the tomb-stone inscriptions were broken up the name of the dead monarch might be lost; and thus his ghost would have to wander about, untended and unsustained by the pious prayers of the priests of the necropolis. This fear led to much thought being given to the question; and we can easily understand that the method of burial in a conspicuous pyramid had to be abandoned as being almost an invitation to robbery.

The trouble was, however, that if the Pharaoh's body was to be hidden away in some remote spot in order to secure its safety, the ancient custom of placing funeral offerings and saying prayers at the tomb would have to be given up, for these offerings and ceremonies would reveal the position of the hiding-place. In the earliest times such offerings had been placed at the east side of the tomb, that being the side on which the spirit came out to greet the rising sun, and in the age of the pyramids this custom had led to the erection of a temple on the east side of each pyramid, where the mortuary services on behalf of the dead monarch were held. Here food and drink for his spirit were placed; and thus it had not to make a ghostly journey of any distance in search of its material needs.

In the case of the tomb of Senusert III at Abydos, the mortuary temple had been erected about half a mile to the east of the rock-cut sepulchre: the temple stood at the edge of the fields, but the tomb was up in the desert at the foot of the cliffs. There was, however, a little shrine under the cliffs where special services were perhaps conducted and offerings made. The concealed entrance of the royal sepulchre was surrounded by the conspicuous tombs of the chief nobles of that reign; and at the fall of the dynasty thieves had thus found their way in and had broken open the sarcophagus.

Ahmose I saw the destruction which had been wrought, yet wished to be buried near his great predecessor, more especially since Abydos was the burial place of the earliest Pharaohs, and was a city sacred to Osiris, the God of the Dead. He, therefore, laid his plans so that the tomb itself should be absolutely concealed and yet that the offerings to his spirit might be made close to it.

He carried out his scheme in the following manner. In the open desert, less than a mile south of the tomb of Senusert III, he caused a long tunnel to be excavated in the rock which underlies the sand of the surface. From a small and rough entrance this tunnel wound its way down to a large eighteen-pillared hall, and thence passed on to a rough chamber deep in the bowels of the earth, wherein he was to be buried. The mouth of the tomb was insignificant, and could easily be hidden and lost under the sand of this open plain; nor did he allow any of his nobles to be buried near him, lest this might give a clue to his whereabouts. Close to it, at the foot of the cliffs, he erected a terraced temple wherein his spirit could receive its food and drink. Then, to deceive possible robbers, he carried all the chippings from the tunnel down to the edge of the fields, the best part of a mile away, and enclosed them in a dummy-pyramid which would, of course, be mistaken for the actual tomb.

Whether he was ever buried here is not known. His mummy was found in a hiding-place at Thebes, whither it had been carried several hundred years later by pious hands; but whether it was taken there from Abydos or elsewhere cannot at present be decided. This tomb at Abydos contained several fragmentary pieces of gold, when it was discovered some years ago by Mr. C. T. Currelly; but, on the other hand, there was no trace of a stone sarcophagus. The place had been entirely plundered, for its secret location had become known by a circumstance which the King had left out of his calculations: the roof of the underground hall had fallen in, thereby leaving a gaping pit in the sandy plain above.

The successor of Ahmose I was Amenhotep I, and to this Pharaoh occurred the novel idea of hiding his body away on the top of the cliffs of Thebes when he should come to die. He chose for the site of his tomb, therefore, a dip or shallow ravine in the undulating surface of the summit, just behind that part of the necropolis now known as Dêr el-Medineh. The entrance, cut in the slope of the hill, was a rough pit in which was a steep flight of steps leading down to a tunnel in the hillside, which brought one first to a small chamber and thence to a fair sized burial-hall and a further chamber.

On the edge of the fields, rather over a mile due south of the tomb, he erected his mortuary temple, at a place now called Medinet Habu. This was a long way for his spirit to go to receive its offerings of food and drink; but this disadvantage was evidently considered worth enduring in order that the secret of the position of his tomb might be kept and his body might thus obtain immunity from pillage.

Amenhotep I appears to have constructed a tomb for his mother, Queen Ahmose-Nefertari, and this has recently been found by Mr. Carter in Dra Abu'l Negga, a part of the necropolis farther to the north. The tomb was situated on the top of the hills, and was entered by a pit from which a passage led to a well or shaft some 30 feet deep. This well served both to deceive and balk possible robbers, and also to carry off any rainwater which might percolate through the filling of the entrance pit. Beyond it the passage continued, leading to a burial-hall, the ceiling of which was originally supported by one pillar. In this tomb Mr. Carter found numerous fragments of vases, three of which had the cartouches of Ahmose I on them, eight had the name of Queen Ahmose-Nefertari, that monarch's wife, and nine were inscribed with the name of Amenhotep I. Another fragment bore the name of King Ausserra Apepi of the Seventeenth Dynasty and his daughter Herath, which may perhaps indicate that the tomb had been usurped by Amenhotep I from this earlier king. It is not likely that Amenhotep I was buried with his mother: he was far more probably buried in the tomb on the top of the cliffs; but he did not thus escape the robbers, for the place was plundered in ancient times, and now it lies open, and is generally called simply No. 39, being regarded as the tomb of an unknown person.

My reasons for identifying it as that of Amenhotep I are rather interesting, and may be mentioned here. It is certainly a royal tomb, judging by its size and shape; and the absence of a well or shaft in it, as will presently be seen, dates it to some period before the reign of Thutmose III.   In the Abbott Papyrus an account is given of the inspection of certain royal tombs in the time of Rameses X, which had been said to be plundered.   The first tomb on the list is that of Amenhotep I, the reference reading as follows:—"The Tomb of King Amenhotep I, which lies 120 cubits down from the buildings (?) belonging to it which are called 'The Height,' north of the temple of 'Amenhotep of the Garden.'"

Now the temple of "Amenhotep of the Garden" may well be the later name of the King's mortuary temple at Medinet Habu, which is known to have had a garden, the site of which, with its artificial lake, can still be seen.   If we take a line due north of this, as the inscription tells us, we come to the well-known pathway leading over the hills behind Dêr el-Medineh; and at the highest point of this track there are the ruins of a number of ancient huts, once occupied by watchmen, which may have been appropriately called "The Height."   From this eminence one commands a striking view of the King's temple at Medinet Habu; and if we measure 120 average cubits of 20.63 inches, which is the regular cubit of the period, down the hill westward from the near side of this group of buildings, we find that the tape brings us exactly to the mouth of this tomb No. 39.   Mr. Carter thought that the tomb which he found at Dra Abu'l Negga as mentioned above, was the sepulchre referred to in the Abbott Papyrus, but the 120 cubit measurement cannot be made to tally with it, except by means of some very improbable calculations, nor do the other directions agree.

The next Pharaoh was Thutmose I; and he decided to make a tomb for himself close to that of his father.* Going a few yards westward from No. 39, that is to say into the desert, away from Thebes, one drops down into the southern corner of the great valley which is now famous as the Valley of the Tombs of the Kings, but which was at that time a remote and desolate ravine. It is a magnificent amphitheatre surrounded by precipices or steep hillsides, dominated to the south by a mountain which rises up like a pyramid into the sky. This valley passes behind the great barrier-wall of the cliffs which face Thebes, and, with many twists and turns, comes out at last amongst the low hills at the extreme north end of the necropolis. It had been created by some long-forgotten prehistoric torrent which had here rushed down from the heights of the Sahara; and in the time of Thutmose I its whole length was strewn with water-worn boulders and stones, nor was there any pathway along it.

There was not a blade of grass nor a trace of scrub in this deserted valley. The sun beat down on its lifeless rocks all through the morning, and in the afternoon it lay in deep shadow, utterly silent except for the sighing of the wind and the occasional cry of a jackal. Although shut off from the necropolis and the Nile valley by no more than a single wall of cliffs, it seemed to be infinitely remote and unearthly: a sterile, echoing region like a hollow in the hills of the Underworld.

Here, in the cul-de-sac at its south end, close to, and below, the tomb of Amenhotep I, the Pharaoh Thutmose I caused his tomb to be excavated in the cliff face at

* Its proximity to No. 39 is a further indication that the latter is the tomb of Amenhotep I.

the foot of a precipice. The idea of cutting the tunnel straight into the face of a cliff was new, for in the case of the tombs of Senusert III and Ahmose I, described above, a pit in the level ground had led down to the entrance; but the tomb of Amenhotep I (i.e. No. 39) gives the link between the old and the new type, for, as has been said, it is cut into the sloping side of a gully.

This tomb of Thutmose I had, for the sake of secrecy, an entrance which was small and roughly hewn—a mere hole, just high enough to admit a man standing upright. A flight of steps led down to a square room cut out of the rock, and thence a second flight led on to the burial-hall, the roof of which was supported by one central column, as in the tomb of his grandmother, Ahmose-Nefertari described above. The walls of this hall were smoothed over with plaster, and a small sarcophagus of quartzite sandstone was dragged down and placed here for the reception of the King's coffin.

This tomb was made for the Pharaoh under the direction of a great noble named Anena, who was Overseer of the Granary of Amon, Superintendent of the workmen in the Treasury of Karnak, and Superintendent of the Royal Buildings; and in the mortuary chapel of this personage an inscription was found in which occur these significant words: "I arranged for the hewing of a rock tomb for his majesty, alone, no one seeing, no one hearing." Thus we are able to realise that the burial of the Pharaohs of this period was conducted in absolute secrecy, so that their bodies might escape the attentions of the robbers. When Thutmose I was buried here in B.C. 1501, the funeral must have been conducted in the greatest possible privacy, the workmen and priests being sworn to silence by the most terrible oaths. The mouth of the tomb was filled in with stones, and boulders were probably placed over the surface so that the site might have a natural and undisturbed appearance. The chippings from the interior were dumped at some distance, and were likewise covered with rocks and gravel.

The mortuary services for the King's spirit were conducted in the temple erected by Amenhotep I at Medinet Habu, that building being enlarged and newly decorated for the purpose. It must have been thought, however, that the spirit's daily journey down to the temple to receive its food and drink imposed considerable inconvenience upon it; and thus we find at about this period the custom of placing embalmed joints of meat in the tomb, each joint being enclosed in a separate box. Food had been placed in earlier tombs in small quantities, but originally the main supplies of this kind had been left outside the sepulchre, and, as we have seen, in more recent ages they have been deposited in the mortuary temples.

The next Pharaoh, Thutmose II, had a tomb made for him close to that of Thutmose I, at the bottom of the cliffs.* A rough flight of steps led down to the entrance of the tunnel, which sloped downwards to a small chamber and thence to a curious oval hall, the ceiling of which was supported by two pillars. The walls of this hall were plastered and tinted a sort of drab-colour to represent papyrus; and at the far end was a plain sarcophagus of quartzite sandstone, which,

* Tomb No. 42. It has no inscription and is therefore generally regarded as an unidentified tomb; but the following facts show pretty certainly that it was made for Thutmose II:—It is close to the tombs of Thutmose I and Thutmose III, and is similar in style to the latter, which is the only other tomb having an oval burial-hall. Like the tombs of Thutmose I and Hatshepsut, it has no well, but those of Thutmose III and his successors all have wells, so that it seems to be earlier than Thutmose III. It is evidently a king's tomb, by its size and shape.

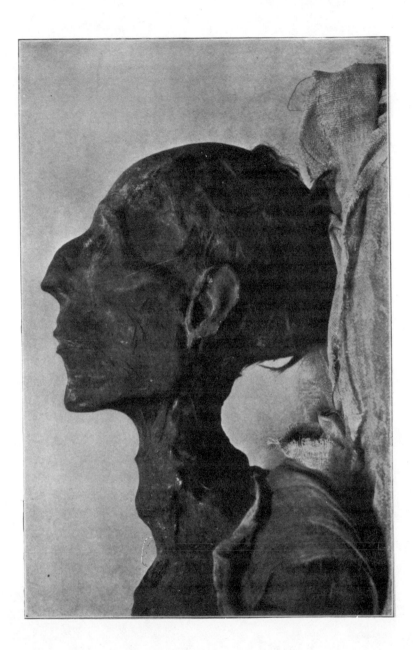

THE MUMMY OF RAMESES THE SECOND

like the sarcophagus of Senusert III and other early
kings, was uninscribed. Thutmose II added his name
to the inscriptions on the wall of the temple of Amenhotep I and Thutmose I at Medinet Habu, and did not
erect a new building as his mortuary temple.

So far only these two tombs, those of Thutmose I
and II, were situated in the afterwards famous valley,
and there was thus no thought as yet of this place being
a regular royal necropolis. It was simply a hiding-
place for the bodies of these two Pharaohs, just as the
summit of the cliff above had been the hiding-place of
the mummy of Amenhotep I; and we are to picture the
valley, therefore, as still being a wild and desolate spot,
apparently untrodden by the foot of man. All this part
of the desert was dedicated to the goddess Hathor, who
was visualised as a spotted cow living somewhere inside
these western hills; and in order to discourage persons
from entering this particular valley it was probably said
to be an area sacred to the goddess, upon which no man
must on any account trespass. In some such manner,
at any rate, the hiding-place must have been kept
inviolate.

Thutmose II was still alive when the power passed
into the hands of Queen Hatshepsut; and she, knowing
that she had many enemies in her own family, and fear-
ing both them and the robbers of some future date,
decided to hide her tomb in a far more remote part of
the desert. A distant valley, deep in the hills to the
west, was selected as the site; and here she caused her
sepulchre to be hewn out of the rock high up in the pre-
cipitous face of a cliff, over 200 feet above the bed of
the valley below, and some 137 feet down from the top.
A flight of steps and a long tunnel led down to the

burial-chamber, and here a fine sarcophagus of quartzite sandstone was, with infinite labour, hauled and dragged into position. It is the most astonishing tomb in Egypt; and its clearance a few years ago was due to the skill and daring of Mr. Carter.

Meanwhile, however, the Queen was erecting for herself the magnificent mortuary temple which is now known as Dêr el-Bahri. It was set against the eastern face of the cliffs overlooking the Theban necropolis and the city of Thebes on the opposite bank of the river; and it was, in its original conception, a development of the idea which Ahmose I had carried into execution near his tomb at Abydos, as recorded above, that is to say it was a terrace-temple wherein the mortuary services for the royal spirit might be conducted. But when the Queen began to feel her position more secure, perhaps after the death or deposition of Thutmose II, she decided to make another tunnel-tomb for herself which should run in under this temple, in somewhat the manner in which the tomb of Ahmose I had penetrated underground towards his terrace-temple.

Now, the silent and untrodden valley at the far end of which the tombs of Thutmose I and II were situated, passed just behind or on the west side of the cliffs which formed the background of her temple; and she therefore decided to cut a tunnel from this valley, which should run right under these cliffs and should end in a hall deep in the rock underneath her temple. In this hall she would be buried; and thus the mortuary services for the benefit of her spirit would be held directly above her mummy as it lay in its secret tomb beneath. Her spirit would rise up each day through the solid rock to greet the sunrise on the terraces of her temple; and the entrance to the tunnel would be so well hidden in the valley behind that her mummy would lie secure from robbery.

The actual tunnel which was made was some 700 feet in length and over 300 feet in depth, but it curved off to the right, either owing to the workmen having lost their sense of direction as they laboured in the dim light of their lamps, or owing to the poor quality of the rock, which obliged them to swerve aside. In the burial-hall, the rough walls of which were lined with limestone blocks inscribed with religious texts, the Queen placed a fine quartzite sandstone sarcophagus for herself and another for her father, Thutmose I. Part of the floor of the hall was sunk somewhat lower than the rest, this being an innovation afterwards copied in later tombs. It is not known whether the Queen actually disinterred Thutmose I from his own tomb and re-buried him here; but it is pretty certain that she herself was laid to rest in this extraordinary sepulchre; for when it was excavated some years ago by Mr. Carter, after it had been plundered by ancient thieves, many fragments of the funeral-paraphernalia were found.

Meanwhile, Thutmose III, Hatshepsut's brother, who had reigned by her side, was making for himself a sepulchre close to that of Thutmose II. It was cut into the rock in an almost inaccessible chimney in the cliffs, high above the tomb of Thutmose II, and not far below the tomb of Amenhotep I, that is to say right in the south corner of the valley. Hatshepsut had modelled her tomb on that of Ahmose I at Abydos, but Thutmose III copied and elaborated the plan of the tomb of Thutmose II. A flight of steps led down through a small rough entrance, easily able to be concealed, to a sloping passage and another staircase. Then came a deep shaft or well, like that in the tomb of Queen Ahmose-Nefertari, hewn out of the rock, completely cutting off the interior chambers.

Its purpose, as in this earlier instance, was two-fold. Firstly, it served to carry off any rainwater which might penetrate through the filling of the entrance, since the place chosen for the tomb, in this rocky chimney, was very liable to become the bed of a torrent upon the rare occasions of a downpour. Secondly, it was a deterrent to robbers, for the entrance to the further chambers and passages on the opposite side of the well was blocked up and covered with plaster, so that only a blank wall was visible. The robbers, if they were without tackle, would thus abandon their godless work here; or, if they had ropes, would descend the shaft and, finding it empty, would think that the tomb had never been used.

Beyond the well there was a pillared hall, upon the walls of which a long list of nearly 750 gods and demi-gods was inscribed. In the floor there was a flight of steps leading down to a magnificent oval-shaped burial-hall, like that in the tomb of Thutmose II; but this stair-case was planned so that it could be filled up to the top and thus concealed. In the burial-hall stood the stone sarcophagus, and on the walls were texts and illustra-tions from the "Book of That Which is in the Under-world," painted in outline like an enlargement of a roll of papyrus. It will be remembered that the walls of the oval hall in the tomb of Thutmose II were also painted to represent papyrus, but the religious inscrip-tions had never been written, probably owing to the tomb having been left unfinished.

Thus, Thutmose I, Thutmose II, Hatshepsut, and

Thutmose III, were all buried in this one valley; and though the exact location of each tomb was a profound secret, this desert ravine must now have been pretty generally known to be the royal burial-ground, and was no doubt talked about as such in awed whispers. Thutmose III had built his mortuary temple on the other side of the barrier of cliffs, near the edge of the fields, far away from his hidden tomb; and thus all possible precautions had been taken to secure secrecy and to avoid robbery.

Besides these four royal sepulchres, there were also in this valley a few small tombs, each consisting of a single shaft, from the bottom of which the burial-chamber led out. These were the burial-places of the Vizirs or other great men of the land, who had been allowed to rest near their royal masters. Most of the great men of the period were buried at the bottom of somewhat similar shafts in a hill now known as Shêkh abd'el-Gurneh in the main Theban necropolis; and above these shafts there were two or three rock-cut chambers which served as their mortuary chapels. But in certain instances these upper chambers are found to have no burial-pits belonging to them; and I think that where this is the case we may suppose the owner to have been buried in the royal valley, near his sovereign. It is not always certain where the queens, princes, and princesses were interred at this period; but in certain cases they were undoubtedly laid to rest in the tomb of the Pharaoh of their day, for some of their bodies have been found in the royal sepulchres.

The next king was Amenhotep II (B.C.1447-1420); and he followed the family custom, and excavated his tomb in the valley, choosing a place for it in the western side of the south end, about a hundred yards from the

tomb of Thutmose I, and cutting it into the base of the
precipice as that Pharaoh had also done. The entrance
was small and rough, as in the case of the earlier tombs
of this dynasty; and a flight of steps brought one to a
sloping passage which descended to a second staircase,
leading to a well, copied from the tomb of Thutmose
III. There was some decoration on the walls of this
well, in order to suggest the false idea that it was the
burial-place. Beyond this, concealed behind a blocked
doorway in the opposite wall, was a two-pillared hall,
through the floor of which, again as in the tomb of Thutmose III, a hidden stairway descended into the six-
pillared burial-hall. The walls of this hall were painted,
as before, like papyrus, and were inscribed with texts
and scenes from the "Book of That Which is in the
Underworld." Upon the pillars the King was shown
in the presence of various gods, drawn in outline. At
the far end of this hall, the floor of which is here at a
deeper level, as in the tomb of Hatshepsut, the quartzite
sandstone sarcophagus was placed. This King's mortuary temple was erected on the edge of the fields just
to the south of that of Thutmose III.

The succeeding Pharaoh was Thutmose IV (B.C.
1420-1411), who chose for his sepulchre a site close to
that of Hatshepsut, and for his mortuary temple a site
some distance to the south of the temple of Amenhotep
II. The tomb followed much the same plan as that of
Amenhotep II, but the quartzite sandstone sarcophagus
was larger, and the painting on the walls of the burial-
hall and well were more elaborate, the figures being no
longer shown in outline, but being completely painted.
A young boy, perhaps one of the king's sons who had

died during his father's lifetime, was buried with the
Pharaoh in this tomb.

Amenhotep III (B.C. 1411-1375) was the next king;
but it seems that he regarded this valley as being now
too obviously a royal necropolis to be safe from robbery.
There were at this time five royal sepulchres in it: those
of Thutmose I, II, and III, Hatshepsut, and Amenhotep II, as well as a number of small tombs wherein the
vizirs and other great personages were buried; and the
new king therefore decided to make his own tomb elsewhere. Immediately behind this valley there was
another ravine, and here, in virgin ground, he caused
his tomb to be excavated, amidst the boulders which lay
heaped about the base of a precipice. The entrance was
larger and more carefully hewn than those of his predecessors, but the chambers, passages and well in this
sepulchre followed pretty closely the plan of the tombs
of Thutmose IV and Amenhotep II; and the sarcophagus was placed at the far end of the pillared hall in a
depression in the floor similar to that first introduced
by Hatshepsut. The walls of this hall and of the well
were painted with the figures of the King and the gods,
and were inscribed with religious texts as before, all
these being more elaborately executed than had previously been the case. His mortuary temple was erected
on the edge of the fields to the south of the temple of
his predecessor, and two great seated figures of the King
were erected in front of its main entrance. These figures, now known as "The Colossi," still at the present
day sit facing the city of Thebes, though the temple
behind them has almost entirely disappeared.

During this Pharaoh's lifetime the death occurred of
his parents-in-law, Yuaa and Tuau, the father and

mother of Queen Tiy; and since the valley where his ancestors lay had now been abandoned by him, he was not unwilling to allow them to be buried in it. He therefore caused a new type of tomb to be made for them, which should be larger than those of the viziers and smaller than those of the kings. A flight of steps led down to the entrance, and then a short subterranean passage sloped down to a single undecorated chamber, some 30 feet long and 11 feet broad, in which the two mummies were laid to rest, surrounded by a mass of funeral-furniture.

An almost similar tomb was made for Queen Tiy during her lifetime, a short distance from this sepulchre of her parents. One descended by a flight of steps to a passage which sloped down to a single chamber, rather smaller than that of Yuaa and Tuau, since it had to accommodate only one mummy. The walls were undecorated, but were more carefully smoothed and shaped than those in her parents' tomb.

Akhnaton (B.C. 1375-1358) was the next king, but, for religious reasons, he removed his residence from Thebes to Tell-el-Amârna in Middle Egypt, where he was ultimately buried in a sepulchre amongst the desert hills some seven miles to the east of his city. A flight of steps led to the entrance, beyond which was a sloping passage terminating in another stairway. At the bottom of this was the well, and beyond it was the burial-hall in which the red granite sarcophagus stood, part of the floor being made at a lower level to receive it. One of the King's daughters died during his lifetime, and he therefore caused some extra rooms to be made for her leading off the corridor of his tomb. Akhnaton having abandoned the worship of the old deities, the walls of his tomb were not decorated with religious texts or paintings of the gods, but funeral and other scenes were substituted.

Before his death he associated Smenkhkara on the throne with him, but this king's tomb is not known, though it may be one of two tombs which were made in the vicinity of Akhnaton's. Then came Tutankhamen (B.C. 1358-1351) who brought the court back to Thebes, and abandoned Tell-el-Amârna; but he did not think it safe to leave Akhnaton's body lying in its remote sepulchre, and he therefore brought it back to Thebes. Having nowhere else to put it,—the position of the earlier tombs being now forgotten—he opened the tomb of Queen Tiy, where that lady had been laid to rest a few years previously, and placed the mummy of Akhnaton, her son, beside her.

He then began to make a sepulchre for himself; but the religious revolution of Akhnaton, and the abandonment of Thebes, had swept aside all traditions. The only tomb he had seen belonging to the old order was that of Queen Tiy, for the earlier tombs in the valley were deeply buried and their exact position lost; and he therefore modelled his tomb on hers, selecting a position not more than twenty or thirty paces from it. The usual flight of steps led to a sloping passage, at the end of which was an undecorated chamber; but wishing to make the tomb more imposing than that of ·Queen Tiy, he sank the floor level at one end of this chamber, in the manner he had observed in the tomb of Akhnaton (who had copied earlier tombs in this respect); and he then enlarged this lower part, and ultimately it was partitioned off by a built wall. Two small store-rooms were added, one leading from the outer chamber and one from the inner. The walls of the tomb of Akhnaton had been decorated with funeral scenes, and Tutankhamen therefore caused some paintings representing his own funeral, and some figures of the sacred apes of the sun, to be executed on the walls of his burial-chamber; but the outer room and passage were left undecorated as in the tomb of Queen Tiy. He does not seem to have built a mortuary temple for himself, but perhaps he used the now destroyed temple of Amenhotep III.

Queen Tiy's coffin had been placed inside a gilded wooden shrine; and the fact that all the royal tombs from that of Hatshepsut to that of Akhnaton had had a sunken area at one end of the burial-hall may perhaps indicate that a similar shrine or series of shrines had encased the sarcophagus of each monarch. Tutankhamen followed this custom, and made arrangements for his coffin to be enclosed in this manner; but we do not know whether the magnificent shrine or tabernacle recently found in his tomb was of large or small size as compared with those of his predecessors. Personally I should think it was not so big as that of, say, Amenhotep III.

King Ay, the father-in-law of the late Akhnaton, succeeded (B.C. 1351-1346); but, regarding his position as insecure, he decided to hide his tomb more effectually, at some remote spot where his body might escape the revenge of his enemies or the cupidity of thieves. He therefore selected a site in the valley to the west, where Amenhotep III was buried, but a considerable distance further up it. The entrance was hidden amongst a group of tumbled boulders; and the steps leading down to it were wider and more imposing than those of Tutankhamen's sepulchre. In general the tomb was mod-

elled on that of Akhnaton, at Tell-el-Amârna, but it
was on a larger scale. At the bottom of the first stairway a passage sloped down to another stairway, beyond
which was an ante-room, leading on the burial-chamber,
where stood a large sarcophagus of pink granite. The
walls of this room were painted with scenes representing
the King hunting wild-fowl amongst the reeds of the
marshes, and there were also some figures of the sacred
apes of the sun; but the main passage was undecorated.
He does not appear to have had a separate mortuary
temple.

Next came Horemheb (B.C. 1346-1315), a reaction-
ary Pharaoh whose great desire was to re-establish the
religious customs of the earlier kings of the Eighteenth
Dynasty. For this reason, and also perhaps because,
being a usurper, he wished to rest in the company of
the great Pharaohs of the past, he caused his tomb to
be made in the main valley, choosing a site between
the sepulchres of Tutankhamen and Amenhotep II.
Now, during the troubled times of the Akhnaton
"heresy," the tomb of Thutmose IV had been discovered by thieves and plundered; and an inscription has
been found which states that Horemheb "re-buried"
that king. He thus knew what that tomb looked like,
and he had also seen the sepulchre of his predecessor,
Ay. He therefore modelled his tomb on the scale of
the latter, but introduced many of the features of the
former, especially in the decoration.

Flights of steps and sloping passages, like those of
the tomb of Ay, led down to a well, as in the tomb of
Thutmose IV, beyond which there was the hall with the
concealed staircase in its floor, leading down to the large,
pillared room where stood the sarcophagus of pink

granite. The walls of the well were painted with figures of himself and the gods, as in the tomb of Thutmose IV; and on the sides of the burial-hall were inscriptions and scenes from the "Book of That Which is in the Underworld." Just before he died he gave orders that these paintings should be sculptured into reliefs, an innovation which had only begun to be carried out when it was interrupted by his death. The bones of four persons were found in his tomb, and it seems, thus, that other members of his family were buried with him. His mortuary temple is unknown.

I must not omit to mention that in the early years of his reign his hatred of the religious "heresy" of Akhnaton became so intense that he caused the tomb of Queen Tiy, in which that King had been deposited by Tutankhamen, to be opened and his name to be erased from his mummy and coffin. The tomb being contaminated by the presence of the "heretic," he then removed Queen Tiy's mummy elsewhere, and, leaving Akhnaton's body alone and bereft of its name, closed the sepulchre once more.

The next king was Rameses I, founder of the Nineteenth Dynasty (B.C. 1315-1314), but as he only reigned for one year he had no time to complete his tomb, which was situated a few paces from that of Horemheb, and which was evidently intended to be on the same scale. A fine flight of steps led down to a sloping passage and a second staircase, at the bottom of which there was to have been a well; but the King's death here interrupted the work, and instead of a well, a chamber was made in which the large pink granite sarcophagus was placed. The walls of this chamber were then decorated with paintings representing the King in the presence of the gods. When, some time later, this Pharaoh's widow died she was buried in a tomb specially made for her in another valley, some distance to the south, now called the Valley of the Queens; and from that time onwards for some generations, the queens were buried there, together with the royal princes.

The next Pharaoh was Sety I (B.C. 1313-1292), and he planned for himself a huge sepulchre very similar to that of Horemheb. It was situated close to the tomb of Rameses I, and the entrance is very similar, being now very much larger than the rough little entrances of the sepulchres of the earlier kings of the Eighteenth Dynasty. A flight of steps led down to a sloping passage, which was followed by another flight and a further continuation of the passage. Then came the well (now filled up), beyond which was a pillared chamber, with the usual concealed stairway in its floor. Another passage and another stairway then led down to the great hall in which stood the sarcophagus, on this occasion made of alabaster.

But no longer was the King satisfied with the old form of decoration: this tomb was sculptured from end to end with richly coloured reliefs and long religious inscriptions. The mortuary temple was erected to the north of those of his predecessors, not far from the mouth of the valley; and it is possible that at about this period some sort of roadway was made leading up to the royal burial-place.

The tomb of Rameses II, the succeeding king (B.C. 1292-1225) is so smashed up, and blocked with rubbish, that one cannot now say what it was like. It was situated but a few paces from that of Rameses I, and was evidently a large sepulchre, probably much like that of

Sety I. This King's mortuary temple, now known as the Ramesseum, was erected in the open ground between those of Amenhotep II and Thutmose IV.

The next Pharaoh, Merenptah (B.C. 1225-1215), made his tomb close to that of Rameses II; and one of these two was the first large royal tomb since the days of Hatshepsut, in which the well was dispensed with, nor was it again used. The hidden stairway in the floor of the wall beyond the well was also given up. But these protections against robbery being abandoned, it became necessary to find some other means of safeguarding the body; and this King, therefore, ordered an enormous outer lid of granite to be placed over his granite sarcophagus. So large was it, however, that the workmen failed to drag it into position, and it was left lying in one of the passages. The Pharaoh's mortuary temple was erected just to the north of that of Amenhotep III.

The next king Amenmeses (B.C. 1215), excavated a tomb for himself near by; but he appears to have been dethroned, and all the figures and inscriptions on the walls of the sepulchre were carefully obliterated. Septah and Sety II followed, each making a tomb for himself in the valley; and then came Setnakht, the founder of the Twentieth Dynasty. He began a tomb for himself a few yards from that of Amenmeses; but the latter must have been hidden and its situation forgotten, for the new tomb was driven straight into it and had to be abandoned. Queen Tausert, wife of Setnakht, being for some time sole ruler of Egypt, had a large tomb in this valley; and she allowed her vizir, the Chancellor Bey, to make an imposing sepulchre here for himself, which was an innovation.

Rameses III (B.C. 1198-1167), the succeeding king, deviated the course of the forsaken tomb of Setnakht, and made it into a very presentable sepulchre for himself; while his magnificent mortuary temple was erected at Medinet Habu, close to that of Amenhotep I.

An interesting sketch-plan of the tomb of Rameses IV, made by its architect, has come down to us; and in this it is interesting to notice that the sarcophagus is enclosed in five frame-like oblongs, one outside the other, these being painted to look like wood. It is probable that these represent a series of shrines or tabernacles built over the coffin, such as were found in the tomb of Tutankhamen.

After the reign of Rameses III the Pharaohs seem no longer to have taken much trouble to hide their tombs, and as they ceased to build mortuary temples for themselves at the edge of the fields, it is possible that the services on behalf of their souls were now performed at the mouths of the sepulchres themselves, for these mouths were now large and imposing, and the entrance passage was no longer a little rabbit-hole sloping at a steep angle, as in the case of the tombs of the earlier Pharaohs of the Eighteenth Dynasty, but was a fine level corridor of palatial proportions. Much bigger sarcophagi, with huge lids, were now used, as a protection against robbers; and thus each Pharaoh's body lay under several tons of granite.

The remaining Pharaohs of this dynasty were each called Rameses, and all of them, except one, were buried up here in the valley, Rameses XII (B.C. 1118-1090), who ended the Twentieth Dynasty, being the last king to make himself a tomb in this royal necropolis, which was no longer the wild and lonely ravine of earlier times, but a place that echoed with the voices and footsteps of priests and workmen.

But though these later tombs were no longer made in secret, the sepulchres of the earlier kings were well hidden; and it is obvious, for instance, that Rameses VI (B.C. 1157) did not know of the existence of the tomb of Tutankhamen (B.C. 1358); for he cut his sepulchre into the rock immediately above it, the earlier tomb being hidden under tons of chippings dumped there from the excavation of other tombs.

These later Ramesside kings lived in very troubled times, and they were quite unable to deal with the systematic robbery of the tombs which was now taking place here in the royal valley and also throughout the Theban necropolis. The tombs of the Pharaohs must have contained at this time a vast treasure of gold and semi-precious stones; and we can easily realise that since the small sepulchre of Tutankhamen, who was quite a minor king, has been found to contain so much gold, the larger tombs of the more important kings must have been huge storehouses of ancient wealth. A great conspiracy for robbing the tombs was detected in the reign of Rameses IX, and in another chapter I shall give an account of the trial of the culprits.

At length, some two centuries later, a devoted band of priests or nobles undertook the removal of all the endangered mummies which they could find, to a private tomb near Hatshepsut's mortuary temple, where they thought they would be safe; and here the royal coffins were ranged in a double row, the entrance being so effectually concealed that it remained lost and untouched until modern times. At some other period the

THE ENTRANCE TO THE TOMB OF TUTANKHAMEN
Cut into the hillside below the later tomb of Rameses VI.

tomb of Amenhotep II was discovered and opened, and another group of royal mummies was hidden in it.

During the centuries which followed the robbers ransacked the abandoned valley, stealing the gold and valuables, smashing the vases and utensils, and using the furniture for fuel: until, so far as we know, only three tombs remained undevastated—those of Queen Tiy, Yuaa and Tuau, and Tutankhamen. The two latter had both been slightly robbed shortly after the burials; but the tomb of Tiy, in which was the body of Akhnaton, remained intact until it was found by Mr. Davis and myself a few years ago.

I must now go back for a few moments to relate the subsequent history of the burials of the Pharaohs after the royal valley had been abandoned. On the death of Rameses XII, the priest-kings of the Twenty-first Dynasty held the throne until B.C. 945; but the necropolis in which they were buried has never been traced. The mummies of some of these Pharaohs were found in modern times in the hiding-place to which the ancient priests had carried the royal bodies for better protection, as related above; and it is clear, therefore, that the endangered tombs from which they were taken could not have been situated at any great distance. It is almost inconceivable that a group of royal tombs, each with its separate entrance, could have escaped the eye of native plunderers or of excavators, even though they were situated in some distant and remote desert valley; and I am therefore inclined to think that these kings must have been buried in one large mausoleum, like the Serapeum at Sakkâra, having but a single small entrance. Perhaps some day we shall hit upon this entrance in one of these desert valleys, and shall descend

into a great corridor from which the various royal sepulchres lead off, as in the case of the tombs of the Apis
bulls in the Serapeum, and shall find them full of magnificent funeral-furniture, not more damaged by the
ancient thieves than was the furniture of Tutankhamen.

The native Pharaohs who reigned over Egypt from
the Twenty-second to Thirtieth Dynasties (B.C. 945-
342) lived mainly in the Delta, and their tombs are lost
under the fields of that densely cultivated region. Herodotus states that the tombs of the Pharaohs of the
Twenty-sixth Dynasty were built in the temple at Sais,
close to the sanctuary; but the ruins of that city, near
Sâ el-Hagar in the Delta, offer little promise to the
archæologist. The sarcophagi of two kings of the Thirtieth Dynasty are preserved, one at Cairo and one in
the British Museum; but their tombs are lost.

The kings of the Ptolemaic Dynasty (B.C. 304-30)
were buried around the tomb of Alexander the Great at
Alexandria; and the ill-starred Cleopatra, the last
queen of Egypt, is stated by Plutarch to have built a
mausoleum for herself adjoining the temple of Isis in
that city. It was in this building that Antony died, and
here also the queen killed herself, thus bringing the
history of Egypt's royal tombs to an end in a tomb.

But to return to the Valley of the Kings at Thebes.
In Greek and Roman times tourists used to visit this
necropolis in considerable numbers, descending by
torchlight into such of the tombs as lay open, and they
were wont to scratch their names or scribble their com-
ments upon the sculptured walls. It is interesting to
notice that two of these sight-seers, Dionysios and Po-
seidonax, hailed from Marseilles, while some came from
other distant places. There is an inscription stating

that one Apollophanes of Lycopolis visited the tombs
in the seventh year of Antoninus; another visitor records
a date in the reign of Augustus; and there are a few
other dates to be seen.   There is the record of a certain
Jasios, who says: "I have seen the peculiarly excellent
workmanship of these tombs, which is unutterable to
us."   A Roman official named Januarius states in Latin
that he came with his daughter Januarina, and that he
"saw and marvelled"; and he says, "Valete omnes."   A
curious Christian prayer is: "O God Almighty, and
Saint Kollouthos, and Saint Father-Patermouthis, and
Saint Father-Ammonios the Anchorite, intercede with
God that He may grant life to Artemidora with Paph-
nuce for a little time . . . . " And the following is
rather amusing: "I, Philastrios the Alexandrian, who
have come to Thebes, and who have seen with my eyes
the work of these tombs of astounding horror, have
spent a delightful day."

In the time of Strabo some forty tombs were known
to exist, and Diodorus speaks of seventeen being open
in his day, but says that forty-seven were recorded in
the official register kept by the priests, which would
mean that they counted in several of the small pits
wherein the vizirs had been buried.   Napoleon's archæologists mention eleven; in 1835 twenty-one were open;
and at the present day, counting the small pits, over
sixty are known.

In 1881, the hiding-place wherein the ancient priests
had secreted the bodies of the kings, was found near
Hatshepsut's mortuary temple at Dêr el-Bahri.   A pit
some forty feet deep led to a passage about 220 feet
long, at the end of which there was a chamber containing the royal mummies.   Here were the bodies of

Ahmose I, Amenhotep I, Thutmose II and III, Sety I, Rameses II and III, and many others; some of them lying in their original coffins, some in coffins which did not belong to them. They were all taken to the Cairo Museum, where, sad to relate, some of them are "on show" in glass cases, to be jibed at by flippant visitors.

For the last five and twenty years extensive excavations have been conducted in the Valley. In 1899, M. Loret, who was then Director-General of Antiquities in Egypt, discovered the tombs of Thutmose I, Thutmose III, and Amenhotep II; and in the last named he found the bodies of Thutmose IV, Amenhotep III, Merenptah, Rameses IV, Rameses V, and Rameses VI, which had been taken there by the priests, as mentioned above, in order to save them from the robbers. Large numbers of antiquities were found, but these tombs had all been much pillaged, and presented a spectacle of great devastation, the objects being broken up and scattered and the bodies in most cases much knocked about.

In 1902, Mr. Howard Carter, at the expense of Mr. Theodore M. Davis, excavated the tomb of Thutmose IV, and found many antiquities therein, mostly smashed up. In the following year he found the tomb of Queen Hatshepsut, but hardly anything had been left in it by the plunderers. In 1905, Mr. Quibell and I, working at the expense of Mr. Davis, found the tomb of Yuaa and Tuau, the parents of Queen Tiy, and here at last a burial was brought to light which had not been much damaged by thieves, though the bodies had been disturbed and the jewellery taken. Here were wonderful chairs, beds, tables, chests, and so forth, which are described in my *Glory of the Pharaohs*.

In 1907, Mr. Davis's excavations, under my super-vision, led to the discovery of Queen Tiy's tomb, in which the body of Akhnaton was found wrapped in sheets of gold. In a hiding-place under a rock, not far away we found a blue-glazed cup bearing the cartouche of Tutankhamen, and in a tomb-pit we discovered a number of fragments of gold, probably torn from funeral-furniture, inscribed with the cartouches of that king and his wife, and with the name of Ay as a private individual, that is to say before he came to the throne. These were probably the remains of a robbed tomb of a vizir or noble. The same excavations laid bare the tomb of Horemheb in 1908, but this had been badly plundered and not much was found.

Five years ago these excavations in the Valley were taken over by the late Lord Carnarvon and Mr. Carter, who were rewarded by the discovery of the tomb of Tutankhamen, the greatest "find" ever made in Egypt. Only a very small portion of this wonderful valley now remains to be examined, and perhaps there are no more royal tombs to be found, though it may be hoped that one or two will still be discovered—the tomb of Smenkhkara, for instance.

At the present time, visitors from all over the world come to Luxor, the modern town built upon the site of ancient Thebes, to see the ruins left by the Pharaohs; and, crossing the Nile to the West bank, they go up to the royal necropolis by the road which has now been made along the winding valley, or they walk over the cliffs by the bridle-path which passes across the hills above Hatshepsut's temple. Seven of the most im-portant tombs are lit by electricity, and sixteen are open to the public. The once desolate and lonely gorge, how-

ever, would hardly be recognised in the present well-
kept and well-guarded tourist-resort, with its tidy roads
and neat walls and its many tombs each protected by
iron gates.

CHAPTER III

THE TOMB OF TUTANKHAMEN

IN the year 1915 Mr. Howard Carter, working at
the expense, and with the help, of Lord Carnarvon,
began the excavations in the Valley of the Tombs
of the Kings which resulted, in 1922, in the discovery
of the tomb of Tutankhamen. During these years he
made a systematic examination of the sides and bed of
the valley hidden under the tons of rock-chippings
thrown out in ancient times by the workmen employed
in tunnelling the royal tombs into the hillsides. This
mass of debris deeply covered the lower surfaces of the
cliffs and slopes around the valley; and it was Mr. Carter's object to leave no single portion of the rock-face
unexamined, lest the entrance to some buried tomb
might be overlooked. During previous excavations on
this site, only certain promising sections of the valley
had been fully examined; and I may mention that in
the work financed by Mr. Davis, between 1905 and
1912, we had cleared the areas on both sides of the spot
at which the new discovery was afterwards made, but
we had here left a small section untouched, because at
this point there was the large tomb of Rameses VI, and
we did not think it likely therefore that any other
sepulchre would be found within that area of the hillside.

Mr. Carter, however, during the course of his complete clearance of the valley, removed the accumulations
of debris from the slopes of the hill just below this

tomb; and the thoroughness of his work was justified and rewarded by the discovery one day of the lintel of a doorway of a sepulchre which evidently passed into the hillside exactly under this Rameside tomb. When the tons of chippings and rocks were cleared away, a flight of some sixteen steps was laid bare, leading down to a walled-up doorway; and it was apparent from the shape and style of this entrance that he had found a tomb of the Eighteenth Dynasty.

He at once telegraphed to Lord Carnarvon, who was then in England, informing him of the discovery; and, at the end of November, 1922, when the latter had arrived at Thebes in answer to the welcome summons, the sealed doorway was opened, and an entrance was effected by the excavating party, who then found themselves in a plain, rock-cut passage, leading down at a steep angle into the darkness.

With beating hearts the excavators walked down this sloping way, which was just high enough to permit of their standing upright, and which proved to be about five-and-twenty feet in length.

At the bottom there was another wall, built across a doorway, and covered with plaster, stamped with the seal of the necropolis; but there were indications that robbers had entered through a small hole which later had been blocked up and re-sealed, probably by the ancient officials of the necropolis. When this hole had been pierced, Mr. Carter, holding an electric torch, thrust his head and arm through, while Lord Carnarvon and his companions waited breathlessly to hear what he saw.

"Wonderful! Marvellous!" Mr. Carter exclaimed; and soon Lord Carnarvon was pulling at his arm, cry-

ing: "Hi! let me have a look!" But Mr. Carter, lost in
the wonder of all he saw, could not be moved, and for
some moments Lord Carnarvon was obliged to wait
with such patience as he could command.

At last Mr. Carter was pulled from the hole, so the
scene was jestingly represented to me, "like a cork
from a bottle," and Lord Carnarvon took his place,
afterwards vividly describing what he saw as looking
like the property-room behind the scenes at a panto-
mime, so full of strange figures and furniture was the
dark chamber.

Presently Mr. Carter squeezed himself through the
aperture, and dropped into the silent room beyond,
where no footstep had trod for some three thousand
years; but once inside he could not be persuaded to
come back: he was like a ferret gone into a hole. His
hollow voice bade them wait, and they heard only his
exclamations echoing in the darkness, and saw the flash
of his torch as it passed from one group of shining
objects to another. At length he returned with the
news that the tomb was undoubtedly that of Tutankhamen, whose cartouche was inscribed on many of the
articles; and, after the entrance had been somewhat
widened, the other members of the party were able to
climb into the chamber. The scene which they beheld
was bewildering in its magnificence and its strangeness.
The room, which was hewn out of the limestone rock
and was undecorated, was about 25 feet long from north
to south, 12 feet broad from east to west, and 9 or 10
feet in height, the entrance being at about the middle
of the east side. It was stacked with gorgeous funeral-
furniture, so well preserved that the enormous gulf of

time between the present day and the era of the Pharaohs was bridged in an instant.

The north wall, which was a built partition, covered with pink plaster, was at once seen to shut off a further chamber, or an extension of this room; and in the middle of the wall there was a doorway blocked up by stones entirely covered with grey cement whereon were stamped the royal seals. This did not seem to have been touched, but on the other hand, the chamber in which they now stood showed evident signs of having been hastily ransacked in ancient times by tomb-robbers, who had probably entered it a few years after the burial, or perhaps in the troubled times of the later Ramesside kings.

To those who saw this blocked-up doorway, as I did, while yet the sealing was unbroken, the thought was awe-inspiring that in the darkness on the other side of the wall the Pharaoh for whom the sepulchre had been made lay slumbering in his coffin, and would soon be aroused. One wondered whether his sleep of three thousand years and more was already being disturbed by the voices and the footfalls of the excavating party, or whether, deep in oblivion, he had not yet heard the sounds in the outer chamber.

But while the sealed doorway showed at once that the full extent of the discovery could not be ascertained for a long time to come, the extraordinary collection of objects in this first chamber was sufficient to defeat the comprehension and to overwhelm the brains of those who now stood staring about them in amazement. All around the room the funeral-furniture was stacked against the walls or lay upon the floor in confusion, so that there was little space in which to move about. The ancient robbers had roughly heaped beds, chests, and chairs on top of one another during their search for objects of intrinsic value, and had emptied the contents of caskets and boxes on to the floor. Then had come the officials of the necropolis, who had hastily attempted to tidy the place up, and had crammed some of the scattered clothes and miscellaneous articles back into these boxes again, but had not touched the disordered heaps piled up against the walls.

The chamber looked, indeed, as Lord Carnarvon said, like a full store-room at a theatre, in which actors in a hurry had been wildly searching for some lost article, and had heaped the boxes, the furniture and the bizarre stage-properties out of their way.

It was difficult for the brain to take in the fact that these shining pieces of furniture had been placed in the tomb centuries before ancient Rome was heard of; and the excavators were conscious of a feeling of fantastic unreality as they crept about the room, the electric lights which they carried casting their shadows like black phantoms upon the walls.

Two life-sized and awe-inspiring wooden statues of the Pharaoh guarded the sealed doorway in the north wall, one at either corner, facing each other. In each case the figure wore a headdress covered with gold-leaf, a gold-collar, gold bracelets, gold skirt or kilt, and gold sandals. In the left hand was a long, gold walking-stick or staff, in the right a mace; and the left foot in each case was thrust forward as though the figures were walking, staff in hand, to meet one another. The eyes and eyebrows were inlaid, the latter in pure gold, and the bare flesh of the face, trunk, and limbs was painted with a dark substance like bitumen. Each figure stood upon an oblong pedestal of wood; and so narrow was the room that the front of each pedestal projected some inches beyond the sides of the blocked doorway, leaving a space between them of no more than four or five feet. Thus an ancient robber tampering with the sealed doorway would stand between these lifelike figures, and might well have expected them to step forward and close in on him, glaring at him with glassy eyes, and to strike him down with the heavy mace which each carried.

It may have been for this reason that a linen garment had been tossed over the arms and head of the figure on the right, and now hung there, fallen into decay and full of small holes. In many Egyptian tombs which have been plundered by robbers, the eyes of the statues or of the figures sculptured on the walls have been destroyed by the thieves, so that they should not see the evil work which was being done; and in this case I think one of the robbers must have flung this robe over the statue for a similar purpose.

Between the two figures there were the remains of some reed mats, a basket, and three or four alabaster vases; and, nearby, there were two great bouquets of flowers and leaves, so well preserved that they looked as though but a few weeks had passed since they left the hands of the florist. In front of these there was an exquisite painted wooden casket with an arched lid, which ultimately proved to contain some of the King's robes. On its four sides and on the lid were charming paintings in rich colours, executed in the manner of the finest miniatures, representing hunting scenes in the desert, in which the King in his chariot was shown pursuing ostriches, gazelle, wild asses, and hares. There were also decorative designs here, depicting the Pharaoh in the form of a human-headed lion, clawing at fallen Ethiopians and Asiatics.

Close by there was a long narrow wooden box standing on four legs: it was painted black and white, and, on being opened, was found to contain the King's undergarments, several staves, many arrows, an ivory-handled whip, and a mace.

The great mass of the funeral-furniture, however, was placed along the west wall of the chamber; and here the most imposing objects were three great funeral-couches, ablaze with gold, the first or northernmost having its sides made in the form of lions, the second in the form of cows, and the third in the form of hippopotami. These couches each consisted of four pieces jointed together, as it was later seen, by surprisingly modern-looking hooks and staples of bronze:—there was the bed itself; there were the two elongated creatures which formed the sides supporting the bed, as it were, slung between them; and, underneath, there was a square frame of woodwork on which the legs stood, this being to prevent the feet wearing holes in the stucco of which Egyptian floors were usually made. They were high, massive constructions, and were too short to carry an averaged sized man lying at full length: a fact which indicated that they were never used as beds, but were simply made for the purposes of the funeral, being, in fact, biers rather than couches.

A couch or bier with sides in the form of lions is often shown in tomb-paintings, with the coffin resting upon it; and the cow and hippopotamus are both animals connected with the Underworld, as may be seen in the Papyrus of Ani, where both are represented standing together at the foot of the hills of the necropolis.

The cow was the form assumed by Hathor, goddess of these hills; and the hippopotamus, usually associated with the goddess Taurt, appears sometimes to have been connected, also, with Hathor. In the tomb of Horemheb we found fragments of three similar couches, with sides made in the form of hippos, lions and cows, and there are representations of three similar couches in the tomb of Sety I; and thus their use seems definitely to be mortuary rather than domestic.

In the case of the lion-couch, the faces were close up to the north wall of the room, and could not at first be seen by the excavators; but the long, thin bodies covered with gold, and the tails which swept up from the foot of the bed in a wide curve, presented a striking sight. Just behind this stood the couch with the cow-sides. The two heads were each surmounted by high horns between which was the disk of the sun; the golden, elongated bodies were dotted all over with shamrock-shaped spots —the usual conventionalised treatment of the markings of the hide; and the tails were fashioned as before in a bold curve. Behind this again was the golden hippo-potamus-couch, the heads of the two creatures being modelled with startling realism. The mouths were open, showing teeth made of alabaster, and tongues of ivory; the ears were pricked up; and, at the other end, the stumpy tails projected stiffly towards the south wall of the chamber.

The room was only just long enough to accommodate these three couches, one behind the other; and it seemed rather as though they had been made exactly to fit into this space. On top of them, and under them, and around them, the other objects were stacked in baffling array.

On the lion-couch there was a wooden bedstead, this being one actually used, or intended for use, and not an article of ritual significance; and here there were also a beautiful little chest, and various other objects, including some candlesticks made in the form of the *ankh,* or sign of life, one of them still holding the tow candle itself. Fayence candlesticks in the form of the *ankh* were found in the tomb of Amenhotep II and elsewhere; but the present examples were of more elaborate workmanship and shape. Underneath this couch there were some charming caskets; a very beautiful and highly decorated armchair of wood inlaid with ivory; and four wonderful alabaster vases each with an amazing tracery of lotus and papyrus stems and flowers carried out with such consummate art that those who saw them exclaimed that they were the most superb objects of the kind ever fashioned in alabaster.

On the middle couch another bed, a box of clothes, an armchair of wood and basket-work, and some delicately carved stools were heaped; and underneath it there was a great pile of thirty or more oval boxes, like immense Easter-eggs, containing embalmed joints of beef, haunches of venison, trussed ducks, liver, and so forth—the food for the King's spirit. In front of these boxes there was a beautiful stool made of ebony, with legs in the form of long-necked ducks' heads, inlaid with ivory, and mounted in gold. The seat was also of carved ebony, inlaid with ivory to represent the spots of a leopard's skin. Here also were a stool made of rushes and basket-work, and two caskets. On the lid of one of these the King's necklace of glazed beads and pendants, was lying; and near it there was a twist of linen on to which a large number of blue fayence finger-rings had been drawn.

Resting on the hippopotamus-couch there was, among other things, a large wooden box or trunk; and underneath the couch there was a magnificent throne or armchair,—one of the finest pieces in the whole amazing collection. It was made of wood covered with gold and silver; the arms were carved to represent winged serpents and were richly inlaid in blue enamel; and the legs were those of lions. On the back were figures of the King and Queen encrusted with semi-precious stones.

At the south end of the room in a confused and gorgeous heap, there were three two-wheeled chariots which had been taken to pieces at the time of the funeral, but had been piled up by the robbers in a disordered mass. The light bodies, or cars, were tumbled at different angles, and four of the wooden wheels, decorated with gold, were stacked against the wall, while others lay underneath the debris, together with the shafts and yokes.

The largest of these chariots was a semi-circular structure, open at the back, made of wood covered with shining gold-leaf, and having delicately embossed decorations and exquisitely inlaid designs in carnelian, malachite, lapis-lazuli, vivid blue glaze, and alabaster—that is to say, browns, greens, blues, and whites, set in gold. At each corner was a small inlaid circle, enclosing the sacred eye, as though to suggest the all-seeing omniscience of the monarch as he drove through the streets of his capital. The inner surface of the car was of gold, with large embossed cartouches of Tutankhamen and his queen. The edges of the car and the handrail around the top were covered with red leather; and between this

A SKETCH OF THE GOLDEN SHRINE IN THE BURIAL CHAMBER
OF TUTANKHAMEN

A reconstruction by the author.

rail and the body were small carved figures of Semitic and Ethiopian captives.

The other cars were somewhat smaller, and were inscribed with the cartouches of the King, but not with those of the Queen. One of them was evidently a sort of triumphal chariot, for there were scenes upon it showing rows of captives roped together, while the human-headed lion, symbolic of the Pharaoh, had its claws in Egypt's enemies.

In front of these chariots there were some alabaster vases, and behind them there were other boxes and caskets and a little wooden shrine, plated with heavy sheet-gold, the doors of which were open, suggesting that a gold statuette had been removed from inside. Near this was a fine *ushabti*-figure of the King, inscribed with four perpendicular lines of hieroglyphics.

Here, also, there was an almost lifesize bust carved in wood and painted in a lifelike manner. The face and neck were coloured that brownish-yellow which, in the main periods of Egyptian history, was the conventional hue used to represent feminine skin, but which was sometimes employed also for male figures. On the head was a crown which might have been a shortened form either of the Pharaoh's crown of Lower Egypt or of the crown first worn by Nefertiti, the mother of Tutankhamen's wife. The features of the face showed that soft, languorous expression which the artists of the period 'loved to portray, and the mouth was slightly smiling in a tired, rather bored manner. It was hard to say whether the face was that of a woman or a man, and the colour of the skin and the shape of the crown were those of either sex. The lobes of the ears were pierced as though to receive jewels; but this, again, did not determine the sex, earrings being worn by both men and women. The body was cut off at the waist, and was covered with a tight-fitting white robe which revealed a figure more like a man's than a woman's. Only the stumps of the arms were shown, as in the case of a bust.

This curious figure was obviously a sculptor's portrait-bust, and called to mind other such busts known in Egyptian art—those of the Twenty-sixth Dynasty for instance, found at Sakkâra and elsewhere, which in each case have the top of the crown, and the arms, cut off in like manner. It was thus, a portrait-bust which had been placed in the tomb in conformity to some ancient custom; but it was hard to decide whether it represented the King himself, or his wife, who is known to have been young and childless, and whose figure, therefore, might have had no pronounced feminine lines.

The strange and beautiful face of this figure, with its large, soft eyes, looked out at the excavators from amidst the shadows cast by an overturned chariot, and held their admiring gaze for some time. But as they stooped to examine it, their attention was attracted by a hole in the wall under the legs of the hippopotamus-couch, close by. This hole proved to be an aperture made by the robbers in the sealed doorway of a small room leading out of the main chamber; and on holding the electric lamp close to the opening they found the chamber within to be crammed with glistening objects, heaped up one upon another. At the time of writing this chamber has not yet been examined, nor the mass of obviously wonderful antiquities in it touched.

Such was the general appearance of the tomb as the excavators saw it; and when they climbed back into the entrance passage, and so went up once more into the

light of the sun, they brought with them the memory of
an experience such as no other living man has enjoyed.
No great royal tomb in anything like an intact condition
has ever been discovered before. The most spectacular
"find" previous to this was that of the tomb of Yuaa and
Tuau, great grand-parents of Tutankhamen's wife: *
in this case the tomb was found to be full of funeral-
furniture, but though the objects were very fine, they
were neither so numerous nor so magnificent as those in
Tutankhamen's sepulchre.

A close examination of the new discovery, during
the next day or two, revealed still more wonders. There
were some superb sticks or staves, one of ebony with a
golden handle carved in the form of the head of an
Asiatic, and another decorated with an exquisite pattern
of beetle's wings. In one of the boxes there was an inlaid gold buckle made in the form of the King's cartouche: the first sign, *Ra,* being of carnelian; the second
sign, *Kheper,* of chased gold; the third, the three plural
strokes, of lapis-lazuli; and the fourth, *Neb,* of green
enamel. In another box the excavators found a pair of
wonderful sandals, of which the part which passed over
the instep was exquisitely designed in inlaid gold: a
lotus flower in the middle, with a duck's head and a
cluster of little rosette-like flowers on either side, all
inlaid in semi-precious stones. Elsewhere, there were
two boomerangs of gold and fayence; many utensils in
beautiful blue glaze; gold-covered sticks; all manner of
robes, unfortunately in a very fragile condition; and so
forth.

One little box contained a lock of plaited hair, such
as youths wore at the side of their head before they

* Described in my *Glory of the Pharaohs.*

reached manhood; and on this box there was an inscription, reading: "The sidelock which his Majesty wore
when he was a boy." In another box there was a little
hood or cap, with a flap hanging down to protect the
neck from the sun. It was made of fine linen covered
with gold sequins, and was of a size to fit a young child.
A child's gauntlet-glove of linen was also found, which
was startling in its modern appearance. Both the hood
and the glove may have belonged to the King when he
was a child, or perhaps to his girl-wife, the little daughter of Akhnaton, who became queen when she was but
nine years of age. There was also another pair of gloves
lined with fleece.

On the floor of the chamber there had been baskets
of grain, but most of it had been upset by the robbers
and was lying about in small heaps. In one of the boxes
there were several squares of folded material which
looked like papyrus, and at first the excavators thought
that these might be letters or documents of some kind;
but on examination they proved to be simply folded
napkins.

Lord Carnarvon and Mr. Carter were at first bewildered by the extent of their discovery, and their
anxieties, both as to the handling of the objects and as
to their safety from robbery, weighed heavily upon
them. The first thing to be done was to take photographs of the interior of the tomb; but their efforts in
this regard met with failure, and, indeed, they risked a
conflagration by using flash-light. Electric light had
then to be installed in the tomb, the current being taken
from the engine which supplied the light in the neighbouring show-tombs. A burglar-proof doorway had to
be affixed to the entrance of the sepulchre, and arrange-

ments had to be made for a guard of soldiers to remain stationed at the mouth, night and day.

It was decided that the work would have to be undertaken in the following manner. First, these objects in the front room would have to be treated one by one with chemical preservatives, and carried across the valley to one of the large, open tombs which would serve as a workshop. Then, when the room was clear, the sealed doorway into the burial-chamber could be opened; and later on the mass of objects in the store-chamber leading from the first room could be tackled.

Mr. Carter, and his assistant, Mr. Callender, could not do the work by themselves; and the director of the neighbouring excavations of the Metropolitan Museum of New York very kindly, therefore, placed at Lord Carnarvon's disposal two English members of his staff, Mr. Mace and Mr. Burton, the former an expert in handling fragile objects, and the latter a first-rate photographer. The services of Mr. Lucas, an English chemical analyst, were also engaged to deal with the preservative treatment of the objects. The work being thus arranged, Lord Carnarvon returned to England, promising to come back to see the opening of the sealed burial-chamber, some time in February.

A few weeks later the long business of bringing up the objects began, and daily the sight-seers from the hotels and river-steamers at Luxor gathered at the mouth of the tomb to see the transportation of these wonderful antiquities to the workshop. I arrived at about this time; and for several weeks I rode up to the Valley almost every day to watch the progress of the work, going down into the tomb, by the courtesy of the Egyptian Government, on two or three occasions.

It was an extraordinary experience to leave the dazzling sunshine and to descend into the stillness of the rock-hewn passage which led down into the first chamber. Suddenly the light and warmth of the sun were gone, the sounds of the living world outside were silenced, and one passed in a moment from the Twentieth Century after Christ into the Fourteenth Century before Christ, from the strident active present into the mute and paralysed past. It was as though the mind had taken a strange backward leap, and had swept swiftly across the centuries like the eye of a god.

But equally dramatic it was to sit on the wall of the parapet above the mouth of the tomb, and to watch the pieces being brought up from the depths into the sunlight which they had not seen for nearly thirty-three centuries. Perhaps the most spectacular arrivals were those of the three great ceremonial couches, described above, each of which came up in four sections—first the actual bed; then the two elongated creatures which formed the sides; and lastly the rectangular frame of wood on which the legs stood.

In the case of the lion-couch the heads of both were sculptured with great artistic feeling and boldness, the gaunt cheeks, the hungry eyes, the pricked-up ears, and the conventionalised yet ragged mane conveying an instant and vivid impression of a sort of ferocious power. The legs were thin and the clawed feet large and clumsy like those of a big puppy; and the tail swept over the back in a bold and spirited curve which was obtained by using the flexible wood of the vine, as we observed in the case of the fragments of a similar lion-couch found in the tomb of Horemheb. The dramatic effect of the arrival of these two lions up from the Underworld was perhaps somewhat lessened by the fact that Mr. Carter brought them out tail first in each case, but presently he considerately turned them round, so that their haggard golden faces stared into the noonday sun.

The second couch, that with the Hathor cow on either side, was brought up on another day; and the arrival of these two bizarre creatures, whose expression was one of astonishment as they emerged into the sunshine after their thousands of years in the darkness, caused a murmur of excitement amongst the assembled sight-seers. The expression on the faces of the hippopotami which formed the sides of the third couch, was, on the other hand, one of frank laughter when they came up from the tomb into the daylight and saw the strange company of tourists gathered to greet them; but their ears were pricked up as though they were alert and listening—as indeed they well might be after nearly thirty-three centuries of silence.

Day after day the crowd which assembled to watch the removal of the different objects increased in size. Now it was a glistening chariot that was taken to the workshop; now a gilded chest or casket, and now a tray bearing bouquets of flowers or a collection of odds and ends. As each of these loads was carried along the valley, soldiers armed with rifles marched behind it, and pressmen and visitors ran by the side clicking their cameras and scribbling their notes. Thus, almost daily, there was some little triumphal procession to the workshop to delight the spectators; and the interest was maintained all through January and the first half of February.

At last the preparations for the opening of the burial-chamber were complete, and nothing remained in the first room except the two statues which stood on either side of the sealed doorway. On Friday, February 16th, just before half past one, when the deserted valley was ablaze with the mid-day sun, and a police sentry yawned at his post, the little party of those who were to make the opening, silently filed down into the hollow in which is the mouth of the tomb. The opening of the first chamber had taken place in comparative privacy; but now at the unsealing of this inner doorway there were about twenty persons present altogether, consisting of the excavators, and a number of distinguished individuals, including two or three Egyptians.

Down they went into the pool of blue shade, like the Forty Thieves descending into the magic cavern; and silently they removed their coats and hats in preparation for their adventure. There was something very solemn, and even tragic, in this awakening of the once great king now when his empire was long fallen to pieces and his glory departed; and as I took my place at the mouth of the tomb I felt, if I may say so without affectation, a sense of deep sadness weighing upon me.

The wind suddenly got up as the party went down the steps, and it blew the hot, white dust about, sending it up into the air in angry little scurries. One might almost have thought it to be connected in some way with the spirit of the dead Pharaoh, petulant and alarmed at being disturbed, or perhaps annoyed at the jokes and laughter of some of the resurrection men, who had abandoned their silence and had become jocular as they went into the sepulchre. A number of cane chairs had been taken down into the bare first room, so that the party could watch while the sealed wall was broken down; and Lord Carnarvon, perhaps somewhat overwrought by the excitement of the moment, made the jesting remark that they were going to give a concert down there in the sepulchre. His words, though of little moment, distressed me, for I was absorbed, as it were, in my own thoughts, which were anything but jocular; and I turned to the man next to me, and said: "If he goes down in that spirit, I give him six weeks to live." I do not know why I said it: it was one of those curious prophetic utterances which seem to issue, without definite intention, from the sub-conscious brain; but in six weeks' time, when Lord Carnarvon was on his deathbed, the man to whom I had addressed the words reminded me of them.

The proceedings were opened with a speech by Mr. Howard Carter and a few remarks by Lord Carnarvon, at the end of which there was some nervous applause from the scantily clad company seated upon the chairs, who were already perspiring in the heat of the small chamber, lit by the glaring arc-lamps. Then a hammer and chisel were produced, and the wall which had tantalised us all for so long was cautiously attacked.

This was at 1.50 p.m., and as the first blows reverberated through the room, a thrill shot through me like something that burnt in my veins, and I seemed to see the Pharaoh in the darkness on the other side of the doorway suddenly wake from his long slumber, and listen. It was the ancient Egyptian belief that the sleep of Death lasted three thousand years, and thus the time was up, and it might well have seemed to him that the day of resurrection was come, and that the jackal-headed Anubis had arrived at long last to carry his soul to the Judgment Hall of Osiris, there to weigh his heart in the balances against the symbol of Truth, that he might be vindicated or found wanting.

Tap-tap went the hammer, and outside in the sunlight another gust of wind, wailing through the valley, violently spun the dust into the air. Tap-tap: and as the first stone of the wall which blocked the doorway was displaced, I felt with peculiar intensity that there must be some message to give to the Pharaoh, if only I could find it, some word of comfort to fortify him at this solemn hour of his summons from the sleep of oblivion.

Perhaps it was because I deem him to be the Pharaoh of the Exodus, or perhaps it was the strange event of the disentombing itself, which directed my groping thoughts; but somehow, of a sudden I knew that the message to be given to the awakening dead was that the Ancient of Days was still Lord of men's lives, that the passage of the years which had changed so much had left Him still the unchanged hope of the world. I suppose my Egyptological colleagues will call me a sentimentalist; but nevertheless I will admit that I was overwhelmingly conscious of the presence of God at that hour, and with all my heart I wanted the awaking King to know that he was safe in His hands, and that there was nothing to fear.

It was at 3.30 p.m., that the doorway was sufficiently cleared to permit of an entrance; and now through the aperture a huge golden shrine could be seen gleaming in the light of the arc-lamps which were directed upon it. This shrine, which stood upon a stone floor three feet lower than the floor of the outer room, seemed to fill almost the entire inner chamber, only a narrow passageway being open upon the front or east side of it; and down into this passage the excavators prepared to

squeeze themselves.   There was silence now in the tomb;
and, in the valley outside, the wind had dropped as suddenly as it had arisen, so that there, too, all was still.

At this moment a hawk, in ancient days the emblem
of the royal house, came swiftly over the hills from the
direction of Thebes, and hovered above the mouth of
the tomb, poised in mid-air against the blue of the sky.
Then it sailed away, down the valley and into the west.

Inside the chamber the company assembled were
staring with wide eyes at that portion of the great
shrine which could be seen standing close up to the inner
side of the partition wall, beyond the now open doorway.   It was a huge box-like structure, made of wood
covered with gold-leaf, and having a very beautiful blue-
green porcelain inlaid between the gilded symbols which
formed the decoration.   Along the side of the curved lid
a winged serpent was represented, whose coils wound
away into the darkness; and beneath this there was a
broad golden band on which was an inscription which
read, so far as I could see it:—"All the gods who are in
the Underworld declare that the King, the Lord of the
Two Lands of Egypt, Lord of the Creations of the
sun, Son of Ra, who loves him, Tutankhamen, is . . ."
The rest of the declaration was lost in the darkness,
owing to the closeness of the shrine to the wall.

Lower down, and immediately opposite the aperture
in the wall, two magical eyes were engraved on the side
of the shrine.   These are often seen on sarcophagi, and
were represented there so that the dead man might look
out through them from his prison inside, and see all that
went on; and if the ancient magic be still potent, Tutankhamen must have been watching every movement of
his disturbers as they broke down the sealed wall.

Mr. Carter, Lord Carnarvon, and, after a while, one or two others, now squeezed themselves round to the front of the shrine; and here they found two great golden doors with heavy bronze hinges, closed and bolted. In the narrow passage-way there was only just room to open these doors in order to see what was inside the shrine; and it was with difficulty that Mr. Carter, working in the intense heat and airlessness of this cramped space, managed to force them open.

Inside there proved to be another and smaller golden shrine of a similar kind, the doors of which were bolted and sealed with the unbroken seals of the royal necropolis. Over this inner shrine a pall of fine linen spangled with gold was thrown; and I recalled that in the intact tomb found by Professor Schiaparelli some years ago at Dêr el-Medineh a linen pall, but of a plainer kind, was lying over the sarcophagus in just this manner. The inside surfaces of the outer shrine were covered with religious texts and decoration; but little of this could now be seen.

No attempt was made to open these inner doors, for it was clear that inside them there would probably be found a sealed sarcophagus, within which there would be an outer and an inner coffin; and only after all these had been opened would the mummy of the Pharaoh be reached. It was at once realised that the taking to pieces of the outer shrines (which had evidently been put together after the body had been laid to rest) and the removal of the lids of the sarcophagus and coffins would be the work of months; and thus, though one might imagine the Pharaoh's rest to have been disturbed by the noise of the breaking down of the entrance to the burial-chamber, by the creaking of the hinges of the golden doors of the shrine as they swung open for the first time for nearly thirty-three centuries, and by the clattering footfalls and excited voices of the excavators, the hour of his actual awakening was seen at once to be postponed for many months or even years. As the great doors of the shrine were closed and bolted once more, it was as though he had been bidden to sleep on yet a little while, and to fear nothing.

The excavators now turned their attention to the walls of the chamber in which the shrine stands. Upon them there were many paintings and inscriptions of a religious character, but the narrow space between the shrine and rock-hewn sides of the room only permitted the wall which faces the golden doors to be seen with clearness. Here there was a large painted scene representing the mummy of the King resting on a funeral barque, which was being drawn upon a sledge by priests or nobles, each wearing a white band around his head. Representations of a funeral such as this are common in the tombs of the nobles, but are unique in a Theban king's tomb; but we must remember that Tutankhamen was the first king to be buried after the Tell-el-Amârna heresy, which had swept all traditions aside, and that the scenes and texts from the Book of the Dead which are to be found on the walls of earlier royal tombs were not in use at this epoch.

In the dim light at the other end of the chamber behind the back of the shrine, one could just see a painting on the wall, representing one of the sacred apes of the sun, like those which are to be seen in the tomb of Ay, the Pharaoh who succeeded Tutankhamen. Both this and the funeral scene mentioned above were somewhat roughly painted, and had little artistic merit.

Leaning up against the wall at the back of the shrine there was a gold-covered standard of the jackal-god who was called "Opener of the Paths" for the dead. I could not see it closely, but it was certainly unique. On the floor, at the side of the shrine, lay seven golden oars, finely decorated, these having a significance connected with the belief that the soul of a dead king sailed like the sun-god across the heavens in a golden barque. Oars of this kind have been found in other royal tombs.

On the right side of the passage in front of the shrine in which the Pharaoh lies, there was, just beyond the golden doors, an opening hewn in the rock, which led into a small chamber; and, looking into this, the excavators beheld a sight indescribable in its magnificence. Here a marvellous collection of funeral-furniture was seen, and the electric lights directed upon it revealed objects of shining gold and bright colours piled up almost to the ceiling.

Near the entrance was a figure in black and gold, representing the jackal-god Anubis resting upon a sledge. Similar figures have been found in other royal tombs, but not, like this, in perfect condition. Behind it was the head of an ox, carved in wood, somewhat similar to one found in the tomb of Amenhotep II. On the right side of the little chamber were great numbers of boxes of various shapes and sizes, some of them gilded and coloured, but most of them painted black with bitumen. These were all sealed, and their contents could not yet be ascertained; but, judging by those found in the tomb of Yuaa, they contain *ushabti*-figures, vases, religious symbols, and possibly papyrus and jewellery. Here, too, there was a shrine-like chest with doors standing open; and inside there were two golden statuettes of the King, one wearing the crown of Upper Egypt, the other of Lower Egypt, and each standing on a leopard beautifully carved. The fragments of similar figures were found in the tomb of Amenhotep II.

At the end of this chamber there was a most beautiful gilded chest, surmounted by rows of royal cobras. At its four sides were exquisite figures of four goddesses, their faces turned towards the chest, and their arms extended as though pleading to be left unharmed. Their figures were slight and childlike, and golden robes or shawls were draped over their outstretched arms. This wonderful chest probably contains the four "canopic" jars, in which the internal organs taken by the embalmers from the body of the King, are separately preserved.

Behind it more boxes were stacked; and to one side there was another group of caskets, made of ivory and wood, some inlaid with enamels and semi-precious stones, others decorated with gold. Here, too, was yet another chariot, and near it there were models of sacred boats.

Amongst the mass of other objects, two alabaster vases of exquisite workmanship must be mentioned. One of these, made of beautiful translucent stone, was in the form of a chalice with two delicately curved lotus stems projecting from the sides and supporting two flower-like cups. There was some exquisitely carved open-work around the base and sides of the chalice. Another object worthy of note was a very fine scarab, perhaps the most beautiful ever found.

The number and richness of these objects were overwhelming, and it was at once apparent that it would take three or four seasons' work to deal with them. One season will be occupied in removing the as yet untouched mass of objects stacked in the chamber which leads from the first room; another season, or perhaps two, will be spent in taking the great shrine to pieces and opening the sarcophagus and coffins; and yet another will be required for the handling of the funeral-furniture in this new store-chamber. And, when all these articles have been taken from the tomb, there will remain a couple of years' work in their cataloguing and photographing. Thus the story has but begun; and year by year there will be fresh wonders to relate.

It was already 4.30 p.m. when the excavators' party left the tomb and climbed up the stairs into the daylight. Lord Carnarvon, always a delicate man, looked pale and exhausted as he came up out of the depths; and on the face of all those who had been present there were marks of fatigue and over-excitement. It had been a day of days; and as I drove down the long desert road back to Luxor in the dim light my thoughts were all of that royal sleep which had been disturbed, and of the littleness of man's life, and of the mightiness of that Power in Whose eyes a thousand ages are as the twinkling of an eye.

On the next day, Saturday 17th, little work was done; and on Sunday 18th, there was the official ceremony of the opening to be faced. This ceremony was very different in character from that of the previous Friday. Then it had been to most of us an eerie and tense business; but on Sunday it was a noisy affair. The valley was crowded at an early hour, and at mid-morning the Dowager-Sultana arrived with her ladies.

There were soldiers springing to the salute; officers with clanking swords shouting orders; kinema operators

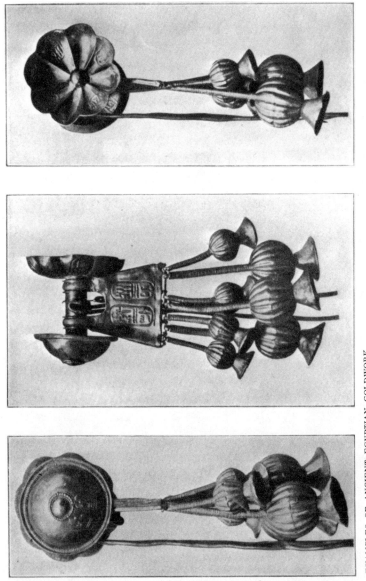

EXAMPLES OF ANCIENT EGYPTIAN GOLDWORK

The gold ear ornaments of Sety the Second, found near the TOMB OF TUTANKHAMEN

running up the hillsides, while native boys climbed behind them carrying their apparatus; crowds of European and American visitors in every kind of costume
from equestrian to regatta; Egyptian notables looking
very hot in western clothes and red tarboushes; tall
black eunuchs in long frock-coats; dragomans in bright
silken robes; and so forth.

The Sultana was taken into the tomb to look over
the broken-down barrier-wall into the chamber beyond;
and everybody photographed her as she went in and
again as she came out, while the soldiers saluted and the
dogs barked.

After she had gone her royal way with mounted
policemen trotting behind her, half smothered in dust,
various other important personages were taken down
into the tomb. Then came picnic luncheons; and presently the Queen of the Belgians and Field-Marshal
Lord Allenby, the British High Commissioner of
Egypt, arrived; and once more the soldiers lined up
and cameras clicked. It was a gay and animated scene.

As for myself I sat for the greater part of the day
upon a stone, like an old owl, brooding upon the strangeness of life, and, as on the Friday, my heart was heavy
and my head full of dreams of other days. The opening
of this tomb still presented itself to my mind as the
disturbing of a sleeping man, and the forcing of some
sort of ordeal upon him; and my feeling for him was
one of intense pity. It was as though he were somebody
who had been left behind by mistake after all his friends
and loved ones had become dust; someone who was alone
in an alien age, and who was being awakened to face
thousands of staring eyes not filled with reverence but
with curiosity.

But when the day's events were over, and all the throng departed, I went over to the mouth of the tomb and stood there for a while in the gathering dusk. There was not a sound in the valley except the distant and subdued murmur of the voices of the watchmen and the police who were crouched around the evening fire, the smoke of which went up into the still air in a thin line. The haze of approaching night lay over the cliffs and hillsides around, enfolding them in a soft and muted peace.

There came into my mind the words of Neferhotep, a minstrel who had lived in the time of Tutankhamen; and in the stillness of the twilight it was almost as though they were coming up to me out of the tomb. "I have heard those songs that are inscribed in the ancient sepulchre, and what they tell in praise of life on earth and belittling the region of the dead. Yet wherefore do they this in regard to the land of Eternity, the just and the fair, where fear is not? Wrangling is its abhorrence, nor does any there gird himself against his fellow. That land, free of enemies!—all our kinsmen from the earliest day of time rest within it. The children of millions of millions come thither, every one. For none may tarry in the land of Egypt; none there is that passeth not thither. The span of our earthly deeds is as a dream; but fair is the welcome that awaits him who has reached the hills of the West."

CHAPTER IV

TUTANKHAMEN: THE HISTORICAL PROBLEMS

THE enormous number of objects found in the tomb of Tutankhamen * have advanced our knowledge of ancient Egyptian arts and crafts in an unexpected and quite astonishing manner; but historically the discovery has left us as we were. So far no important new facts have been forthcoming to add to the information we already possess in regard to this most interesting period; but the great "find" has, of. course, focussed our minds upon this particular epoch of Egyptian history, and thus certain avenues of speculation have been opened up, which might otherwise have remained unnoticed for yet some years to come. I propose here to direct the reader's attention to some of these unexplored lines of thought, with the purpose more of stimulating discussion than of reaching definite conclusions. When the objects in the inner chambers are examined, and when the body has been taken from its sarcophagus, and studied by anatomical experts, we may come upon various facts which will substantiate or refute these theories and suggestions.

The history of Tutankhamen rises out of that of Akhnaton, the famous "heretic king," whose reign from B.C. 1375 to 1358 stands as the first great landmark

* Amen, Amon, Amun, Ammon are all readings of the same name, the pronunciation being probably Amoon.

99

in the higher development of the human brain; and we must therefore begin by considering this period. Akhnaton was the son of Amenhotep III and Queen Tiy, in whose life-time Egypt was at the height of her power, and was mistress of the chief parts of the civilised world. The wealth of Thebes, the capital of this empire, was enormous, and life had reached a condition of luxury which has never been surpassed in the East.

At this time, however, the whole country was under the heel of the priesthood of Amon, the proudest and most conservative community which conservative Egypt ever produced. It demanded implicit obedience to its strict and ancient conventions, and the worship of the host of gods, of which Amon was king, had become a complicated and exacting business, as intellectually low and primitive as its state of organisation was high and pompous. As is so often the case, a luxurious civilisation had brought with it a great increase in the outward ceremonial and inward emptiness of the state religion; and gross superstition was everywhere to be seen.

Then the young Pharaoh Akhnaton, a mere boy, filled with an overwhelming zeal for truth and sincerity, set himself to overthrow the entire structure. As soon as he came to the throne he began to direct men's eyes to the worship of the true God, almost as we understand Him now, under the name of Aton, a deity having very close connections with Ra-Horakhti, the sun-god of Heliopolis. Aton, he declared, was the intangible, formless, omnipresent Father of mankind, the controller of that remote, yet proximate Force, which, for want of a better definition, was called the life-giving energy behind the power of the sun. He was the tender and merciful "Father and Mother of all that He had made," the "Lord of love," the "Comforter of them that weep," in Whose eyes even the chicken in the egg and the smallest fish in the river were creatures to be watched over and made to rejoice in His love. Akhnaton called upon his followers to search for Him not in the confusion of battle nor behind the smoke of sacrifices but amidst the everyday scenes and events of nature, and in the heart's happiness. The sunlight being His most obvious manifestation on earth, sun-worship was an outward aspect of the new religion; but Akhnaton again and again explained that God was not the sun itself but the "Master of the Sun," the energy which sustained it and all creation.

In the fourth year of his reign, abandoning the city of Thebes with its many temples dedicated to Amon and the old gods, the young King founded a new capital at Tell-el-Amârna, which he called the "Horizon of Aton." Here a beautiful palace was prepared for him; a splendid temple dedicated to Aton was set up amidst an extensive garden; fine streets were laid out; and in the neighbouring hills the tombs and mortuary chapels for himself and his nobles were cut out of the rock. In this city of his dream he preached his astonishingly enlightened monotheism, a doctrine of truth and love, moving about freely amongst his people and personally directing the carrying out of his plans. He himself, so the records say, originated the new canons of art of which such exquisite examples have come down to us; he himself taught his people to walk in the way of truth; and he himself wrote the religious hymns, amongst which there is the undoubted original of our 104th Psalm, many of the verses of which in the hieroglyphic script are almost word for word those of the Hebrew version.

The foremost law of Akhnaton's religion was identical with the first Mosaic commandment, namely that no graven image either of the true God or of the older gods was to be made or worshipped; and towards the end of his reign he even went so far as to cause the word "gods" to be cut out of the religious inscriptions upon the old temples.   In particular he issued orders that the name of Amon, the arch-enemy of his new religion, should be erased from every inscription in the land: a drastic measure which was carried out in the minutest manner, so that the ruins to-day everywhere bear traces of these erasures, and even tombs were opened in search of the hated name.

His doctrines were of an entirely pacific character. He did not believe that warfare or military domination over other countries was compatible with his creed of universal gentleness and love; and when revolts broke out in his Syrian provinces he seems to have refused to fight.   There is no more pathetic page of history than that which tells of his soldiers' desperate efforts to hold the nations of the empire faithful to their King.   Some of the letters imploring him to take action were discovered at Tell-el-Amârna some years ago, and the tragedy of the fall of the Egyptian power in Syria can still be read.   Akhnaton sacrificed all glory and dominion to his ideals, and before his short life drew to a close he had lost the fruits of all the conquests of his fathers.   He reigned seventeen years, thirteen of which were spent at Tell-el-Amârna, and his age at his death was thirty years at most.

His queen, Nefertiti, bore him seven daughters, but

no son. The eldest of these daughters, Merytaton, he
married to a noble whom, in the last years of his reign,
he associated on the throne with him, under the name of
Smenkhkara. The second daughter, Meketaton, died
as a child; the third, Ankhsenpeaton, was afterwards
married to Tutankhamen; the fourth, Neferneferuaton,
was married to the son of the King of Babylon; and the
remaining three, of whom we know practically nothing,
were still very young when their father died, the last
having been born some two years before his death.

We know nothing as to the origin or as to the fate
of Smenkhkara. He seems to have been one of Akhnaton's devoted followers, and he generally wrote after
his name the words "Beloved of Akhnaton," indicating
that the King's love for him was his title to the throne.
He disappeared from the scene at about the same time
as Akhnaton, and his place was taken by Tutankhamen
or Tutankhaton as he was called at his accession.

I will suggest the following possibility as to Tutankhamen's origin. During the reign of Akhnaton the
most important courtier was a certain Tutu, who held
the position of court chamberlain. As in the case of
all important nobles of the period, a tomb was prepared
for him, during his lifetime, in the hills of Tell-el-
Amârna; and from the scenes and inscription upon its
walls a considerable amount of information regarding
his career can be gleaned. He explains that he was the
"supreme mouth-piece of the entire land," and that his
particular duty was to introduce foreign envoys and
ambassadors to the court. "My voice," he says, "was
not loud in the King's house, nor my walk swaggering
in the palace. The King rose early every day to teach
me, because of my zeal in carrying out his teaching."

And he adds that he grew wealthy, thanks to the bounty of his master, and received many rewards from him.

When this tomb was made for him he appears to have been unmarried or a widower, for there is no mention of a wife; nor are his parents referred to. In the Tell-el-Amârna letters we find him called Dudu, which is evidently the same name as Tutu, and we see that he was the close friend of a certain Amorite prince, named Aziru, who ultimately proved traitorous to Akhnaton and joined the rebels in Syria. Aziru addresses Tutu as "My lord" or "My father," which suggests that Tutu was an elderly man. As his particular work was that of introducing foreigners to the court it may be that he was an Asiatic himself. The name Tutu or Dudu is probably a form of Daoud, which we call David.

Now, since there was no male heir to the throne, it is highly probable that the most important and powerful man in the kingdom would seize it on the death of Akhnaton; and when we recollect that the most powerful man at the time was named Tutu, and that the new king was named Tutankhaton, "Tut, living in Aton," one is much tempted to identify *"Tutu,"* the court chamberlain, with *"Tut*-living-in-Aton," the Pharaoh.* We know, as mentioned above, that Tutu had no wife while he was chamberlain; we know that Tutankhaton, the king, was married to Akhnaton's daughter, Ankhsenpeaton; and thus we are justified in surmising that Tutu was either married to the princess towards the close of Akhnaton's lifetime and hence had a claim, through her, to the throne, just as had Smenkhkara,

* The word *Tut* must not be pronounced as though it rhymed with *but:* it more probably rhymes with *rude*, being, in fact, indistinguishable from Daoud, the native form of David.

the other son-in-law of the King, or that Tutu married her at Akhnaton's death to legitimise his accession.

When the body now lying in the newly discovered tomb is examined we shall probably learn the age of this king at his death. The so-called "dummy" found in the tomb represents a youthful face, and if it be a portrait of the King it would certainly indicate that he was but a lad; but, on the other hand, the Cairo statue is that of a much older man. If an examination of the mummy shows him to have been a young man, then his identification with Tutu will become improbable, unless we are to suppose that the court chamberlain of a youthful king could be also but a youth, and that the term "My father" used towards him by Aziru is only a meaningless title of honour; but if the mummy is found to be that of a middle-aged or elderly man, I think we may safely make the identification. The suggestion that he was the son of Akhnaton by a concubine has no fact to support it. In a certain inscription Amenhotep III is referred to as his "father," but the word here probably means "predecessor." For the present the problem must remain in abeyance.

Tutankhaton did not remain long at Tell-el-Amârna. The priesthood of Amon had once more raised its head at the death of Akhnaton, and, finding the country ready to revolt against the mismanagement of affairs by the Tell-el-Amârna government, it persuaded the new king to abandon his late father-in-law's Utopian city and to bring the court back to Thebes. The King realised that a compromise between Amon and Aton was the only way to save the country; and therefore, changing his name to Tutankhamen, and his wife's to Ankhsenamen, he returned to the ancient metropolis, leaving Akhnaton's temples and palaces, villas and gardens, to become the haunt of jackals and the home of the owls. Akhnaton's body was carried back to the old capital, and was laid to rest in the Valley of the Tombs of the Kings, in the tomb of his mother, Queen Tiy; and, a few yards from it, Tutankhamen caused a tomb to be prepared for himself.

He celebrated his return to Thebes by building the famous colonnade in the Temple of Luxor, afterwards appropriated by the Pharaoh Horemheb. This colonnade is the most imposing part of the temple, and was at that time about the biggest building of its kind in Egypt. He caused its walls to be decorated with scenes showing the wild enthusiasm of the populace at his return and the first celebration of the great Amon festival; and the modern visitor may still see representations of the people dancing, beating drums, and blowing trumpets, in their excitement.

During Akhnaton's reign the temples of Amon and of the old gods had been neglected; and in the last years an absolute persecution of the old priesthoods had taken place; but the new Pharaoh restored these buildings and re-established their revenues, and in a great inscription at Karnak he tells us in vivid phrases how he did so. "The temples of the gods," he says, "had come upon bad times. Their courts were a road for common feet. The land was overridden with plagues, and the gods were neglected." But "His Majesty searched for what was useful for Amon," made his image in pure gold, raised monuments to other gods, filled their buildings with foreign slaves, and multiplied their estates.

He reigned at least six years, for the sixth year is mentioned on a piece of linen found in the Valley of the

Tombs of the Kings some years ago, but to the end of his life he seems to have hovered uncertainly between the Amon and Aton religions, though now there was no longer any thought of monotheism. He was succeeded by Ay, the maternal grandfather of his queen, who, after a brief reign, gave place to Horemheb, formerly commander-in-chief of the army. Horemheb legitimised his accession by marrying Ay's daughter, Nezemmut, sister of Akhnaton's queen Nerfertiti; but later in his reign he turned upon the whole Akhnaton brood, and erased from the records the names of Akhnaton, Smenkhara, Tutankhamen, and Ay, vilifying particularly the memory of Akhnaton and calling him "that criminal." His reign came to be dated from the death of Amenhotep III, Akhnaton's father, these intermediate kings being ignored; and thus we find in the tomb of Mes at Sakkâra a reference to his 59th year, although actually he did not reign for more than about 30 years, while in the famous list of kings at Abydos he is given as the immediate successor of Amenhotep III.

In his book, *Contra Apion,* the ancient Jewish historian, Josephus, quotes a long passage from the now lost works of Manetho, the Egyptian historian who lived in the second century B.C.; and in my opinion this passage, which has been more or less ignored by Egyptologists as legendary and fanciful, actually gives a fairly correct account of the Tell-el-Amârna episode as viewed by those who were opposed to it.

A certain Pharaoh Amenophis (Amenhotep), says Manetho, wished to hold communion with the gods, and he therefore asked the advice of Amenophis-son-of-Papis, a wise man, who told him that he must first clear the country of all impure persons. Some 80,000 unclean people were therefore collected and sent to certain quarries on the east bank of the Nile that they might be separated from the rest of Egypt, but no violence was offered to them. This wise man, however, saw into the future that these unclean persons would obtain dominion over the whole land for thirteen years; and this he so dreaded that he committed suicide, leaving behind him a letter of warning to the King, who was much grieved.

After a few years the city of Avaris, in Lower Egypt, was also assigned to these polluted people, and there they found a leader in the person of a certain priest of Heliopolis. They made a law for themselves that they would not worship the old gods of Egypt, nor reverence the sacred animals; and, deciding to open hostilities against the rest of Egypt, they invited certain wandering Semitic people to their aid, who came to them in great numbers. The Pharaoh Amenophis was afraid to fight them at first, because he thought that would be to war against the gods; so he went to Memphis, took the sacred Apis bull from the temple there, sent his little son Rameses, a boy of five, into hiding, and marched into Ethiopia, where he lived in exile under the friendly care of the King of Ethiopia. Meanwhile, the confederacy of unclean Egyptians and Asiatics destroyed the images of the old gods, slaughtered the sacred animals, and committed every kind of outrage on orthodoxy; but at length the King returned from Ethiopia, overthrew them, and chased them out of Egypt.

Such is Manetho's story of what Josephus calls "the fatal thirteen years," and though it is confused it is evident to me that it describes the thirteen years of the Aton "heresy" at Tell-el-Amârna. The wise old Amenophis-son-of-Papis is a well-known historical character who died at the end of the reign of Amenhotep (Amenophis) III, Akhnaton's father. He must have been an enemy of the rising Aton-worship, for he was Overseer of the Sacred Cattle of Amon and Leader of the Amon Festival. He was certainly a man whom the King would have consulted, and such a matter as the removal of a multitude would come within the scope of his official work, for he is known to have organised the whole country, and particularly to have had the management of all foreign slaves. How he died we do not know, but that the King took his death to heart is shown by the fact that he personally established the old man's mortuary temple in the 31st year of his reign, which is just about the time of the rise of the Aton religion.

The 80,000 unclean people I take to be the heretic Aton-worshippers, and their removal to the quarries on the east bank of the Nile corresponds very strikingly to the historic transference of the whole capital of Akhnaton from Thebes to Tell-el-Amârna, a district on the east bank of the river, famous at that date for its quarries, then known as Hetnub. We know from the inscriptions from the tomb prepared for Horemheb at Sakkâra before he came to the throne, that Akhnaton allowed Asiatics to settle in Egypt. We know also that the Tell-el-Amârna heresy lasted exactly thirteen years, as Manetho here says, for Akhnaton in one of his inscriptions speaks of it beginning in the fourth year of his reign, and he died in the seventeenth.

The persecution of the orthodox Egyptians is exactly in accordance with the known facts; and it is highly probable that when this persecution became intense, towards the end of the fatal thirteen years, those who were faithful to the old gods would have been obliged to fly southwards to Nubia and the borders of Ethiopia, just as the Mamelukes fled thither before the wrath of Mohammed Ali. That the Nubian princes were friendly is known from the paintings and inscriptions in the tomb of Huy, Tutankhamen's Viceroy in those regions; and the sovereign of the land of Maam in Nubia is there given the honourable title of "the good prince," which is most unusual.

Manetho makes all the events occur under one Pharaoh, whom he calls Amenophis. Actually, they began under Amenophis or Amenhotep III; but, as has been mentioned above, Horemheb dated his reign from the death of this Amenhotep, and this may partly explain why Manetho mentions only one king. Manetho states that the King of Egypt was told that he must turn out the impure people if he wished to hold converse with the gods. On the great stela of Tutankhamen at Karnak that monarch tells us that he restored the old temples because he had found that the gods would not hold converse with him, which is a remarkable corroboration of Manetho's statement. With reference to the mention of the Apis bull it is interesting to note, too, that Tutankhamen is known to have buried one of these sacred creatures in the Serapeum at Sakkâra with full honours.

This same Pharaoh, though still linked to some extent with the Aton heresy, made war on the Asiatics, and we read of "that day of the slaying of the Asiatics"; but it was Horemheb who finally thrust them out of Egypt. Horemheb's successor (not son) was Rameses

I, who may well have been only five years old, as
Manetho states, at the time when the orthodox Egyptians went into exile. We do not know from the monuments anything about this exile, but, as has been said,
it is very probable. Horemheb was once loyal to the
heretic Akhnaton, but the persecution begun at the
close of that reign may have caused him to leave Egypt
for a short time. If the little boy, Rameses, was then
five years of age he would have been nearly fifty years
of age at his accession on the death of Horemheb in
B.C. 1315, which is quite in accord with the known historical facts.

I think it is clear, therefore, that we have here without question Manetho's account of the Aton heresy; but
now comes the interesting point in regard to Tutankhamen. Manetho states that the priest of Heliopolis, who
led the confederacy of unclean people at Avaris was
none other than Moses.

If he is correct we may suppose that Moses was
born in the reign of Amenhotep III; that he fled to the
land of Midian in the reign of Akhnaton; that Akhnaton's death is referred to in Exodus ii, 23, in the words:
"And it came to pass in process of time that the King
of Egypt died"; and that Tutankhamen was the Pharaoh under whom Moses returned to Egypt and organised the exodus of his enslaved countrymen.

How does this accord with the known facts? Until
now the all-important date of the Exodus has never
been decided by Egyptologists; and tradition has
simply associated these events with the Pharaoh best
known to it—Rameses the Great. The Biblical evidence is contradictory. In Kings vi, 1, it is stated that
480 years elapsed between the Exodus and the building

of the temple at Jerusalem. The latter date is fixed at
B.C. 973, which would give B.C. 1453 as the date of the
Exodus. But, on the other hand, in Exodus i, 11, the
Israelites are said to have built the treasure cities of
Pithom and Raamses before they left Egypt, and
these cities are generally thought to have been built
under Rameses II, the Pharaoh who came to the throne
in B.C. 1292, though actually, as Dr. Gardiner has
pointed out,* their identification with earlier cities is
likely. The only piece of Egyptian evidence in regard
to early Israel occurs in an inscription in the fifth year
of the Pharaoh Merenptah, B.C. 1220, in which there is
a list of foreign conquests, including that of Israel; but
all we can gather from this is that the Jews were then
a recognised nation apparently outside Egypt.

The genealogies given in 1 Chronicles vi, however,
supply yet another date; for they give eleven or twelve
generations between the time of Exodus and that of
David (B.C. 1000). One generally allows three generations to the century, as, for example, in the case of the
genealogy of the Pharaohs of the Eighteenth Dynasty
down to Amenhotep III; and this takes us back to somewhere between B.C. 1360 and 1330 for the Exodus.
Tutankhamen reigned from B.C. 1358 to about 1350;
and therefore these genealogies bring us just to the
required date.

There is another computation which brings us to
somewhere about the same date for the Exodus. We
read in the Book of Exodus that the whole period of
the sojourn of the Israelites in Egypt was 430 years,
and a rabbinical tradition states that 190 years of this
period were passed before the oppression and 240 years

* Part No. 234 of the *Bibliothèque de l'Ecole des Hautes Etudes.*

THE HALL BUILT BY TUTANKHAMEN IN THE TEMPLE OF LUXOR

after it. In the Book of Genesis the prophecy is made that the Israelites shall pass 200 years in bondage; but as there is no means of saying whether this 200 years or the 240 years is the correct figure, we may as well split the difference and reckon that the bondage lasted somewhere about 220 years. Now most scholars are agreed that the oppression began when Ahmose I, the first King of the Eighteenth Dynasty, conquered the Asiatics who had been living in Lower Egypt all through the Hyksos period, and made himself master of Syria. This conquest took place somewhere about B.C. 1570, about ten years after the accession of Ahmose I; and, reckoning the bondage from that date, we reach about B.C. 1350 for the Exodus, which thus falls within Tutankhamen's reign. It may be, however, that the oppression started when the kings of the Seventeenth Dynasty first began their wars against the foreigners, somewhere about B.C. 1590; and if the 240 years is the correct figure, we would thus again reach B.C. 1350 as about the date of the Exodus.

The Tell-el-Amârna letters, however, afford the most striking testimony to Manetho's correctness in assigning the days of Moses to this period. From these letters we learn that Akhnaton's last years were overcast by the revolts in Syria, and we obtain a vivid picture from them of events in that country. We see the Hittites pressing down from the north; we see the Amorites in arms under their prince Aziru; and we see a horde of tribesmen, called the Khabiri, pushing into Palestine from the south and east. In one case we have a letter from Ninur, a queen of part of Judea, who calls herself Akhnaton's handmaid, and entreats him to save her from the Khabiri, who have captured one of her cities. There is another letter, this time from Ribaddi, King of Byblos, in which he says that the fortress of Simyra has fallen into the hands of the Khabiri. A letter from a certain Ebed-tob says that the Khabiri are capturing his forts, and another letter from him states that they are laying everything waste. Other letters show that Aziru, the Amorite, was in league with these Khabiri against Akhnaton.

Various scholars have hazarded the suggestion that the Khabiri are to be identified with the Hebrews, as the similarity of the names may indicate; and if this be so we must suppose that at this time hordes of Semitic peoples—Hebrews—related to the children of Israel resident in Egypt were pouring into Palestine and carrying all before them. Now, Moses conceived the idea of the Exodus while he was living in Midian, one of the centres from which the Khabiri are thought to have been moving northwards into Palestine; and thus if he lived at this period we can see how he was there told of this land flowing with milk and honey which his fellow-Semites were conquering, and how he determined to go back to Egypt and to raise his oppressed countrymen, urging them to march out of Egypt and to join the other Hebrews, the Khabiri, in their attack on Palestine. The Exodus of the Israelites from Egypt therefore becomes simply part of the great movement of the Semitic tribesmen, which was taking place at this period; and thus it is a far more understandable event than it can ever be if it is regarded as an isolated adventure. Those who are willing to believe that Moses had sufficient to inspire him in the word of God given from the burning bush, may be able to think of the decision of the Israelites to march out of Egypt as being justified; but those of us who have been unable to accept the recorded divine intervention as fact, have had to regard the Exodus as the extreme of recklessness. Now, however, by fixing it at this date when these tribesmen were all on the march northwards, we can see clearly what induced the Israelites in Egypt to set out across the desert and what made the adventure seem certain of success. In this case it is quite possible that the Biblical story of the invasion of Palestine under Joshua is to be identified with the invasion of the Khabiri as told in the Tell-el-Amârna letters, and that these events occurred before the Exodus and wanderings of the Israelites, and not after. Indeed the leader of the Khabiri, so often referred to in these letters as "that dog," may be Joshua himself.

The Biblical narrative suggests that although the Egyptians were using the Israelites extensively as slaves in their building operations, they were ultimately not unwilling to let them go, and indeed in Exodus xi, 1, and xii, 39, the latter are described as being "thrust out of Egypt." This accords well with the suggestion that Tutankhamen was on the throne at the time, for we know from his Karnak inscription that he was employing Asiatic slaves in his great work of rebuilding the temples ruined by Akhnaton, and at the same time representations of him chasing Asiatics out of Egypt have been found. I need not point out how wide an area of thought is opened up by this supposition that Moses lived through the Aton heresy; for the question as to what connection there was between the Hebrew monotheism and this earliest known monotheism of the Egyptians will at once present itself to the reader. It is a subject which deserves the fullest study.

With reference to the plagues, it is interesting to notice that Tutankhamen in the same inscription speaks of Egypt as being plague-ridden in his reign. In regard to the death of the first-born, it is to be noticed that Tutankhamen had no son to succeed him. The Pharaoh of the Exodus, by the way, was not himself drowned in the Red Sea; for the hymn of Moses, given in Exodus xv, makes that clear.

Let us now look for a moment at the traditional stories of the Exodus given in the Jewish Talmud. This ancient book states that the Pharaoh under whom Moses fled to Midian was afflicted with leprosy; but it is possible that the story originated in the fact that the King was religiously unclean, like the 80,000 who in Manetho's account left Thebes, that is to say, he was a heretic. If this interpretation of "leprosy" be correct, we have here a fact which points clearly to Akhnaton as the monarch in question. The Talmud further states that this Pharaoh fell from his chariot and was badly injured, but survived as an invalid for three years. Have we here the record of an accident which occurred to Akhnaton?—and does this explain why it was that Smenkhkara was associated on the throne with him during these last years of his reign?

Another curious statement is made in the Talmud. It is said that when this Pharaoh died he left two sons and three daughters, and that the son who succeeded him was a dwarf. Now Akhnaton, when he died, left two sons-in-law, and, apart from their wives, three little daughters, as mentioned above, one other daughter having died, and another having gone to Babylon. Was

Tutankhamen, then, a dwarf? We must leave the answer until his body is examined; but it is interesting to recall the fact that in his tomb were found a very small glove and cap, and some very small stools, while his statue in the Cairo Museum is only about five feet in height. Moreover, the word *Tut* may be regarded as an Egyptian word, and not as the Asiatic *David,* in which case it means a figure, or statuette, or puppet, and is the sort of name a man of small stature might be expected to have. This, however, is merely an amusing speculation.

Another interesting problem which I may here touch upon in conclusion is that relating to the fate of Tutankhamen's queen, Ankhsenpeaton, afterwards called Ankhsenamen. She was born in or about the eighth year of the reign of her father, Akhnaton, and was only nine years old when he died. She was married to Tutankhamen, therefore, at about that age, which is by no means uncommonly young for marriage in Egypt; and when her husband died, some seven years later, she was still only about sixteen, and was childless.

Among the Hittite archives, discovered at Bohaz Keui, there is a letter written by a Hittite king in which he gives the following curious information. During the reign of his father, he says, the King of Egypt, Tutankhamen, died, and the widowed queen, whose name was Dakhamun, wrote to him saying that her husband was dead and that she had no children, and therefore that if the Hittite king had a grown-up son she would like to marry him. An ambassador was at once sent to Egypt to report, and especially to find out how it was that she had no heir.

Owing to a lacuna the remainder of the letter is not

easy to understand, but it appears that the queen explained that no man had had seed by her, and that if she now married the Hittite prince she would be able to make him King of Egypt. She then selected one of the Hittite king's sons, but the letter does not tell us whether she ever actually married him, nor do we know from other sources what happened to her.

It is hard to reconcile the name Dakhamun with Ankhsenamen, yet we must do so, since the latter had been Tutankhamen's sole queen; and thus we see how this sixteen-year-old widow was fending for herself. At the death of her husband the throne had passed to Ay, the father (not foster-father, as some Egyptologists have thought *) of Nefertiti, Akhnaton's queen. Ay was thus Ankhsenamen's grandfather; but that fact did not deter her, it seems, from attempting to oust him from the throne and to put a Hittite in his place in order to save herself from retirement. It is significant that the next king, Horemheb, fought the Hittites, as shown on his pylons at Karnak; and we are left wondering whether Tutankhamen's ambitious widow was the cause of the war.

These are some of the problems which present themselves to the mind in regard to the reign of Tutankhamen; but we must wait some time yet before more light can be shed upon them from the tomb.

* Compare his titles with those of Yuaa, father of Queen Tiy: Ay's wife, Ty, was evidently Nefertiti's step-mother.

CHAPTER V

THE ANCIENT GHOULS OF THEBES

THE ruins of the ancient city of Thebes, once the capital of Egypt, stand on the east bank of the Nile, some 450 miles south of Cairo. On the opposite side of the river there is a two-mile strip of flat, cultivated land, wherein are numerous clumps of trees and groups of native huts; and behind this verdant plain rise the mighty hills of the desert, bounding the view like a wall of gold against the deep blue of the sky. At the back of the first range of hills lies the desolate valley in which the tombs described in the previous chapters are situated, and which is approached either by a road entering this barren region of rocks and cliffs along a gorge where once flowed a primeval torrent, or else by bridle-paths over the heights. In this valley practically all the Pharaohs of Egypt who reigned between the years B.C. 1500 and B.C. 1000 were buried, their sepulchres being cut into the face of the cliffs or hillsides and penetrating deep into the solid rock in a series of passages and halls.

It was the Egyptian custom to bury a large amount of jewellery with their dead, and the Pharaohs selected this remote and unfrequented valley for their necropolis, in order that their sepulchres should not be attacked by robbers, as those of their predecessors had been. Some of these earlier kings, as far back as B.C. 1800, had been buried in small pyramids built at the exposed

119

foot of the hills, at the edge of the cultivated land overlooking the Nile; and already, in B.C. 1500, many of the
tombs had been pillaged. But although the succeeding
Pharaohs hid their sepulchres away so carefully in the
valley behind, the secret was not kept for long, and soon
the new necropolis came to be as insecure from the
plunderers as the old.

About B.C. 1150, when a line of degenerate Pharaohs of the name of Rameses had, for some generations, ruled a nation fast slipping down the road to ruin,
a systematic robbery of the royal sepulchres which were
not well hidden commenced; and such fear for the safety
of the mummies of the Pharaohs was felt that a few
years later the priests entered all the known tombs and
carried off the royal remains, placing them together in
a secret hiding-place, where they lay undisturbed until
they were discovered in 1881 and conveyed to the
museum in Cairo.

This hiding of the Pharaohs was only resorted to
when the corruption of the Government no longer permitted the thieves to be arrested and brought to justice.
When the wholesale robberies first began the police
made some attempt to cope with the danger, and the
prosecution of a large number of culprits was effected;
but there can be no question that several high officials
were generally implicated, and from this and other
causes the ends of justice were defeated. The first and
probably the only effective trials took place in the sixteenth and seventeenth years of the reign of Rameses
IX and in the first years of Rameses X, i.e., about
B.C. 1126-1123.

A record of these trials, fortunately, has been preserved to us, written on papyrus. One roll, known as

the Abbott Papyrus, was discovered at Thebes, and in 1857 was purchased by the British Museum from Dr. Abbott, of Cairo, into whose hands it had passed. Another roll was purchased by the late Lord Amherst, of Hackney. There is a fragment in the Turin Museum, and two other pieces, known as the Meyer Papyrus, now rest in the Liverpool Museum. Several translations of these important documents have been made, but the literature on the subject is not very easy of access, and the story which the documents tell has to be pieced together. It is a narrative of much interest just now, when the discovery of the tomb of one of the Pharaohs, by Lord Carnarvon, has turned the eyes of the world to the Valley of the Kings.

At the time of the robberies thus recorded, the Government of Thebes, and of all Upper Egypt, was in the hands of the Vizer Khamwast. Under him at Thebes, there were two mayors, one presiding over the great city on the east bank of the Nile, and the other in charge of the necropolis and the various temples and religious buildings on the west bank. The former, the Mayor of the City, was a presumably honest man, named Paser; the latter, the Mayor of the Necropolis, was a plausible scoundrel of the name of Pauraa. These two men had evidently quarrelled with one another, and, as is the Egyptian custom, each was eager to obtain any piece of information which might be derogatory to the other and might lead to his downfall. To this day Egyptian officials spend a great deal of their time in this kind of intrigue, and the only saving grace in this aspect of their lives is the fact that they treat these incidents very lightly, and when the rage of the moment is passed they smile and make friends in the happiest manner.

The quarrel was probably in full swing when news was brought to Paser, sitting fat and resplendent in his house in the city, that a certain royal tomb in the necropolis under the care of his rival Pauraa had been entered by thieves and plundered under the noses of the police. The tomb which was reported to have been robbed was that of a Pharaoh named Sebekemsaf and of Nubkhas, his queen, who had lived somewhere about B.C. 1700. The thieves, eight in number, seem to have been living in the city, and Paser was therefore able to seize them and to extract a confession from them. The first part of this document is now lost, but the second part, which records how the thieves had entered the tomb of the king and queen, has been preserved.

"We penetrated through the masonry and mortar of the tomb," runs the confession, "and we found the queen lying there. We opened the coffin and the coverings in which it was. Then we found the august mummy of the king. There were numerous amulets and golden ornaments at his throat, his head had a mask of gold upon it, and the mummy itself was overlaid with gold throughout. Its coverings were wrought with gold and silver within and without, and were inlaid with every splendid and costly stone. We stripped off the gold which we found on the august mummy of this king, and the amulets and ornaments which were at its throat, and the coverings in which it rested. We found the queen likewise, and we stripped off all that we found on her in the same manner. We then set fire to the coffins, and carried away the funeral-furniture which we found with them, consisting of gold, silver, and bronze. We divided the booty, and made the gold, amulets, ornaments, and coverings into eight parts."

This confession, together with the list of the eight names, Paser at once despatched to the Vizir, who was living in Thebes. The Vizir very wisely took no action until he had heard what the Mayor of the Necropolis, Pauraa, had to say; and he at once sent across the river to that personage, ordering him to send in a report. Pauraa, realising the gravity of the matter, thought it best to assume an attitude of complete innocence, and he therefore requested the Vizir to send an official commission of inspectors over to the necropolis to enquire into the truth of the so-called confession. This was done, and accompanied by Pauraa and a detachment of police, the inspectors made a thorough examination of ten royal tombs, all of which were found to be uninjured; but when they came to the sepulchre which had been the subject of the scandal they found that it had been ransacked exactly as the eight thieves had described. They then proceeded to examine the tombs of the queens of more recent date, and they found that two of them had been robbed, while of the sepulchres of the nobles, which they next examined, not one remained intact. "It was found," says their report, "that the thieves had broken into them all, that they had pulled out the occupants from their coverings and coffins and had thrown them to the ground; and that they had stolen the articles of furniture which had been given to them, together with the gold, the silver, and the ornaments."

When the commission returned to the Vizir things must have looked very black for Pauraa and his necropolis officials, while Paser must have chuckled with pleasure at the imminent downfall of his rival. By this time the whole of his household no doubt knew what

was afoot, and all were eager to win their master's
favour by routing out further evidence of the negligence
or guilt of the Mayor of the opposite bank of the Nile.
But in such matters Egyptians are, to this day, very
apt to defeat their own ends by overloading the case for
the prosecution with worthless evidence; and this fatal
blunder was now made by Paser. One of his servants
or agents reminded him that a certain coppersmith,
named Pakharu, son, by the way, of a woman called
Little-Cat, had languished in prison for nearly two
years on a charge of having been connected with suspected thefts from the tomb of Queen Isis, the wife of
Rameses III: and the suggestion was made that he
might be able to furnish further information concerning
the robberies. Paser, therefore, caused the man to be
brought to him, and having satisfied himself that the
information likely to be obtained was of value to the
case, he sent him to the Vizir, and thereafter, one may
suppose, sat down in his house to await the inevitable
discomfiture of Pauraa.

Upon the next day the Vizir examined this coppersmith and the eight other thieves who had made the
original confession to Paser; and, to quote the subsequent report, "having been examined by beatings with
a double rod upon their hands and feet, they told the
same story as before," the coppersmith's confession
being to the effect that he "had entered the sepulchre
of Queen Isis, and had carried off a few things from it
and had retained them." When torture is employed in
extracting a confession, however, the statements of the
victims have to be tested in order to ascertain whether
they are not merely lies told to obtain temporary relief
from pain. The Vizir, therefore, ordered the prisoners

to accompany him to the other side of the river, and to identify the tombs which they said they had robbed.

The cavalcade set out on its excursion a day or two later. At the head of the procession the nine prisoners were led along by the police; and behind them came the Vizir riding in his chariot, accompanied by the Pharaoh's Chief Butler, a very important personage, named Nesuamon. Then followed a number of secretaries and officials, and a mixed company of servants and soldiers. When they had traversed the road leading across the fields and had reached the desert at the foot of the towering hills, the Vizir seems to have decided first to test the evidence of the coppersmith in regard to the tomb of Queen Isis; and it appears that he left the eight other thieves in the charge of some of his men, intending to hold the enquiry as to the veracity of their confession later in the day. The tomb of Queen Isis, which the modern tourist knows as No. 51, is cut into the hillside at the southern end of the necropolis, in what is now known as the Valley of the Queens, but which was in those days called the Place of Beauty. It was approached by a road which passed up into the hills behind the great temple of Rameses III; and as the party proceeding along it came into view of the royal burial-ground they blindfolded the coppersmith, only removing the bandage when they had placed him on the rocky terrace along which the more important sepulchres were situated.

The man was then told to identify the tomb which he had said he had entered, and no doubt he was hurried into a decision by the sticks of his captors. Dazed and terrified, he led the party to the mouth of a tomb which, unfortunately, proved to be an empty sepulchre never used for a burial at all. A sound beating followed this error, and the coppersmith, still more confused, then admitted his mistake and pointed to another cavernous opening in the cliff. The officials hastened forward, only to find that the place was simply a cave inhabited by one of the workmen of the necropolis. The coppersmith was thereupon "examined in this great valley with a severe examination," so the report tells; that is to say, he was stretched upon the ground in the customary fashion and beaten with stout sticks. No further information, however, could be obtained from him, and at last he swore an oath in the name of the Pharaoh, saying, "I know not any place here amongst these tombs except these which I have pointed out," and declaring that his nose and ears might be cut off if he were proved to have lied.

Thoroughly disgusted, the Vizir then drove northwards along the edge of the desert towards the pyramid-tombs which were said to have been robbed by the other prisoners; and his wrath may be imagined when he received the news that all the eight had managed to escape from their guards and had fled into the hills. The Vizir seems to have vented his fury on the over-zealous Paser, the Mayor of the City, who had instigated the proceedings, and, in the case of the coppersmith, had certainly sent the party on a wild goose chase. On the return journey the friends of Pauraa, the Mayor of the Necropolis, seemed to have approached him to ask permission to come across the river to Thebes that afternoon as a deputation in favour of their master; and this the Vizir, doubtless having received heavy *bakshish,* readily granted, apparently indicating that they could go and jeer at Paser to their hearts' content.

Pauraa, meanwhile, had been working at high speed, and by threats and bribes had obtained the names of a number of persons implicated in the robberies; and now he hastened to send the list to the Vizir, of course, with further presents, and he made it appear that he himself had been the instigator of the investigations which had taken place, and that the confessions extracted by Paser were faked up, the real thieves having been detected by himself alone. The failure of the coppersmith to corroborate his written confession materially strengthened Pauraa's position; and the general opinion amongst the Vizir's entourage seems now to have been that the Mayor of the City had obtained possession of some of the facts about to be revealed by the Mayor of the Necropolis, and had attempted to forestall him.

That same afternoon, in accordance with the sanction given in the morning, a number of officials connected with the necropolis, together with the various members of Pauraa's household, and a crowd of workmen from that side of the river, crossed over to Thebes and made a demonstration against Paser under the guise of a deputation to the Vizir. It is probable that they marched through the streets of the city, and they seem to have paused in front of Paser's house to groan and swear at him in the usual Egyptian manner. Paser's chagrin at this turn of events knew no bounds; and by the time that the demonstration had broken up he was in a state of such uncontrolled fury that he was hardly responsible for his actions.

In the evening he drove along the great avenue of sphinxes to the Temple of Karnak, probably to discuss matters with the High Priest or some great dignitary of

the priesthood of Amon-Ra; and while he was standing
at the doorway of the little Temple of Ptah, at the north
end of the sacred precincts, he met the Chief Butler,
Nesuamon, who was probably at Karnak for a similar
purpose. The two men fell into conversation, and
Nesuamon, pretending to be the disinterested spectator
of the affair, no doubt bewailed Paser's ill fortune and
admonished him for his over-zeal. They were thus
engaged when three of the demonstrators, who had not
yet returned to the other side of the river, happened to
pass by. At sight of them Paser was quite unable to
contain his anger, and he called across to them, using a
wealth of language which at once brought them, shaking
with rage, over to him. A lively exchange of highly-
flavoured vituperation ensued, and at length the Mayor
of the City broke into real accusations against the Mayor
of the Necropolis.

"As for this deputation which you have made," he
roared, "it is no deputation at all. It is simply your
jubilation at my expense. You exult over me at the
very door of my house. O indeed! Remember I am a
Mayor and I make my reports direct to the Pharaoh,
and thus you exult over *him*. You were there when the
tombs were inspected, were you?—and you found them
uninjured! I tell you the tomb of Sebekemsaf and of
his queen Nubkhas *was* broken into, though you make
ten reports to the contrary. I invoke the severity of
Amon-Ra, King of the Gods, upon you in defence of
these sacred tombs, here where I stand this day in his
halls."

One of the men replied that all the other tombs, at
any rate, were undamaged, and he added that they were
under the care of the Pharaoh, a remark which was

meant to indicate that any suggestion that they had
come to harm was a slight upon the king. Paser re-
torted: "Are your deeds as good as your words?"
Then, his passion getting the better of his discretion,
he flung a further accusation at them. "Look," he
cried, "the scribe of the necropolis, Horishere, came to
my house the other day, and made three very serious
accusations against you all. And the scribe of the
necropolis, Pebes, also told me of two other matters,
making in all five accusations. I had them put in writing. God forbid that he who possesses such information
should keep silent concerning it; for they are great and
capital crimes worthy of the utmost penalty of the law.
And I am going to write about them to Pharaoh, so
that he may send someone to take you all in charge."
Then he swore ten round oaths, and said solemnly, "So
will I do."

Having launched this bolt at the Mayor of the
Necropolis and his creatures, he returned to his house,
fuming with apparently justifiable rage. The Chief
Butler, Nesuamon, who had been present during this
episode, and who had his own axe to grind, hurried next
morning across the river to Pauraa, and told him all
that had occurred. "It were a crime," said the hypo-
critical wretch, "for one like me to hear such words and
to conceal them; and therefore I report them to you."
Pauraa immediately sat down and wrote a long letter
to the Vizir, accusing Paser of slander; and this document Nesuamon seems to have taken back with him to
Thebes when he returned to the city, together with any
further presents which may have seemed suitable to the
occasion. Paser had certainly been very indiscreet, and

should not have lost his temper as he did, though one can hardly blame him for doing so.

To the Vizir, however, his conduct seemed unpardonable, and worthy of public reprimand. He appears, therefore, to have sent for Paser and to have ascertained from him the nature of the five accusations of which he had spoken; and having learnt that these concerned some other coppersmiths who were said to have committed further robberies, he seems to have caused the immediate arrest of this new gang, and to have held a rapid enquiry which led him to doubt the truth of their evidence. He then sent a message to the Mayor of the City to attend at the trial of the coppersmiths, which was fixed for the next day, and the unfortunate Paser must have realised that the men would certainly be proved not guilty, and that he himself would be found to be in the wrong.

The trial was held the next morning in "the great court of the city near the gate called *Praise,*" the judges who presided being the Vizir, the Chief Butler, the High Priest of Amon-Ra, the High Steward of the House of the Divine Votress of Amon-Ra, the Chief Standard-bearer of the Navy, a Scribe of the Temple-of-Millions-of-Years-of-the-Pharaoh, another high official whose title is now illegible, and, of course, Paser himself, who had a seat on the judicial bench, as being Mayor of the City.

The Vizir, in addressing the court, said: "The Mayor of the City here, Paser, spoke a few words to certain officials of the necropolis in the presence of the Chief Butler, Nesuamon, making slanderous statements concerning the tombs which are in the necropolis. Now, I, the Vizir of the Land, have been there with Nesuamon; and we inspected the tombs where Paser said the robbers had been. We found them uninjured, and therefore all that he said is shown to be untrue. See now, the accused coppersmiths themselves stand before you: let them tell all that has occurred." The prisoners were forthwith examined, and were soon proved to the satisfaction of the court to be innocent of the charges brought against them. "It was found," says the report, "that they did not know any of the tombs in the necropolis about which the Mayor of the City had made these accusations. He was found to be in the wrong in this matter." The Vizir then seems to have admonished Paser, and having caused the coppersmiths to be released, he dismissed the court. Pauraa had completely triumphed, although, in view of the evidence which the modern excavator's spade has revealed, it is pretty certain that wholesale robberies were taking place at this time; and the unfortunate Paser suffered the penalty of meddling in the affairs of the other bank of the river. It is surprising that he ever expected to be thanked for opening up to public view a scandal which would have been injurious to the Vizir's reputation had the accusations been substantiated, and, indeed, it is this flying in the face of the powers above him which makes one feel certain that he was an honest man.

About a year later the eight thieves who had escaped into the hills during the Vizir's inspection of the tombs appear to have been recaptured; and a confession seems to have been extracted from them that the tomb of Queen Isis had really been robbed, and that they, and not the coppersmiths originally suspected, had committed the crime. The Vizir therefore made another journey to the Valley of the Queens, and this time he

decided to remove the stones which blocked the entrance
of the sepulchre in the usual way, so that he might see
for himself whether the burial was intact. For this
purpose he brought some workmen with him and these
men soon effected an entrance into the tomb. The Vizir
and his officers then crawled into the subterranean passage probably muttering prayers to the shade of the
dead queen and calling her attention to the not very
apparent fact that they were honest men bent only on
securing the safety of her earthly remains; but when
they reached the burial-chamber at the end of the
passage they found that the thieves "had wrought evil
destruction on all that was therein." The lid of the
granite sarcophagus had been prised off, the mummy
had been pulled out of the inner coffin and had been
much damaged, and the funeral-furniture had been
thrown about the chamber. Three thousand years later
I myself made a similar official inspection of this tomb
which had been re-opened by the Italian Egyptologist,
Professor Schiaparelli, but nothing now remained of
the burial except a few broken fragments of the woodwork and the damaged granite sarcophagus. Unfortunately the documents which have been preserved to us
do not relate the subsequent proceedings, but it is to be
supposed that the result of the investigation placed a
feather in the cap of the ill-used Mayor of the City,
Paser.

Two years now elapsed, and the Vizir Khamwast
was succeeded in his office by a certain Nebmara-Nakht,
who does not seem to have been quite so prejudiced in
favour of the Mayor of the Necropolis, Pauraa. That
personage, therefore, felt it necessary to show greater
activity in the detection of the robberies, and he hastened

to send in the names of forty-five persons suspected of similar crimes. Six of these thieves were brought to trial a month later, and fortunately we have a full account of the proceedings. They were accused of robbing the sepulchres of the great Pharaohs Sety I and Rameses II, two enormous tombs which are situated in the Valley of the Kings behind the first range of the Theban hills. It appears from the evidence that the robbers had first obtained access to the tombs many years previously, and since that time they had paid regular visits to their secret treasure trove, in the manner of the forty thieves in the Arabian Nights.

The mouths of the sepulchres were blocked with stones, but the thieves had doubtless tunnelled their way into the interior in such a manner that the hole could be entirely concealed.

These ghouls must have been men of very strong nerves thus to penetrate into the subterranean halls and passages where the spirits of the dead monarchs were thought to roam at large. It is not as though they could climb in, snatch up some article of value, and scramble back to safety; they had to penetrate more than 500 feet into the hillside and to descend nearly 150 feet. In the case of the tomb of Sety I, for example, the thieves had first to descend a long flight of steps, then pass along a passage leading to a second flight and a further passage. This brought them into a room opening out into a large hall, the roof of which was supported by four great columns. From a corner of this echoing hall a stairway descended into another long passage, at the end of which a shorter flight of steps led down into two further passages. Then came a large columned hall from which four rooms opened, and at last, down some more steps, they reached the actual place of burial. From end to end of this vast subterranean palace of the Pharaoh's spirit the walls were covered with sculpture and paintings representing the gods and demons of the Underworld; and the figure of the king they were outraging was to be seen on all sides in communion with the deities whose wrath they were incurring. Sometimes when I have been sitting at work alone at the bottom of this great tomb, I have been oppressed by the silence and the mystery of the place; and if, after this lapse of three thousand years, one is still conscious of the awful sanctity of these dark halls cut into the heart of the hills, one wonders what must have been the sensations of the ancient thieves who penetrated by the light of a flickering oil lamp into the very presence of the dead.

The trial of the robbers was conducted by the new Vizir, the Overseer of the White House, the Herald of Pharaoh, and the Steward of the Court. It appears that the Chief of the Police had been informed that the robbers were wont to enter the tombs every now and then, and his agents had managed to give him the date of their next visit. He therefore hid himself with some of his men near one of the sepulchres, and thus managed to catch the thieves red-handed. This official now gave his evidence, describing what had occurred, after which the prisoners were each brought in and bastinadoed until they confessed their guilt. In the case of each of the wretches, the report says, "The examination was conducted by beating with a rod, the bastinado was applied to the hands and feet, and the oath of the king was administered that the speaker might be put to death if the truth were not told."

The first prisoner was a herdsman in charge of the

sacred cattle of Amon-Ra, the second was an official of the necropolis, the third a watchman of the temple, the fourth a priest, the fifth a weaver, and the sixth a woman who was the mistress of another priest also implicated. The evidence mostly relates to the objects stolen from these tombs, which were discovered in the possession of the prisoners when their houses were searched. Articles made of gold and copper had been found, and most of the prisoners did their best to explain how they had obtained them innocently from other hands. The evidence, however, was damning; and although the end of the trial is not recorded, it is unlikely that any of the prisoners escaped with their lives.

Two days later the trial of five other suspected persons was conducted, but in their case the evidence was not conclusive and they were all found not guilty. A few months afterwards the trial of twenty-two further prisoners is briefly noted, one of whom was convicted of having broken into three royal tombs. Another document contains a long list of names of persons afterwards arrested on suspicion, but their evidence is not recorded.

These wholesale disclosures must have caused the downfall of the Mayor of the Necropolis, and it is to be hoped that his enemy, the Mayor of the City, received ample compensation for the slights inflicted upon him; but, sad to relate, there is nothing to tell us what occurred, and for all we know, Paser may have died in unmerited disgrace in the interval between the first and second investigation.

CHAPTER VI

THE MALEVOLENCE OF ANCIENT
EGYPTIAN SPIRITS

DURING the recent excavations which led to
the discovery of the tomb of Tutankhamen,
Mr. Howard Carter had in his house a canary
which daily regaled him with its happy song. On the
day, however, on which the entrance to the tomb was
laid bare, a cobra entered the house, pounced on the bird,
and swallowed it. Now, cobras are rare in Egypt, and
are seldom seen in winter; but in ancient times they
were regarded as the symbol of royalty, and each
Pharaoh wore this symbol upon his forehead, as though
to signify his power to strike and sting his enemies.
Those who believed in omens, therefore, interpreted this
incident as meaning that the spirit of the newly-found
Pharaoh, in its correct form of a royal cobra, had killed
the excavator's happiness symbolised by this song-bird
so typical of the peace of an English home.

At the end of the season's work, Lord Carnarvon
was stung mysteriously upon the face, and died.

Millions of people throughout the world have asked
themselves whether the death of the excavator of this
tomb was due to some malevolent influence which came
from it, and the story has been spread that there was a
specific curse written upon a wall of the royal sepulchre.
This, however, is not the case.

There are very few such curses known during the Eighteenth and Nineteenth Dynasties in ancient Egypt, that is to say, during the century or two before and after the time of Tutankhamen, and they are not at all common at any Pharaonic period.

Whenever they do appear, their object is simply to terrify the would-be tomb-robbers of their own epoch, who might smash up the mummy in their search for jewellery, or damage the tomb, thereby causing that loss of the dead man's identity which the Egyptians thought would injure the welfare of his spirit in the Underworld. The mummy and the tomb were the earthly home of the disembodied spirit, and to wreck either was to render the spirit homeless and nameless.   On the other hand, to enter a tomb for the purpose of renewing the dead man's memory was always considered by the Egyptians to be a most praiseworthy proceeding; and inscriptions are often found on the wall of a sepulchre stating that some friendly hand had been at work there, setting things to rights after a lapse of many years.

As an example of one of these curses, I will give here the translation of an inscription which is written upon a mortuary-statue of a certain Ursu, a mining engineer who lived less than a hundred years before the time of Tutankhamen.   "He who trespasses upon my property," he says, "or who shall injure my tomb or drag out my mummy, the Sun-god shall punish him.   He shall not bequeath his goods to his children; his heart shall not have pleasure in life; he shall not receive water (for his spirit to drink) in the tomb; and his soul shall be destroyed for ever."   On the wall of the tomb of Harkhuf, at Aswân, dating from the Sixth Dynasty, these words are written: "As for any man who shall enter into this tomb . . . I will pounce upon him as on a bird; he shall be judged for it by the great god."

The fear is that the tomb or the body will be broken up; and thus the scientific modern excavators, whose object is to rescue the dead from that oblivion which the years have produced, might be expected to be blessed rather than cursed for what they do. Only the robber would come under the scope of the curse. If we are to treat these questions seriously at all, it may be said that in general no harm has come to those who have entered these ancient tombs with reverence, and with the sole aim of saving the dead from native pillage and their identity from the obliterating hand of time.

The large number of visitors to Egypt and persons interested in Egyptian antiquities who believe in the malevolence of the spirits of the Pharaohs and their dead subjects, is always a matter of astonishment to me, in view of the fact that of all ancient people the Egyptians were the most kindly and, to me, the most loveable. Sober and thoughtful men, and matter-of-fact matrons, seem to vie with the lighter-minded members of society in recording the misfortunes which have befallen themselves or their friends as a consequence of their meddling with the property of the dead. On all sides one hears tales of the trials which have come upon those who, owing to their possession of some antiquity or ancient relic, have given offence to the spirits of the old inhabitants of the Nile valley. These stories are generally open to some natural explanation, and those tales which I can relate at first hand are not necessarily to be connected with black magic. I will therefore leave it to the reader's taste to find an explanation for the incidents which I will here relate.

In the year 1909 Lord Carnarvon, who was then conducting excavations in the necropolis of the nobles of Thebes, discovered a hollow wooden figure of a large black cat, which we recognised, from other examples in the Cairo Museum, to be the shell in which a real embalmed cat was confined. The figure looked more like a small tiger as it sat in the sunlight at the end of the pit in which it had been discovered, glaring at us with its yellow painted eyes and bristling its yellow whiskers. Its body was covered all over with a thick coating of smooth, shining pitch, and we could not at first detect the line along which the shell had been closed after it had received the mortal remains of the sacred animal within; but we knew from experience that the joint passed completely round the figure—from the nose, over the top of the head, down the back, and along the breast—so that, when opened, the two sides would fall apart in equal halves.

The sombre figure was carried down to the Nile and across the river to my house, where, by a mistake on the part of my Egyptian servant, it was deposited in my bedroom. Returning home at dead of night, I here found it seated in the middle of the floor directly in my path from the door to the matches; and for some moments I was constrained to sit beside it, rubbing my shins and my head.

I rang the bell, but receiving no answer, I walked to the kitchen, where I found the servants grouped distractedly around the butler, who had been stung by a scorpion and was in the throes of that short but intense agony. Soon he passed into a state of delirium and believed himself to be pursued by a large grey cat, a fancy which did not surprise me since he had so lately assisted in carrying the figure to its ill-chosen resting-place in my bedroom.

At length I retired to bed, but the moonlight which now entered the room through the open French windows fell full upon the black figure of the cat; and for some time I lay awake watching the peculiarly weird creature as it stared past me at the wall. I estimated its age to be considerably more than three thousand years, and I tried to picture to myself the strange people who, in those distant times, had fashioned this curious coffin for a cat which had been to them half pet and half household god. A branch of a tree was swaying in the night breeze outside, and its shadow danced to and fro over the face of the cat, causing the yellow eyes to open and shut, as it were, and the mouth to grin. Once, as I was dropping off to sleep, I could have sworn that it had turned its head to look at me; and I could see the sullen expression of feline anger gathering upon its black visage as it did so. In the distance I could hear the melancholy wails of the unfortunate butler imploring those around him to keep the cat away from him, and it seemed to me that there came a glitter into the eyes of the figure as the low cries echoed down the passage.

At last I fell asleep, and for about an hour all was still. Then, suddenly, a report like that of a pistol rang through the room. I started up, and as I did so a large grey cat sprang either from or on to the bed, leapt across my knees, dug its claws into my hand, and dashed through the window into the garden. At the same moment I saw by the light of the moon that the two sides of the wooden figure had fallen apart and were rocking themselves to a standstill upon the floor, like two great empty shells. Between them sat the mummified figure of a cat, the bandages which swathed it round being ripped open at the neck, as though they had been burst outward.

I sprang out of bed and rapidly examined the divided shell; and it seemed to me that the humidity in the air here on the bank of the Nile had expanded the wood which had rested in the dry desert so long, and had caused the two halves to burst apart with the loud noise which I had heard. Then, going to the window, I scanned the moonlit garden; and there in the middle of the pathway I saw, not the grey cat which had scratched me, but my own pet tabby, standing with arched back and bristling fur, glaring into the bushes, as though she saw ten feline devils therein.

I will leave the reader to decide whether the grey cat was the malevolent spirit which, after causing me to break my shins and my butler to be stung by a scorpion, had burst its way through the bandages and woodwork and had fled into the darkness; or whether the torn embalming cloths represented the natural destructive work of Time, and the grey cat was a night-wanderer which had strayed into my room and had been frightened by the easily-explained bursting apart of the two sides of the ancient Egyptian figure. Coincidence is a factor in life not always sufficiently considered; and the events I have related can be explained in a perfectly natural manner, if one be inclined to do so.

My next story tells how a little earthenware lamp once in my possession brought misfortune upon at least two persons.

It sometimes happens that people who have visited Egypt and have there purchased a few trifling antiquities are suddenly seized with the fear that these relics are bringing them bad luck; and, in a moment of frenzy, they pack up their Egyptian purchases, and post them back to the Nile. When I was Inspector-General of Antiquities they not infrequently used to address these parcels to me or to my office at Luxor; and without further consideration the objects were laid away on the shelves of the store-room, where soon the dust gathered upon them and they were forgotten.

Now it chanced that a little earthenware lamp was once returned to me in this manner; and, happening to mention the fact to some friends, I learnt that it had been returned by a lady who declared herself dogged with misfortune ever since it came into her possession, and who had often stated that she intended to get rid of it by sending it back to the unoffending official in charge of antiquities. I cannot now recall the series of misfortunes which had occurred to the owner of the lamp, but I remember that they included little incidents such as the spilling of a bottle of ink over her dress. I paid, of course, small attention to the matter, and the lamp lay unnoticed on the shelf for a year or more.

One day, a certain royal lady who was travelling in Egypt asked me to give her some trifle as a souvenir of her visit; and, without recalling its history to my mind, I gave her the unlucky lamp, which, so far as I know, did not bring any particular ill-fortune to its owner. There the matter would have tamely ended, had it not been for a chance conversation on the subject of unlucky antiquities, which occurred one night at a dinner-party in London. One of the ladies present told me a long story of the ill-luck from which she had suffered during the whole time in which she was the owner of a little earthenware lamp which came from Egypt. To such a state of apprehension had she been brought, she said, by the intuitive feeling that this little antiquity was the cause of her troubles, that at last she went down to the Embankment and hurled it into the Thames.

Vague recollections of the story of the unlucky lamp which I had given to our illustrious visitor began to stir in my mind, and I asked with some interest how she came into possession of the malevolent object. Her reply confirmed my suspicions. The lamp had been given to her by the royal lady to whom I had presented it as a souvenir!

Most people have heard the story of the malevolent "mummy" in the British Museum. As a matter of fact, it is not a mummy at all, but simply a portion of the lid of a coffin. It was bequeathed to the museum after it had wrought havoc wherever it went, but now it is said to confine its dangerous attentions to those visitors who are disrespectful to it. A lady of my acquaintance told me that she had "been rude" to it, with the startling result that she fell headlong down the great staircase and sprained her ankle. There is also the well-known case of a journalist who wrote about it in jest, and was dead in a few days.

The originator of the whole affair was the late Mr. Douglas Murray, who told me the following facts. He purchased the coffin some time in the 'sixties, and no sooner had he done so than he lost his arm, owing to the explosion of his gun. The ship in which the coffin was sent home was wrecked, as also was the cab in which it was driven from the docks; the house in which it was deposited was burnt down; and the photographer who made a picture of it shot himself. A lady who had some connection with it suffered great family losses, and was wrecked at sea shortly afterwards, her life being saved, so she told me, only by the fact that she clung to a rock for the greater part of a night. The list of accidents and misfortunes charged to the spirit which is connected with this coffin is now of enormous length, a fact which is not surprising, since persons who have seen the coffin attribute all their subsequent troubles to its baneful influence, and misfortunes in this life are not so rare that they can be counted on the five fingers. Personally, I think that, if these matters are to be considered at all, we should attempt rather to incur this restless spirit's benediction by refusing to credit it with an evil purpose.

The veracity of the next story cannot be questioned. A photograph in my possession, about which there is no fake, tells the tale more accurately than could any words of mine; and there can be no getting away from the fact that a shadowy human face has come between the camera and the object which was being photographed. The facts are as follows.

Some years ago we were making excavations in the tomb of a Great Vizir of about B.C. 1350, when we came upon a highly decorated coffin of a certain priest, which, by the style of the workmanship, appeared to date from some two hundred years later, and evidently must have been buried there by unscrupulous undertakers who opened up the original tomb for its reception in order to save themselves the trouble of making a new sepulchre. Now this act of desecration might be thought to have called down upon the intruding mummy the wrath of the Vizir's spirit, whose body was probably ousted to make room for the newcomer; but, whether this be so or not, those who believe in these powers might

THE FAMOUS STATUE OF SEKHMET AT KARNAK AFTER
HAVING BEEN SMASHED BY A NATIVE WHO BELIEVED IN
ITS MALEVOLENCE

It was later restored.

have reason to suppose that the priestly usurper lay restlessly in his coffin, retaining, in place of the usual quiescence of the dead, a continued activity which caused an atmosphere of malignity to linger around his mortal remains.

As soon as the coffin and mummy were deposited in my store-room, I began to feel an unaccountable sense of apprehension whenever I stood in its presence; and every time I opened the door of the room to enter its dark recesses I glanced uneasily at the embalmed figure which lay in the now lidless coffin, as though expecting it to do me some injury. This appeared to me to be remarkable, for I had long been accustomed to the presence all around me of the embalmed dead. I had slept night after night in the tombs, sharing their comfortable shelter with the human remains which still lay therein; I had, during a *dahabiyeh* trip in the south, filled the cabin bunkers with the skulls and bones of the dead and had worked and slept contentedly in their company; I had eaten many a luncheon on the lid of a not empty coffin. But this particular mummy seemed to draw my eyes towards it, so that when I was at work in the room in which it lay, I caught myself glancing over my shoulder in its direction.

At length I decided to unwrap the bandages in which the mummy was rolled, and to look upon the face of the dead man who had now begun to haunt my thoughts, after which I proposed to send both it and the coffin down to the Cairo Museum. The process of unwrapping was lengthy, for of course many notes had to be taken and photographs made at the different stages of the proceedings; but at last it was completed, and the body was placed in the packing-case in which it was to travel.

Some of the linen cloths which had covered the face were of such beautifully fine texture that I took them into the house to show them to the friends who were staying with me at the time; and one of the servants, shortly afterwards, placed them upon a shelf in a bedroom wardrobe.

Now it happened that this room was occupied by a lady and her little girl, and a day or two later, while the body still lay in the portico outside the house, and the ancient linen still rested upon the shelf inside the room, the child was seized with violent illness. There followed some days of anxiety, and at length one morning, when the doctor's visit had left us distraught with anxiety, the mother of the invalid came to me with a haggard face, holding in her hands the embalmer's linen. "Here," she cried, with an intensity which I shall not soon forget, "take this horrible stuff and burn it; and for goodness' sake send that mummy away, or the child will die."

The mummy and its linen went down to Cairo that night, and the little girl in due course recovered; but when, a month or two later, I developed the photographs which I had taken of the unwrapped body, there, between it and my camera, stared a shadowy face. It is possible that I took two photographs upon one plate; I do not remember, but that, and the state of my nerves, due to overwork, may account for all that happened.

I am minded now to relate an experience which befell me when I was conducting excavations in the desert behind the ancient city of Abydos. The tale does not deal with any very particular malevolence of any spirit of the past, but it bears sufficiently closely upon that subject to be recorded here. We were engaged in clearing out a vertical tomb-shaft which had been cut through

the rock underlying the sandy surface of the desert.
The shaft was about ten foot square; and by the end of
the second day's work we had cleared out the sand and
stones, wherewith it was filled, to the depth of some
twenty feet. At sunset I gave the order to stop work
for the night, and I was about to set out on my walk
back to the camp when the foreman came to tell me that,
with the last strokes of the pick, a mummied hand had
been laid bare, and it was evident that we were about
to come upon an interred body.

By lamplight, therefore, the work was continued;
and presently we had uncovered the sand-dried body
of an old woman, who by her posture appeared to have
met with a violent death. It was evident that this did
not represent the original burial in the tomb, the bottom
of the shaft not yet having been reached; and I con-
jectured that the corpse before us had been thrown
from above at some more recent date—perhaps in Roman times—when the shaft was but half full of debris,
and in course of time had become buried by blown sand
and natural falls of rock.

The workmen were now waiting for their evening
meal, but I, on the·other hand, was anxious to examine
the body and its surroundings carefully, in order to see
whether any objects of interest were to be found. I
therefore sent all but one of the men back to the camp,
and descended into the shaft by means of a rope ladder,
carrying with me a hurricane lamp to light my search.
In the flickering rays of the lamp the body looked particularly gruesome. The old woman lay upon her back,
her arms outstretched upwards, as though they had
stiffened thus in some convulsion, the fingers being
locked together. Her legs were thrust outwards rigidly,

and the toes were cramped and bent. The features of the face were well preserved, as was the whole body; and long black hair descended to her bony shoulders in a' tangled mass. Her mouth was wide open, the two rows of teeth gleaming savagely in the uncertain light, and the hollow eye-sockets seemed to stare upwards, as though fixed upon some object of horror. I do not suppose that it is often man's lot to gaze upon so ghastly a spectacle, and it was only the fact of the extreme antiquity of the body which made it possible for me to look with equanimity upon it; for the centuries that had passed since the occurrence of this woman's tragedy seemed to have removed the element of personal affinity which sets the living shuddering at the dead.

Just as I was completing my search I felt a few drops of rain fall, and at the same time realised that the wind was howling and whistling above me and that the stars were shut out by dense clouds. A rain storm in Upper Egypt is a very rare occurrence, and generally it is of a tropical character. If I left the body at the bottom of the shaft, I thought to myself, it would be soaked and destroyed; and since, as a specimen, it was well worth preserving, I decided to carry it to the surface, where there was a hut in which it could be sheltered. I lifted the body from the ground, and found it to be quite light, but at the same time not at all fragile. I called out to the man whom I had told to wait for me on the surface, but received no reply. Either he had misunderstood me and gone home, or else the noise of the wind prevented my voice from reaching him. Large spots of rain were now falling, and there was no time for hesitation. I therefore lifted the body on to my back, the two outstretched arms passing over my shoulders and the linked fingers clutching, as it were, at my chest. I then began to climb up the rope ladder, and as I did so I noticed with something of a qualm that the old woman's face was peeping at me over my right shoulder and her teeth seemed about to bite my right ear.

I had climbed about half the distance when my foot dislodged a fragment of rock from the side of the shaft, and, as luck would have it, the stone fell right upon the lamp, smashing the glass and putting the light out. The darkness in which I found myself was intense, and now the wind began to buffet me and to hurl the sand into my face. With my right hand I felt for the woman's head and shoulder, in order to hitch the body more firmly on to my back, but to my surprise my hand found nothing there. At the same moment I became conscious that the hideous face was grinning at me over my *left* shoulder, my movements, I suppose, having shifted it; and, without further delay, I blundered and scrambled to the top of the shaft in a kind of panic.

No sooner had I reached the surface than I attempted to relieve myself of my burden. The wind was now screaming past me and the rain was falling fast. I put my left hand up to catch hold of the corpse's shoulder, and to my dismay found that the head had slipped round once more to my right, and the face was peeping at me from that side. I tried to remove the arms from around my neck, but, with ever-increasing horror, I found that the fingers had caught in my coat and seemed to be holding on to me. A few moments of struggle ensued, and at last the fingers released their grip. Thereupon the body swung round so that we stood face to face, the withered arms still around my neck, and the teeth grinning at me through the darkness. A moment later I was free, and the body fell back from me, hovered a moment, as it were, in mid air, and suddenly disappeared from sight. It was then that I realised that we had been struggling at the very edge of the shaft, down which the old woman had now fallen, and near which some will say that she had been wildly detaining me.

Fortunately the rain soon cleared off, so there was no need to repeat the task of bringing the gruesome object to the surface. Upon the next morning we found the body quite uninjured, lying at the bottom of the shaft, in almost precisely the position in which we had discovered it; and it is now exhibited in the museum of one of the medical institutes of London.

Most people who have visited Upper Egypt will be familiar with the lioness-headed statue of Sekhmet which is to be seen in the small temple of Ptah, at Karnak. Tourists usually make a point of entering the sanctuary in which it stands by moonlight or starlight, for then the semi-darkness adds in an extraordinary manner to the dignity and mystery of the figure, and one feels disposed to believe the goddess not yet bereft of all power. Sekhmet was the agent employed by the sun-god, Ra, in the destruction of mankind; and she thus had a sinister reputation in olden times. This has clung to her in a most persistent manner, and to this day the natives say that she has the habit of killing little children. When the statue was discovered a few years ago, a fall of earth just in front of her terminated the lives of two of the small boys who were engaged in the work, a fact which, not surprisingly, has been quoted as an indication of the malevolence of the spirit which resides in this impressive figure of stone.

One hears it now quite commonly said that those who offend the goddess when visiting her are pursued by ill-fortune for weeks afterwards.

It actually became the custom for English and American ladies to leave their hotels after dinner and to hasten into the presence of the goddess, there to supplicate her and to appease her with fair words. On one of these occasions, a few years ago, a well-known lady threw herself upon her knees before the statue, and rapturously holding her hands aloft, cried out, "I believe, I believe!" while a friend of hers passionately kissed the stone hand and patted the somewhat ungainly feet. On other occasions lamps were burnt before the goddess and a kind of ritual was mumbled by an enthusiastic gentleman; while a famous French lady of letters, who was a victim of the delusion that she possessed ventriloquial powers, made mewing noises, which were supposed to emanate from the statue, and which certainly added greatly to the barbaric nature of the scene. So frequent did these séances become that at last I had to put an official stop to them, and thereafter it was deemed an infringement of the rules to placate the malevolent goddess in this manner. There she stands alone, smiling mysteriously at her visitors, who are invariably careful not to arouse her anger by smiling back. A native, who probably believed himself to be under her ban, burgled his way, one summer's night, into the sanctuary and knocked her head and shoulders off; but the archæologist in charge cemented them on again, and thus she continues as before to dole out misfortune to those who credit her with that ill desire.

During the winter of 1908-9 the well-known Bos-

tonian painter and pageant-master, Joseph Lindon
Smith, and his wife, were staying with my wife and myself in our house on the banks of the Nile, at Luxor, the
modern town which has grown up on the site of the once
mighty "hundred-gated Thebes," the old capital of
Egypt. It was our custom to spend a great part of our
time amongst the ruins on the western side of the Nile,
for my work made it necessary for me to give constant
attention to the excavations which were there being conducted, and to supervise the elaborate system of policing
and safeguarding, which is nowadays in force for the
protection of the many historical and artistic treasures
there on view. Mr. Smith, also, had painting work to do
amongst the tombs; while the ladies of our party amused
themselves in the hundred different ways which are so
readily suggested in these beautiful and romantic surroundings.

Sometimes we used to camp the night amongst the
tombs, the tents pitched on the side of the hill of Shêkh
abd'el Gurneh in the midst of the burial-place of the
great nobles; and at sunset, after the tourists had all
disappeared along the road back to Luxor, and our
day's occupations were ended, we were wont to set out
for long rambling walks in the desert ravines, over the
rocky hills, and amongst the ruined temples; nor was it
until the hour of dinner that we made our way back to
the lights of the camp. The grandeur of the scenery
when darkness had fallen is indescribable. In the dim
light reflected from the brilliant stars, the cliffs and
rocky gorges assumed the most wonderful aspect. Their
shadows were full of mystery, and the broken pathways
seemed to lead to hidden places barred to man's investigation. The hills, and the boulders at their feet, took

fantastic shape; and one could not well avoid the thought that the spirits of Egypt's dead were at that hour roaming abroad, like us, amongst these illusory scenes.

It was during one of these evening walks that we found ourselves in the famous Valley of the Tombs of the Queens, a rock-strewn ravine in which some of Egypt's royal ladies were buried. At the end of this valley the cliffs close in, and an ancient torrent, long ago dried up, has scooped out a cavernous hollow in the face of the rock, into which, as into a cauldron, the waters must have poured as they rushed down from the hills at the back. The sides of the hollow form two-thirds of a circle, and overhead the rock somewhat overhangs. In front it is quite open to the valley, and as the floor is a level area of hard gravel, about twenty-five feet at its greatest breadth and depth, the hollow at once suggests to the mind a natural stage with the rocky valley which lies before it as the theatre. The place was well known to us, and in the darkness we now scrambled up into the deep shadows of the recess, and, sitting upon the gravel, stared out into the starlit valley, like ghostly actors playing to a deserted auditorium. The evening wind sighed quietly around us, and across the valley the dim forms of two jackals passed with hardly a sound. Far away over the Nile we could see, framed between the hills on either side of the mouth of the ravine, the brilliant lights of Luxor shining in the placid water; and these added the more to the sense of our remoteness from the world and our proximity to those things of the night which belong to the kingdom of dreams.

Presently I struck a match, in order to light my

pipe, and immediately the rough face of the rocks around us was illuminated and made grotesque. As the flame flickered, the dark shadows fluttered like black hair in the wind, and the promontories jutted forward like great snouts and chins. An owl, startled by the light, half tumbled from its roost upon a deep ledge high above us and went floundering into the darkness, hooting like a lost soul. The match burnt out, and immediately blackness and silence closed once more about us.

"What a stage for a play!" exclaimed the amateur actor-manager; and a few moments later we were all eagerly discussing the possibility of performing a ghostly drama here amongst the desert rocks. By the time that we had reached our camp a plot had been evolved which was based on the historical fact that the spirit of the above-mentioned Pharaoh Akhnaton was, so to speak, excommunicated by the priests and was denied the usual prayers for the dead, being thus condemned to wander without home or resting-place throughout the years. Akhnaton, the son of the powerful and beautiful Queen Tiy, reigned from B.C. 1375 to 1358; and being disgusted with the barbarities perpetrated at Thebes in the name of the god Amon, and believing that the only true god was Aton, the life-giving "Energy of the Sun," overthrew the former religion and preached a wonderfully advanced doctrine of peace and love, which he associated with the worship of Aton. He removed his capital from Thebes to "The City of the Horizon of Aton," and there reigned with his wife and children, devoting his whole energy to his religion and to the demonstration of his lofty teaching. He died at the age of about thirty years; and thereupon the nation unanimously returned, under Tutankhamen, to the worship of Amon and the old gods, whose priests erased the dead king's name from the book of life.

Here, then, was a ghost ready to hand, and here was our stage. The part of the young Akhnaton should be assigned to my wife, for his gentle character and youthful voice could better be rendered by a woman than by a man. Then we must bring in the beautiful Queen Tiy, who could well be impersonated by Mrs. Lindon Smith. Mr. Smith could take the part of the messenger of the gods, sent from the Underworld to meet the royal ghost. And as for myself, I would be kept busy enough, managing the lights, prompting the actors, and doing the odd jobs. There would have to be some weird music at certain moments; and for this purpose our friend, Mr. F. F. Ogilvie, that painter of Anglo-Egyptian fame, might be commandeered together with his guitar.

On our return to Luxor we busied ourselves during all our spare hours in designing and making the costumes and properties; and it fell to me to write as fast as I could the lines of the play. They have no merit in themselves; but when a few days later they were read over in our desert theatre, beneath the starlit heavens, the quiet, earnest diction of the two ladies, and the strange, hawk-like tones of our celebrated amateur, caused them to sound very mysterious and full of meaning.

We now fixed the date for the performance and invited our friends to come by night to the Valley of the Tombs of the Queens to see the expected appearance of the ghost of the great Pharaoh, and a few days before that date we moved over once more to our desert camp.

We rehearsed the play a few nights later, but alas!

hardly had Mrs. Smith finished her introductory lines, when she was struck down by agonising pains in her eyes, and in less than two hours she had passed into a raving delirium. The story of how at midnight she was taken across the deserted fields and over the river to our house at Luxor, would read like the narration of a nightmare. Upon the next day it was decided that she must be sent down immediately to Cairo, for there was no doubt that she was suffering from ophthalmia in its most virulent form, and there were grave fears that she might lose her sight. On this same day my wife was smitten down with violent illness, she being ordered also to proceed to Cairo immediately. On the next morning, Mr. Smith developed a low fever, and shortly afterwards, I myself was laid low with influenza. Mr. Ogilvie, returning to his headquarters by train, came in for a nasty accident in which his mother's leg was badly injured. And thus not one of us could have taken part in the production of the play on the date announced.

For the next two or three weeks Mrs. Smith's eyes and my wife's life hung in the balance and were often despaired of. Mercifully, however, they were both restored in due time to perfect health; but none of us entertained any desire to undertake the rehearsals a second time. Many of our friends were inclined to see in our misfortunes the punishing hand of the gods and spirits of ancient Egypt; but they must not forget that the play was to be given in all solemnity and without the smallest suggestion of burlesque. For my own part, as I have said, I do not think that the possibilities of that much under-rated factor in life's events, coincidence, have been exhausted in the search for an explanation of our tragedy; but far from me be it to offer an opinion upon the subject. I have heard the most absurd nonsense talked in Egypt by those who believe in the malevolence of the ancient dead; but at the same time, I try to keep an open mind on the subject.

CHAPTER VII

THE PROBLEM OF EGYPTIAN CHRONOLOGY

THE discovery of the tomb of Tutankhamen has aroused extensive interest in Egyptology, and books on Egyptian history and archæology have lately been read by large numbers of people who had hardly given the subject a thought before. But these new readers have been much confused by finding that Egyptologists differ very widely in the dating of the earlier dynasties; and they have been inclined to abandon their reading altogether on learning that two such famous authorities, for instance, as Professor James Henry Breasted, of Chicago, and Professor Flinders Petrie, of London, differ to the extent of over two thousand years in the date they assign to the beginning of the First Dynasty, the former believing it to have occurred about B.C. 3400, and the latter about B.C. 5550.

I think it will be useful, therefore, if I attempt to explain this discrepancy; but I must warn the reader that the subject is extremely complicated and he will require to give his full attention to it if he would understand it. I will endeavour, however, to state the problem as simply as its nature permits.

All Egyptologists agree very closely as to the dating of the reigns on our side of the foundation of the Eighteenth Dynasty, that event being ascribed to B.C. 1587 by Professor Petrie, and to B.C. 1580 by Professor

Breasted; and the reader, therefore, has little to worry
him from this period onwards. But in regard to the
ages before that time, the two schools differ upon two
distinct grounds. The first of these is as regards the
length of the period from the Thirteenth to the Seventeenth Dynasty, inclusive; and the second is in regard
to the length of the period from the First to the Twelfth
Dynasty, inclusive.

Let us first consider the composition of the ancient
Egyptian calendar. The calendar began with five
epagomenal or intercalary days, which were celebrated
as the birthdays of gods, the first being the birthday
of Osiris. The remaining three hundred and sixty days
were divided into three seasons, named *Shat, Pert,* and
Shemut. The name of the first of these seasons, *Shat,*
is no doubt to be identified with the same word which
means "germination," or "growth," and is found with
some frequency in the inscriptions. This season, therefore, is "The Season of Growing the Crops," as is indicated also by the fact that it is introduced by the birth
of Osiris, who is always closely connected with the germination of the crops. The word *Pert* means "to come
forth," or "to go out," and it has generally been assumed
that its use in the calendar has reference to the coming
forth of the crops; but I would suggest another explanation of its origin. All those who have lived in Egypt
will know how the *fellahîn,* or peasants, go out into the
fields and take up their residence there in temporary
booths (in Egyptian, *per*) during harvest-time. To
the agricultural classes it is the great annual event, and
it may well be expected to have given the name to the
season. *Pert,* then, is probably "The Season of Going
Out into the Fields." The word *Shemut* originally

meant the "Inundation," though it came to be used for "summer," and "harvest," and this season is thus nominally "The Season of the Inundation."

This Egyptian calendar is seen, therefore, to be one based on the natural conditions of life in the Nile valley as they affected an agricultural people, such as were the ancient Egyptians. It was a farmers' calendar; the first season being *Shat,* originally from the middle of November to the middle of March, when the floods of the Nile had left the fields, and the sowing of the crops took place; the second being *Pert,* originally from the middle of March to the middle of July, when the harvests were reaped; and the third season being *Shemut,* originally from the middle of July to the middle of November, when the river was in flood and inundated the land.

Each of these three seasons was divided into four months of thirty days. In late Egyptian, or Coptic, times these months were given names; but in the days of the Pharaohs they were called simply the First, Second, Third or Fourth month of one of the three seasons. The calendar was thus, as follows:—

Ancient Egyptian name.   *Coptic name.*

1 First month of *Shat,* or Season of
  Growing .... Mesore
2 Second month of *Shat*........... Thoth
3 Third month of *Shat*........... Paopi
4 Fourth month of *Shat*........... Hathor
5 First mouth of *Pert,* or Season of
  Going Out .... Khoiak
6 Second month of *Pert*........... Tobi
7 Third month of *Pert*............. Mekhir

HE AVENUE OF RAM HEADED SPHINXES IN FRONT OF THE
AIN ENTRANCE OF THE TEMPLE OF KARNAK

Ancient Egyptian name.	*Coptic name.*
8 Fourth month of *Pert*.............	Phamenoth
9 First month of *Shemut,* or Season of Flood	Pharmuth
10 Second month of *Shemut*..........	Pakhons
11 Third month of *Shemut*..........	Paoni
12 Fourth month of *Shemut*........	Epephi

After the Eighteenth Dynasty and down to the Roman period, the epagomenal days were placed between Mesore and Thoth; and Thoth thus would have been identified with the first month of *Shat,* while Mesore would be the fourth month of *Shemut.* But the form of the calendar shown above is that in which the Egyptian of the Eighteenth Dynasty and earlier knew it, though, as I have said, the Coptic names of the months had not yet been applied, so far as we know. The earliest record of the calendar in this form is found in an inscription of the time of King Userkaf, at the beginning of the Fifth Dynasty, and in it the five epagomenal days are shown as coming after the season of *Shemut* and before that of *Shat,* which is placed as the first season.

This ancient agricultural calendar was, except at its beginning, merely a nominal method of recording the months, for, owing to this loss of one day in every four years, it only coincided with actual conditions every 1460 years. But there was another calendar, or, rather, another method of fixing the beginning of the year, which was also in use; for, at an early date, the Egyptian astronomers had discovered that the heliacal rising of the planet Sothis, or Sirius, each summer coincided with the rise of the Nile. It is true that the Sothic year and the ordinary solar year are not absolutely of the same length; but the divergence is so slight that it was then not noticed. The annual festival of the Rising of Sothis, coincidental with the coming of the floods, therefore, came to be celebrated as New Year's Day; but it coincided with the beginning of the nominal Season of Flood in the shifting official calendar only once in every 1460 years.

It will be seen, then, that if we can fix the date of any year in which the annual rising of Sothis, or Sirius, coincides with a definite day in the Egyptian calendar year, we can at once obtain the date of any recorded Sothic rising—with this qualification, however, that the coincidence recurs every 1460 years, and that therefore our date may be 1460 years too early or too late. Fortunately this date can be fixed, for we know from a well-determined observation reported by Censorinus, that in or about that year A.D. 139 the Sothic year began on the first day of the first Egyptian calendar month, at that time Thoth.

Bearing in mind that the month Thoth in earlier times was not the first but the second month, that is to say that the five epagomenal days have to be shifted, which throws the dating back by 120 years, it is not difficult to make the required calculations; and Professor Petrie has published in Volume II of his *Historical Studies* (1911) a diagram made by Mr. E. B. Knobel, by means of which the date in our months and years of any ancient Egyptian calendar date, and any rising of Sothis, can be found at a glance.

Now, there is, in the Ebers Papyrus, a record of the heliacal rising of Sothis occurring on the ninth day of the third month of the season of *Shemut*, in the ninth year of Amenhotep I, of the Eighteenth Dynasty; and this can thus be fixed to about the year B.C. 1548. And in the Kahun Papyrus there is a record of the same event occurring on the seventeenth day of the fourth month of the season of *Pert,* in the seventh year of the reign of Senusert III, of the Twelfth Dynasty; and, similarly, this can be fixed to about B.C. 2000, or else to 1460 years earlier, i.e., B.C. 3460. So little is known about the period between the end of the Twelfth Dynasty and the beginning of the Eighteenth Dynasty, that there is room for question as to which of these two dates for Senusert III is to be adopted. Professor Petrie believes in the longer period; but the majority of Egyptologists believe in the shorter. I, personally, am amongst the latter.

The history of this intervening period is very confused. The ancient historian Manetho, and the list of kings in the famous Turin Papyrus, both point to the longer period; for each records the names of a large number of kings who reigned during this dark age. On the other hand, the small number of monuments now known belonging to this intermediate period, and the similarity of manners, customs, and styles of workmanship prevailing in the latter part of the Twelfth and earlier part of the Eighteenth Dynasty strongly suggest the shorter reckoning. The great stela of Ahmose I, found at Abydos, for instance, shows that the work of the beginning of the Eighteenth Dynasty is remarkably like that of the Twelfth.

Perhaps the short genealogy of some family will be found linking these two dynasties, and thus proving the shorter period to be correct; or perhaps a series of monuments covering a great part of the disputed era will be brought to light, and will settle the question; or, again, excavation in Syria or Mesopotamia may show some early Egyptian dynasty to be contemporaneous with an epoch in those lands, the date of which is known. But, in the absence of such material, Egyptologists are at present on the look-out for some calendar date of a seasonal or astronomical event, which will fit in with, and prove, the one dating or the other. I will give here two instances of the occurrence of such events, in order to show the reader the kind of evidence which is being sought.

In a tomb at El-Bersheh, in Middle Egypt, a certain Thutnakht, who lived at the beginning of the Twelfth Dynasty, records the fact that the flax harvest was reaped in the last quarter of the fourth month of *Shat*. Now, according to the shorter reckoning, the date of the foundation of the Twelfth Dynasty is B.C. 2120; and reference to Mr. Knobel's diagrams shows that the end of the fourth month of *Shat* at that date corresponds to about the tenth of April. According to Professor Petrie's reckoning, the Twelfth Dynasty began in B.C. 3580; and at that time the end of the fourth month of *Shat*, according to the diagram, fell in the last week of March. The flax harvest is generally reaped in Middle Egypt about the end of March, or beginning of April; and thus the balance is here slightly in favour of the longer dating, but the evidence is not very conclusive.

In the Rhind Mathematical Papyrus there is a statement that on the third day of the first month (of *Shat*) in the second year of the reign of Ausserra Apepi I, of the Fifteenth Dynasty, there was rain, and the voice of the god was heard, that is to say, probably, it thundered.

According to Professor Petrie the date is about B.C. 2370, at which time the beginning of the first month fell about February 20th. According to the shorter reckoning the date is about B.C. 1700, at which time the day in question coincides with the middle of September. Professor Petrie argues that rain and thunder are common in February, but are unknown in September, and that therefore we must accept the longer reckoning. But actually the evidence is inconclusive, for I, myself, have known thunder and rain in September in Egypt.

These two instances will show the difficulty of obtaining evidence of this kind, which will settle the question of the length of the period between the Twelfth and Eighteenth Dynasty. Let us now consider the second part of the controversy, namely, that in regard to the length of the period between the First and the Twelfth Dynasty.

The difference of opinion arises in the main from the question as to whether Manetho's lists are to be accepted or not. By adding up the reigns of the kings, with Manetho's history as a basis, Professor Petrie comes to the conclusion that this period covered about twenty-two centuries. Most of the other Egyptologists, on the other hand, disallow many years not accounted for by actual monuments, and make the total period not more than about sixteen centuries. Thus, in dealing with this epoch, the difference of opinion is not confined to the 1460 years of the Sothic cycle, but, added to that, we have another six hundred years or so in dispute.

Let us, as before, take two instances in which seasonal dates recorded in contemporary inscriptions are used as arguments on the one side or the other; but we shall find them once more inconclusive.

Professor Petrie uses an ingenious argument derived from the quarrying-dates inscribed on the stones of the Pyramid of Meidûm. The few stones which were able to be examined were inscribed with dates covering the period from the sixth to the eleventh months of the year. This pyramid was built during the reign of Sneferu, whose date, according to the longer reckoning is about B.C. 4750, and according to the shorter, about B.C. 3000. Now, in B.C. 4750 these Egyptian months coincided with the period between March and August; and Professor Petrie argues that this is the likely time for quarrying, the blocks being thus able to be transported across the floods of the inundation in September and October. But in B.C. 3000 these months corresponded to the period between January and the end of May; and one may just as well argue that that would be the natural time for quarrying, during the cool weather, and that the work would certainly have been shut down during the height of summer. Nothing, therefore, can be derived from these quarry-marks.

In the Sixth Dynasty a certain Una describes how his king, Merenra I, ordered him to quarry a large offering-table of alabaster from the hills near Tell-el-Amârna, and to convey it to the royal pyramid at Sakkâra. The work was executed at express speed, as he states, "in the third month of *Shemut,* although there was no flood-water on the land," over which to float it. According to the shorter reckoning, the event occurred about B.C. 2690, at which time the third month of *Shemut* corresponded to March. The inundation, it will be remembered, is in the autumn. According to the longer reckoning, the season corresponded from the middle of February to the middle of March. Nothing definite, therefore, can be deduced from this argument, although it is often used.

I come now to a very interesting piece of evidence, which though not helping us to decide whether the longer or the shorter reckoning is correct, shows us the state of the calendar at the beginning of the Fifth Dynasty. In the Cairo Museum there is a table of offerings belonging to a Superintendent of the Scribes, named Sethu, which comes from a tomb at Gizeh, numbered by Reisner G.4710. This tomb dates from about the end of the Fourth or beginning of the Fifth Dynasty, which, according to the longer reckoning, is about B.C. 4500, and, according to the shorter, about B.C. 2870.

Cut into this offering-table there is a small tank, having three steps around it. On the lowest step is written: "Season of *Shemut,* height 22 cubits"; on the middle step: "Season of *Pert,* height 23 cubits"; and on the top step: "Season of *Shat,* height 25 cubits." It is obvious that these figures refer to the height of the water in the tank, consequent upon the state of the Nile, and the table must have served, thus, as a petition, or thank-offering, for the best possible river levels throughout the year. But these inscriptions show that, at that date, the lowest river levels occurred in the season of *Shemut,* or Inundation, and the highest flood levels in the season of *Shat,* or Growing.

Referring to the diagrams, we see that in B.C. 4500 *Shemut* corresponded to the period between the middle of March and the middle of July; and in B.C. 2870 to the period between the beginning of March and the end of June. Either of these periods cover the time of the lowest Nile. Again, in B.C. 4500, *Shat* corresponds to the period between the middle of July and the middle of November; and in B.C. 2870 to the period between the beginning of July and the end of October. Both these periods cover the time of the highest Nile.

The point to be observed is that at the beginning of the Fifth Dynasty the calendar had shifted round, by the loss of one day in every four years, until the season of *Shemut,* or Inundation, fell in the time of the actual harvest, and the season of *Shat,* or the growing time of the crops, fell in the period of the actual inundation. This means to say that this calendar must have been first established much earlier, at a time when the beginning of the season of *Shemut,* or Inundation, coincided with the actual rising of the Nile, in July, which it did in B.C. 3400, 4900, and 6400.

Those who accept the longer dating will probably take B.C. 4900 as the date of the establishment of the calendar, which date, according to that reckoning, falls in the middle of the Third Dynasty—quite a likely age for it. Those who believe in the shorter period, will regard B.C. 3400 as the date of the origin of this calendar, which, according to them, falls in the middle of the First Dynasty—an even more likely date for it.

So much for the agricultural calendar; but when did the rising of Sothis, which was coincident with the annual rise of the Nile, come to be regarded as the beginning of the year? It must have been, surely, at a time when the Sothic "New Year's Day" and the New Year's Day of the agricultural calendar happened to be simultaneous, that is to say, when the rising of Sothis and the coming of the floods coincided with one of the five epagomenal days, or with the first day of the first month of *Shat.* This coincidence occurred in about B.C. 2900, 4360, and 5820.

Those who accept the longer dating will attribute this event to B.C. 4360, when, according to them, the Fifth Dynasty was at its height, or to B.C. 5820, when the kings of what is called Dynasty O. (i.e., before the First Dynasty) were reigning. Those who believe in the shorter dating will rather say that it occurred in B.C.2900, which, to them, falls in the reign of Mykerinos, the builder of the Third Pyramid, just after the time of Khephren and the making of the Sphinx. Professor Breasted, however, goes back a cycle of 1460 years, and places it in B.C. 4360,* some 800 years before the beginning of the First Dynasty, a rather improbable conjecture.

If we accept the shorter dating, then, we see that an agricultural calendar was established in the First Dynasty and that it began with the season of *Shat,* the season, nominally, when the flood-waters had left the fields and the work of preparing the ground commenced— which is obviously the natural time for the working year to begin in Egypt. The Sothic year, however, began with the rise of the Nile and the simultaneous heliacal rising of Sothis. We see that towards the end of the Fourth Dynasty and in the early years of the Fifth, the nominal beginning of the agricultural year—the season of *Shat*—had moved round until it coincided with the Sothic rising; and thus this rising of Sothis came to be called "New Year's Day." By the time of the Twelfth Dynasty the calendar had moved round until the end of the season of *Pert,* the time of harvest, co-incided with the rising of Sothis, that is to say, the calendar had nearly completed an entire cycle since its

* The date he gives, actually, is B.C. 4240, for he has not taken into consideration the shift back of 120 years owing to the change of the first month from Thoth to Mesore.

establishment. At the beginning of the Eighteenth Dynasty it had moved on so that now the Sothic rising coincided with the end of the nominal season of inundation; and in A.D. 139 it had completed two whole cycles since the time of the pyramids, and the Sothic rising now coincided once more with the beginning of the calendar year.

The reader, I dare say, will find the whole matter very difficult to understand; but, if that be so, he will the more readily appreciate the difficulty confronting Egyptologists, who find their dates for the Eighteenth and Twelfth Dynasties checked by these astronomical considerations, but yet cannot by this means reach a unity of opinion as to whether an extra Sothic cycle should be added between these two dynasties. Personally, I take the view that three centuries or so is a quite sufficient time to allow for the Thirteenth to Seventeenth Dynasties, and I think it inconceivable that nearly 1800 years could have elapsed between the end of the Twelfth and beginning of the Eighteenth Dynasties, as Professor Petrie would have us think. Let us hope that some new facts, astronomical or otherwise, will soon be found to prove the one school or the other right.

CHAPTER VIII

THE EASTERN DESERT AND ITS INTERESTS

I KNOW a young man who declares that after reading a certain explorer's description of a journey across the burning Sahara, he found to his amazement that his nose was covered with freckles. The reader will perhaps remember how, on some rainy day in his childhood, he has sat over the fire and has read sea-stories and dreamed sea-dreams until his lips, he will swear, have tasted salt. Alas, my little agility in the art of narration is wholly inadequate for the production, at this time of life, of any such phenomena upon the gentle skins of those who chance to read these pages. Were I a master-maker of literature, I might herewith lead the imaginative so straight into the boisterous breezes of Egypt, I might hold them so entranced in the sunlight which streams over the desert, that they would feel, wherever they might be seated, the tingling glow of the sun and the wind upon their cheeks, and would hold their hands to their eyes as a shelter from the glare. The walls of their rooms would fall flat as those of Jericho; and outside they would meet the advancing host of the invaders—the sunshine, the north wind, the scudding clouds, the circling vultures, the glistening sand, the blue shadows, and the rampant rocks. And the night closing over the sack of their city, they would see the moonlight, the brilliant stars, the fluttering bats, the solemn owls; they would hear the wailing of the hyænas and the barking of the dogs in the distant camps. If I only possessed the ability, I might weave such a magic carpet for those who knew how to ride upon it, that, deserting the fallen Jericho of their habitation, they would fly to the land of the invaders which they had seen, and there they would be kept as spell-bound and dazzled by the eyes of the wilderness as ever a child was dazzled by a tale of the sea.

But with this ability lacking it is very doubtful whether the reader will be able to appreciate my meaning; and, without the carpet, it is a far cry to Upper Egypt. Nevertheless, I will venture to give an account, in the next few chapters, of some journeys made in the Upper Egyptian desert, in the hope rather of arousing interest in a fascinating country than of placing on record much information of value to science; although the reader interested in Egyptian archæology will find some new material upon which to speculate.

The Upper Egyptian desert is a country known only to a very few. The resident, as well as the visitor, in Egypt raises his eyes from the fertile valley of the Nile to the bare hills, and lowers them once more with the feeling that he has looked at the wall of the garden, the boundary of the land. There is, however, very much to be seen and studied behind this wall; and those who penetrate into the solitudes beyond will assuredly find themselves in a world of new colours, new forms, and new interests. In the old days precious metal was sought here, ornamental stone was quarried, trade-routes passed through to the Red Sea, and the soldiery of Egypt, and later of Rome, marched from station to station amidst its hills. The desert as one sees it now is, so to speak, peopled with the ghosts of the Old World; and on hidden hill-slopes or in obscure valleys one meets with the remains of ancient settlements scattered through the length and breadth of the country.

The number of persons who have had the energy to climb the garden wall and to wander into this great wilderness is so small that one might count the names upon the fingers. Lepsius, the German Egyptologist, passed over some of the routes on which antiquities were to be met with; Golenischeff, the Russian Egyptologist, checked some of his results; Schweinfurth, the great German explorer, penetrated to many of the unknown localities and mapped a great part of the country; Bellefonds Bey, the Director-General of Public Works in Egypt, under Mohammed Ali, made a survey of the mineral belt lying between the river and the Red Sea; and during the last thirty years various prospectors and miners have visited certain points of interest to them. Before the war, the Government Survey Department was engaged in mapping this Eastern Desert, and most valuable reports were published; while for a few years there existed a Mines Department, whose director, Mr. John Wells, made himself acquainted with some of the routes and most of the mining centres. Thus, most of the journeys here to be recorded have not been made over absolutely new ground; though, except for reports of the Survey Department's explorers, and some papers by Schweinfurth, it would be a difficult matter to unearth any literature on the subject. Even so, however, in describing these journeys I have often been able to indulge in the not unpleasing recollection that I write of places which no other western eyes have seen. The subject is of particular interest just now, because, by the discovery of the tomb of Tutankhamen, the public has been set wondering whence came the gold and ornamental stones which were used by the artists and craftsmen of those days, and some answer will here be found to their question.

Those who have travelled in Egypt will not need to be told how the Nile, flowing down from the Sudan to the distant sea, pushes its silvery way through the wide desert; now passing between the granite hills, now through regions of sandstone, and now under the limestone cliffs. A strip of verdant cultivated land, seldom more than six or eight miles wide, and often only as many yards, borders the broad river; and beyond this, on either side, is the desert. In Upper Egypt one may seldom take an afternoon's ride due east or due west without passing out either on to the sunbaked sand of a limitless wilderness or into the liquid shadows of the towering hills. For the present we are not concerned with the Western Desert, which actually forms part of the great Sahara, and our backs may therefore be turned upon it.

Eastwards, behind the hills or over the sand, there is in most parts of the country a wide, undulating plain, broken here and there by the limestone outcrops. Here the sun beats down from a vast sky, and the traveller feels himself but a fly crawling upon a brazen table. In all directions the desert stretches, until, in a leaden haze, the hot sand meets the hot sky. The hillocks and points of rock rise like islands from the floods of the mirage in which they are reflected; and sometimes there are clumps of withered bushes to tell of the unreality of the waters.

The scenery here is often of exquisite beauty; and

its very monotony lends to it an interest when for a while the grouping of the hills ceases to offer new pictures and new harmonies to the eye. Setting out on a journey towards the Red Sea, the traveller rides on camel-back over this rolling plain, with the sun bombarding his helmet from above and the wind charging it from the flank; and, as noonday approaches search is often made in vain for a rock under which to find shade. Naturally, the glaring sand is far hotter than the shady earth under the palms in the cultivation; but the stagnant, dusty, fly-filled air of the groves is not to be compared with the clear atmosphere up in the wilderness. There are no evil odours here, breeding sickness and beckoning death. The wind blows so purely that one might think it had not touched earth since the gods released it from the golden caverns. The wide ocean itself has not less to appeal to the sense of smell than has the fair desert.

Descending from the camel for lunch, the explorer lies on his back upon the sand and stares up at the deep blue of the sky and the intense whiteness of a passing cloud. Raising himself, the Nile valley may still be seen, perhaps, with its palms floating above the vaporous mirage; and away in the distance the pale cliffs rise. Then across his range of sight a butterfly zigzags, blazing in the sunlight; and behind it the blue becomes darker and the white more extreme. Around about, on the face of the desert, there is a jumbled collection of things beautiful; brown flints, white pebbles of limestone, yellow fragments of sandstone, orange-coloured ochre, transparent pieces of gypsum, carnelian and alabaster chips, and glittering quartz. Across the clear patches of sand there are all manner of recent footprints, and the incidental study of these is one of the richest delights of a desert journey. Here may be seen the four-pronged footprints of a wagtail, and there the larger marks of a crow. An eagle's and a vulture's footmarks are often to be observed, and the identification of those of birds such as the desert partridge or of the cream-coloured courser is a happy exercise for the ingenuity. Here the light, wiggly line of a lizard's rapid tour abroad attracts the attention, reminding one of some globe-trotter's route over Europe; and there footprints of the jerboa are seen leading in short jumps towards its hole. Jackals or foxes leave their dainty pad-marks in all directions, and sometimes there are seen the heavy prints of a hyæna, while it is not unusual to meet with those of a gazelle.

In the afternoon he rides onwards, and perhaps a hazy view of the granite hills may now be obtained in the far distance ahead. The sun soon loses its strength and shines in slanting lines over the desert, so that he sees himself in shadow, stretched out to amazing lengths, as though the magnetic power of night in the east were already dragging in the reluctant darknesses to its dark self. Each human or camel footprint in the sand is at this hour a basin filled with blue shade, while every larger dent in the desert's surface is brimful of that same blue; and the colour is so opaque that an Arab lying therein, clad in his blue shirt, is almost indistinguishable at a distance. Above, the white clouds go tearing by, too busy, too intent, it would seem, on some far-off goal to hover blushing around the sun. The light fades, and the camp is pitched on the open plain; and now the traveller is glad to wrap himself in a large

overcoat, and to swallow the hot tea which has been prepared over a fire of the dried scrub of the desert.

The nights in the desert are as beautiful as the days,
though in winter they are often bitterly cold. With the
assistance of a warm bed and plenty of blankets, however, one may sleep in the open in comfort; and only
those who have known this vast bedroom will understand how beautiful night may be. Turning to the east,
one may stare at Mars flashing red somewhere over
Arabia, and westwards there is Jupiter blazing above
the Sahara. One looks up and up at the expanse of
star-strewn blue, and the mind journeys of itself into
the place of dreams before sleep has come to conduct
it thither. The dark desert drops beneath; the bed
floats in mid-air, with planets above and below. Could
one but peer over the side, earth would be seen as small
and vivid as the moon. But a trance holds the body
inactive, and the eyes are fixed upon the space above.
Then, quietly, a puff of wind brings the mind down
again to realities as it passes from darkness to darkness.
Consciousness returns quickly and gently, points out
the aspect of the night, indicates the large celestial
bodies, and as quickly and gently leaves one again to
the tender whispers of sleep.

When there is moonlight there is more to carry the
eye into the region of dreams on earth than there is in
the heavens; for the desert is spread out around in a
silver, shimmering haze, and no limit can be placed to
its horizons. The eye cannot tell where the sand meets
the sky, nor can the mind know whether there is any
meeting. In the dimness of coming sleep one wonders
whether the hands of the sky are always just out of
reach of those of the desert, whether there is always

another mile to journey and always another hill to climb; and, wondering, one drifts into unconsciousness. At dawn, the light brings an awakening in time to see the sun pass up from behind the low hills. In contrast to the vague night the proceeding is rapid and business-like. The light precedes its monarch only by twenty minutes, or so; and ere the soft colours have been fully appreciated, the sun appears over the rocks and flings a sharp beam into the eyes of every living thing, so that in a moment the camp is stirred and quickened.

During the second or third day's ride the granite regions are generally entered, and the traveller is lost amidst the intricate valleys which pass between the peaks of the hills. Here plenty of shelter may be found from the sun's rays in the shadow of the cliffs; and as the camel jogs along over the hard gravel tracks, or as the dismounted rider sits for refreshment with his back propped against a great boulder, the view which is to be enjoyed is often magnificent. On the one side the dark granite, porphyry, or breccia rocks rise up like the towered and buttressed walls of some fairy-tale city; while on the other side range rises behind range, and a thousand peaks harmonize their delicate purples and greys with the blue of the sky. When the sun sets these lofty peaks are flushed with pink, and, like mediators between earth and heaven, carry to the dark valleys the tale of a glory which cannot be seen. There is usually plenty of scrub to be found in the valleys with which to build the evening fires, and with good luck, the food-supplies may be replenished with the flesh of the gazelle. Every two or three days the camp may be pitched beside a well of pure water, where the camels may drink, and from which the portable tanks may be filled.

Near these wells there are sometimes a few Bedouin to be found tending their little herds of goats; quiet, harmless sons of the desert, who generally own allegiance to some Shêkh living in the Nile valley. The guides and camel-men exchange greetings with them, and pass the latest news over the camp fires. Often, however, one may journey for many days without meeting either a human being or a four-footed animal, though on the well-marked tracks the prints of goats and goatherds, camels and camel-men are apparent.

No matter in what direction one travels, hardly a day passes on which one does not meet with some trace of ancient activity. Here it will be a deserted gold-mine, there a quarry; here a ruined fortress or town, and there an inscription upon the rocks. Indications of the present day are often so lacking, and time seems to be so much at a standstill, that one slips back in imagination to the dim elder days. The years fall off like a garment doffed, and a vast sense of relief from their weight is experienced. A kind of exhilaration, more-over, goes with the thought of the life of the men of thousands of years ago who lived amongst these change-less hills and valleys. Their days were so full of ad-venture; they were beset with dangers. One has but to look at the fortified camps, the watch-towers on the heights, the beacons along the highroads, to realise how brave were the "olden times." One of the peculiar charms of these hills of the Eastern Desert is their im-pregnation with the atmosphere of a shadowy adventur-ous past. The mind is conscious, if it may be so ex-pressed, of the ghosts of old sights, the echoes of old sounds. Dead ambitions, dead terrors, drift through these valleys on the wind, or lurk behind the tumbled rocks. Rough inscriptions on these rocks tell how this captain or that centurion here rested, and on the very spot the modern traveller rests to ease the self-same aches and to enjoy the self-same shade before moving on towards an identical goal in the east.

On the third or fourth day after leaving the Nile, the caravan passes beneath the mountains, which here rise sometimes to as much as 6000 feet; and beyond these the road slopes through the valleys down to the barren Red Sea coast, which may be any distance from 100 to 400 miles from the Nile. Kossair is the one town on the coast opposite Upper Egypt, as it was also in ancient times; and Berenice, opposite Lower Nubia, was the only other town north of Sudan territory. Kossair does a fast-diminishing trade with Arabia, and a handful of Egyptian coastguards is kept mildly busy in the prevention of smuggling. The few inhabitants of the Egyptian coast fish, sleep, say their prayers, or dream in the shade of their hovels until death at an extremely advanced age releases them from the boredom of existence. Those of them who are of Arab stock sometimes enliven their days by shooting one another in a more or less sporting manner, and by wandering to other and more remote settlements thereafter; but those of Egyptian blood have not the energy even for this amount of exertion. There is a lethargy over the desert settlements which contrasts strangely with one's own desire for activity under the influence of the sun and the wind, and of the records of ancient toil which are to be observed on all sides. It must be that we of the present day come as the sons of a race still in its youth; and in this silent land we meet only with the worn-out remnant of a people who have been old these thousands of years.

There was a threefold reason for the activities of the ancients in the Eastern Desert. Firstly, from Koptos, a city on the Nile not far from Thebes, to Kossair, there ran the great trade-route with Arabia, Persia, and India; and from Suez to Koptos there was a route by which the traders from Syria often travelled; from Edfu to Berenice there was a trade-route for the produce of Southern Arabia and the ancient land of Pount; while other roads from point to point of the Nile were often used as short-cuts. Secondly, in this desert there were very numerous gold-mines, the working of which was one of the causes which made Egypt the richest country of the ancient world. And thirdly, the ornamental stones which were to be quarried in the hills were in continuous requisition for the buildings and statuary of Egypt, Assyria, Persia and Rome.

There is much to be said in regard to the gold-mining, but here space will not permit of more than the most cursory review of the information. Gold was used in Egypt at a date considerably prior to the beginning of written history, in Dynasty I, and there are many archaic objects richly decorated with that metal. The situation of many of the early cities of the Nile valley is due solely to this industry. When two cities of high antiquity are in close proximity to one another on opposite banks of the river, as is often the case in Upper Egypt, one generally finds that the city on the western bank is the older of the two. In the case of Diospolis Parva and Khenoboskion, which stand opposite to one another, the former, on the west bank, is the more

ancient and is the capital of the province, and the latter,
on the east bank, does not date later than Dynasty VI.
Of Ombos and Koptos, the former, on the west bank,
has prehistoric cemeteries around it; while the latter, on
the east bank, dates from Dynasty I at the earliest.
Hieraconpolis and Eileithyiaspolis stand opposite to
each other, and the former, which is on the west bank,
is certainly the more ancient. Of Elephantine and
Syene, the latter, on the east bank, is by far the less
ancient. And in the case of Pselchis and Baki (Kub-
bân), the former, on the west bank, has near it an
archaic fortress; while the latter, on the east bank, does
not date earlier than Dynasty XII.

The reason of this is to be found in the fact that
most of the early cities were engaged in gold-mining,
and despatched caravans into the Eastern Desert for
that purpose. These cities were usually built on the
western bank of the river, since the main routes of communication from end to end of Egypt passed along the
Western Desert. Mining stations had, therefore, to be
founded on the eastern bank opposite to the parent
cities; and these stations soon became cities themselves
as large as those on the western shore. Thus the antiquity of the eastern city in each of these cases indicates at least that same antiquity for the mining of gold.

Throughout what is known as the Old Kingdom,
gold was used in ever-increasing quantities, but an idea
of the wealth of the mines will best be obtained from
the records of the Empire. About 250,000 grains of
gold were drawn by the Vizir Rekhmara in taxes from
Upper Egypt, and this was but a small item in com-
parison with the taxes levied in kind. A king of a north
Syrian state wrote to Amenhotep III, the Pharaoh of

Egypt, asking for gold, and towards the end of his letter he says: "Let my brother send gold in very large quantities, without measure, and let him send more gold to me than he did to my father; for in my brother's land gold is as common as dust." To the god Amon alone, Rameses III presented some 26,000 grains of gold, and to the other gods he gave at the same time very large sums. In later times the High Priest of Amon was made also director of the gold mines, and it was the diverting of this vast wealth from the crown to the priesthood which was mainly responsible for the fall of the Ramesside line.

A subject must here be introduced which will ever remain of interest to the speculative. I believe that the southern portion of this desert is to be identified with the Ophir of the Bible, and that the old gold-workings here are none other than "King Solomon's Mines." In the Book of Kings one reads, "And King Solomon made a navy of ships in Ezion-geber, which is beside Eloth, on the shore of the Red Sea, in the land of Edom. And Hiram sent in the navy his servants, shipmen that had knowledge of the sea, with the servants of Solomon. And they came to Ophir, and fetched from thence gold, four hundred and twenty talents, and brought it to King Solomon." Ophir cannot be identified with Arabia, since there is no gold there; and hence one may seek this land of ancient wealth at the southern end of the Eastern Egyptian Desert. If it is argued that the Hebrews would have found difficulties in carrying on mining operations unmolested in Egyptian territory, it may be contended, on the other hand, that King Solomon may have made some bargain with the Pharaoh; for example, that the former might mine in a certain tract of desert if the latter might cut timber in the Lebanon. The purchase of cedar-wood by the Egyptians is known to have taken place at about this period, payment in gold being made; and therefore it does not require an undue stretch of the imagination to suppose that the Hebrews themselves mined the gold. Again, at the time when King Solomon reigned in all his glory in Palestine, the short-lived Pharaohs of Egypt sat upon tottering thrones, and were wholly unable to protect the Eastern Desert from invasion. The Egyptians often state that they encountered hostile forces in this land, and these may not always have consisted of Bedouin marauders.

No savant has accepted for a moment the various theories which place Ophir at the southern end of the African continent; and the most common view is that Solomon obtained his gold from the land of Pount, so often referred to in Egyptian inscriptions. This country is thought to have been situated in the neighbourhood of Suakin; but, as Professor Naville points out, it is a somewhat vague geographical term, and may include a large tract of country to the north and south of this point. One cannot imagine the Hebrews penetrating very far over the unknown seas to the perilous harbours of Middle Africa; one pictures them more easily huddled in the less dangerous ports of places such as Kossair or Berenice, or at farthest, in that of Suakin. It is thus very probable that some of the gold-workings in the desert here described are actually King Solomon's Mines, and that the country through which the reader will be conducted is the wonderful Ophir itself. Certainly there is no one who can state conclusively that it is not.

Work continued with unabated energy during the later periods of Egyptian history, and the Persian, Greek, and Roman treasuries were filled consecutively with the produce of these mines. Several classical writers make reference to these operations, and sometimes one is told the actual name and situation of the workings. Diodorus gives a description of the mines in the Wady Alâgi, and tells how the work was done. The miners each wore a lamp tied to his forehead. The stone was carried to the surface by children, and was pounded in stone mortars by iron pestles. It was then ground to a fine powder by old men and women. This powdered ore was washed on inclined tables, the residue being placed in earthen crucibles with lead, salt, and tin for fluxes, and was there baked for five days.

Agatharchides describes how the prisoners and negroes hewed out the stone, and, with unutterable toil, crushed it in mills, and washed out the grains of gold. The Arabian historian, El Macrizi, states that during the reign of Ahmed ibn Teilûn there was great activity in the mining industry throughout the Eastern Desert, and Cufic inscriptions of this date, found in the old workings, confirm this statement. From then, until modern times, however, little work was done; but in recent years many of the ancient workings have been re-opened, and one must admit that if these are really to be regarded as King Solomon's Mines, that potentate must have had a somewhat lower opinion of Ophir than tradition indicates.

The other cause for the ancient activity in the Eastern Desert was, as has been said, the need of ornamental stone for the making of vases, statues, and architectural accessories. From the earliest times, bowls and vases of alabaster, breccia, diorite, and other fine stones were used by the Egyptians, and the quarries must have already formed quite a flourishing industry. Soon the making of statuettes, and later, of statues, enlarged this industry, and with the growth of civilisation it steadily increased. The galleries of the Cairo Museum, and those of European museums, are massed with statues and other objects cut in stone, brought from the hills between the Nile and the Red Sea.

The breccia quarries of Wady Hammamât were worked from archaic to Roman days; the Turquoise Mountains, not far from Kossair, supplied the markets of the ancient world; white granite was taken from the hills of Um Etgâl; there were two or three alabaster quarries in constant use; and in the time of the Roman Empire the famous Imperial Porphyry was quarried in the mountains of Gebel Dukhân. One may still see blocks of breccia at Hammamât, of granite at Um Etgâl, or of porphyry at Dukhân, lying abandoned at the foot of the hills, although numbered and actually addressed to the Cæsars. The towns in which the quarrymen lived still stand in defiance of the years, and the traveller who has the energy to penetrate into the distant valleys where they are situated may there walk through streets untrodden since the days of Nero and Trajan, and yet still littered with the chippings from the dressing of the blocks.

In the old days the provisioning of the mining and quarrying settlements must have taxed the ingenuity even of the Egyptians; and the establishing of workable lines of communication with the distant Nile must have required the most careful organisation. The caravans bringing food were of great size, for there were often several thousands of hungry miners to be fed. In Dynasty VI, one reads of 200 donkeys and 50 oxen being used in the transport, and in Dynasty XI, 60,000 loaves of bread formed the daily requirements in food of one expedition. In late Ramesside times the food of an expedition of some 9,000 men was carried on ten large carts, each drawn by six yoke of oxen, while porters "innumerable" are said to have been employed. The families of the workmen generally lived on the spot, and these also had to be fed—a fact which is indicated, too, by an inscription which states that in one expedition each miner required twenty small loaves of bread per diem.

Whenever this organisation broke down, the consequences must have been awful. In this quarrying expedition in Ramesside times, consisting of 9,000 men, ten per cent of them died from one cause or another; and later writers speak of the "horrors" of the mines. In summer the heat is intense in the desert, and the wells could not always have supplied sufficient water. The rocks are then so hot that they cannot be touched by the bare hand, and one's boots are little protection to the feet. Standing in the sunlight, the ring has to be removed from one's finger, for the hot metal burns a blister upon the flesh. After a few hours of exercise there is a white lather upon the lips, and the eyes are blinded with the moisture which has collected around them; and thus, what the quarrymen and miners must have suffered as they worked upon the scorching stones, no tongue can tell.

In ancient Egyptian times the camel was regarded as a curious beast from a far country, and was seldom, if ever, put to any use in Egypt. Only three or four representations of it are now known, and it never occurs amongst any of the animals depicted upon the walls of the tombs, although bears, elephants, giraffes, and other foreign and rare creatures, are there shown. It was an Asiatic animal, and was not introduced into Egypt as an agent of transportation until the days of the ubiquitous Romans. Donkeys, oxen, and human beings were alone used in Pharaonic days for transporting the necessities of the labourers and the produce of their work; and probably the officials were carried to and fro in sedan-chairs. Even in Roman days there is nothing to show that the camel was very largely employed, and one may not amuse oneself too confidently with the picture of a centurion of the empire astride the hump of the rolling ship of the desert.

Nowadays, of course, one generally travels by camel in the desert, except along certain routes where the use of an automobile is possible. For an expedition of fifteen days or so, about ten camels are required and one or two guides. Some of the animals carry the water in portable tanks; others are loaded with the tents and camp-beds; and others carry the boxes of tinned food and bottled drinks. The whole caravan rattles and bumps as it passes through the echoing valleys, and one's cook rises from amidst a clattering medley of saucepans and kettles, which are slung around his saddle. The camels are obtained from some Shêkh, who pretends to hold himself more or less responsible for one's safety. With a steady steed and a good saddle, there are few means of locomotion so enjoyable as camel-riding. Once the art is learnt, it is never forgotten, and after the tortures of the first day or so of the first expedition, one need never again suffer from stiffness, though many months may elapse between the journeys. This preliminary suffering is due to one's inability at the outset to adjust the muscles to the peculiar motion; but the knowledge comes unconsciously after a while and ever remains.

One jogs along at the rate of about four and a half or five miles an hour, and some thirty miles a day are covered with ease. The baggage camels travel at about three miles an hour. They start first, are passed during the morning, catch one up at the long rest for luncheon, are again passed during the afternoon, and arrive about an hour after the evening halt has been called. If possible, all the camels drink every second day, but they are quite capable of going strongly for three or four days without water, and, when really necessary, can travel for a week or more through a land without wells.

As has been said, experiments have been tried on certain routes with automobiles and motor bicycles, which were by no means unsuccessful. Many of the main roads in the Eastern Desert pass over hard gravel, and a motor car may be driven with safety over the unprepared camel tracks. If wells were sunk every ten or fifteen miles, there would be no dangers to be feared from a breakdown; and under favourable circumstances the journey from the Nile to the Red Sea, at various points, might be comfortably accomplished in a day. In the future, one may picture the energetic tourist leaving his Luxor or Cairo hotel, whirling over the open plains where now one crawls, rushing through the valleys in which the camel-rider lingers, penetrating to the remote ruins and deserted workings, and emerging breathless on to the golden coast of the sea, to wave his handkerchief to his friends upon the decks of the Indian liners.

The time must surely come when the owners of automobiles in Egypt will sicken of the short roads around Cairo, and will venture beyond the garden wall towards the rising sun. Whether it will be that the re-working of the gold mines and the quarries of orna-mental stone will attract the attention of these persons to this wonderful wilderness, or that the enterprising automobilists will pave the way for the miners and the quarrymen, it is certain that some day the desert will blossom with the rose once more, and the rocks re-verberate with the sound of many voices.

Had I now in my two open hands pearls, diamonds, and rubies, how gladly would I give them—or some of them—for the sight of the misty mountains of the East-ern Desert, and for the feel of the sharp air of the hills! The mind looks forward with enthusiasm to the next visit to these unknown regions, and I cannot but feel that those who have it in their power to travel there are missing much in remaining within the walls of the little garden of the Nile. I hear in imagination the camels grunting as their saddles are adjusted; I feel the tingle of the morning air; and I itch to be off again, "over the hills and far away," into the solitary splendour of the desert.

CHAPTER IX

THE QUARRIES OF WADY HAMMAMÂT

THE so-called Breccia Quarries of Wady Hammamât are known to all Egyptologists by name,
owing to the important historical inscriptions
which are cut on the rocks of the valley. In reality, the
stone quarried there was mainly tuff, or consolidated
volcanic ash, and the real name of the locality is Wady
Fowakhîeh, "the Valley of the Pots"; but such niceties
do not trouble the average archæologist. Many of the
inscriptions were copied by Lepsius, the German
Egyptologist, and further notes were made by Golenischeff, a Russian savant; but except for these two persons, no Egyptologist beside myself has studied the
quarries. They have been seen, however, on a few occasions by Europeans; and, as the caravan road to Kossair passes along the valley in which they are situated,
they are known to all the natives who have crossed the
desert at this point. Some years ago, I found it possible
to visit this historic site, and I was fortunate enough to
obtain the companionship of three English friends who
happened, very opportunely, to be in search of mild
excitement at the time.

We set out from Luxor one morning in November,
our caravan consisting in all of twenty-three camels,
nine of which were ridden by our four selves, my servant, two guards, the Shêkh of the camel-men, and the
guide, while fourteen were loaded with the three tents,

the baggage, and the water-tanks, and were tended by a dozen camel-men, who made the journey mainly on foot. Our road led eastwards from Luxor, past the temple of the goddess Mut, at Karnak, reflected in its sacred lake, and so along the highroad towards the rising sun. The day was cool, and a strong invigorating breeze raced past us, going in the same direction. Before us, as we crossed the fields, the sunlit desert lay stretched behind the soft green of the tamarisks which border its edge. Away to the right, the three peaks of the limestone hills, which form the characteristic background of Thebes, rose in the sunlight; and to the left we could discern the distant ranges behind which we were to penetrate.

On reaching the desert, we turned off northwards towards these hills, skirting the edge of the cultivated land until we should pick up the ancient road which leaves the Nile valley some twenty miles north of Luxor. After luncheon and a rest in the shade of the rustling tamarisks, the ride was continued, and we did not again dismount until, in the mid-afternoon, the Coptic monastery, which is situated behind the town of Qus, and which marks the beginning of the road to the Red Sea, was reached; and here the camp was pitched. The quiet five hours' ride of about twenty miles had sufficed to produce healthy appetites in the party, and, when the sun went down and the air turned cold, we were glad to attack an early dinner in the warmth of the mess-tent—one of the camel-boxes serving as a table, and the four saddles taking the place of chairs.

The next morning we set out soon after sunrise, and rode eastwards into the desert, which here stretched out before us in a blaze of sunlight. The road passed

WADY HAMMAMAT

AN ABANDONED SARCOPHAGUS AT WADY HAMMAMAT

over the open gravel and sand in a series of parallel
tracks beaten hard by the pads of generations of camels.
Gebel el Gorn, "the Hill of the Horn," was passed
before noon; and, mounting a ridge, we saw the wide
plain across which we were to travel, intersected by a
dry river-bed, marked for its whole length by low
bushes. Unable to find shade, and these bushes being
still some distance ahead, we lunched in the open sunlight, at a spot where the wind, sweeping over the ridge,
brought us all the coolness which we could desire.

We were now on the great mediæval highway from
Qus to Kossair, by which the Arabian and Indian trade
with Egypt was once conducted. The quarries of
Hammamât lie on the main road to the sea. Nowadays
the road starts from Keneh; in ancient times it started
from Koptos, now called Quft, about ten miles south of
Keneh; and in mediæval days it started from Qus, about
ten miles south of Quft again. The roads from these
different places join at the little oasis of Lagêta, which
lies some four-and-twenty miles back from the Nile
valley.

Riding into Lagêta in mid-afternoon, the scene was
one of great charm. The flat desert stretched around
us in a haze of heat. In the far distance ahead, the
mountains of Hammamât could be seen, blue, misty,
and indistinct. The little oasis, with its isolated groups
of tamarisks, its four or five tall palms, its few acacias,
and its one little crop of corn, formed a welcome patch
of green amidst the barren wilderness; and the eyes,
aching from the glare around, turned with gratitude
towards the soft shadows of the trees. A large, and
probably ancient, well of brackish water forms the
nucleus around which the few poor huts cluster; and

two or three *shadûfs,* or water-hoists, are to be seen here and there. A ruined, many-domed building, which may have been a caravanserai, or perhaps a Coptic monastery, stands picturesquely under a spreading acacia; and near it I found a fragment of a Greek inscription, in which, like a light emerging momentarily from the darkness of the past, the name of the Emperor Tiberius Claudius was to be seen. The few villagers idly watched us as we dismounted and walked through the settlement, too bathed in the languor of their monotonous life to bother to do more than greet with mild interest those of our camel-men whom they knew; and while we sat under the tamarisks to drink our tea, the only living thing which took any stock of us and our doings was a small green willow-wren, in search of a crumb of food.

The camp was pitched to the east of the oasis, and at dawn we continued our way. The temperature was not more than 38° Fahrenheit when the sun rose, and we were constrained to break into a hard trot, in order to keep warm. Two desert martins circled about us as we went, now passing under the camels' necks, and now whirling overhead; while more than once we put up a few cream-coloured coursers, who went off with a whirr into the space around. After a couple of hours' riding over the open, hard-surfaced desert, we topped a low ridge and came into view of a ruined Roman station, called in ancient times the Hydreuma, and now known as Kasr el Benât, "the Castle of the Maidens." The building stands in a level plain around which the low hills rise, and to the east the distant Hammamât mountains form a dark background. From the outside one sees a well-made rectangular wall, and entering the doorway on the north side one passes into an enclosure surrounded by a series of small chambers, the roofs of which have now fallen in. In these little rooms the weary Roman officers and the caravan masters rested themselves as they passed to and fro between the quarries and the Nile; and in this courtyard, when haply the nights were warm, they sang their songs to the stars and dreamed their dreams of Rome. The building is so little ruined that one may picture it as it then was without any difficulty; and such is the kindness of Time that one peoples the place with great men and good, intent on their work and happy in their exile, rather than with that riff-raff which so often found its way to these outlying posts.

Across the plain, opposite the entrance to the Hydreuma, there is a large isolated rock with cliff-like sides upon which are all manner of inscriptions and rough drawings. Here there are two Sinaitic inscriptions of rare value, and several curious signs in an unknown script, while Ababdeh marks and Arabic letters are conspicuous.

We mounted our camels again at about eleven o'clock, and rode towards the wall of the Medîk es-Salâm hills ahead, passing into their shadows soon after noonday. We halted for luncheon in the shade of a group of rocks, and our meal was enlivened by the presence of two butterflies, which seemed out of place in the barren desert, and yet in harmony with the breezy, light-hearted spirit of the place. Early in the afternoon we rode on, but an hour had not passed when some obvious inscriptions on the rocks to the left of the track, opposite a point where the road bends sharply to the right, attracted my attention. These proved to date from the Middle Empire, about B.C. 2000, and no doubt marked a camp of that period. The names of various officials were given, and a prayer or two to the gods were to be read. Rounding the corner, we had no sooner settled ourselves to the camels' trot, than another group of inscriptions on the rocks to the right of the path necessitated a further halt. Here there were two very important graffiti of the time of Akhnaton, the father-in-law of Tutankhamen; and considerable light is thrown by one of them upon the fascinating period of the religious revolution of that king. There are three cartouches, of which the first is that of Queen Tiy, the second reads "Amenhotep" (IV), and the third seems to have given the name Akhnaton; but both this cartouche and that of Tiy are erased. The three cartouches are placed together above the symbols of sovereignty and below the rays of the sun's disk, thus showing that Akhnaton was but a boy of tender years, under his mother's guidance, when he first came to the throne, and that the Aton worship had already begun.

The shadows were lengthening when we once more mounted and trotted up the valley, which presently led into more open ground; but after half-an-hour's ride, a second Roman station came into sight, and again the grumbling camels had to kneel. The building is much ruined, and is not of great interest to those who have already seen the Hydreuma and other stations. As we continued the journey the sun set behind us, and in the growing moonlight the valley looked ghostly and wonderfully beautiful. The shapes of the rocks became indistinct, and we were hardly aware when the well, known as Bir Hammamât, was at last reached. This well lies in a flat, gravelly amphitheatre amidst the rugged hills, which press in on all sides. It is in all about six hours' ride—i.e., twenty-eight or thirty miles —from Lagêta; but our several halts had spread the journey over twice that length of time. The well is circular and fairly large, and stones dropped into its pitch-dark depths seemed a long time in striking the water. A subterranean stairway, restored in recent years by a mining company, runs down at one side to the water's level; and at its doorway in the moonlight we sat and smoked until the baggage camels came up.

The next morning we rode up a valley which was now tortuous and narrow. This is the Wady Hammamât of the archæologist, and the Wady Fowakhîeh of the natives. Dark, threatening hills towered on either side, as though eager to prison for ever the deeds once enacted at their feet. Our voices echoed amongst the rocks, and the wind carried the sound down the valley and round the bend, adding to it its own quiet whispers. A ride of about half-an-hour's length brought us to some ruined huts where the ancient quarrymen had lived in the days of the Pharaohs. From this point onwards for perhaps a mile the rocks on either side are dotted with inscriptions, from which a part of the history of the valley may be learnt.

The place is full of whispers. As the breeze blows round the rocks and up the silent water-courses, it is as though the voices of men long since forgotten were drifting uncertainly by. One feels as though the rocks were peopled with insistent entities, all muttering the tales of long ago. Behind this great rock there is something laughing quietly to itself; up this dry waterfall there is a sort of whimpering; and here in this silent recess one might swear that the word to be silent had

been passed around. It is only the wind, and the effect
of the contrast between the exposed and the still places
sheltered by the rocks; but with such a history as is writ
upon its walls, one might believe the valley to be
crowded with the ghosts of those who have suffered or
triumphed in it.

Wady Fowakhîeh extends from Bir Hammamât to
another well, called Bir Fowakhîeh, which lies in the
open circus at the east end of the valley. Although the
tuff quarried here is of a blue or olive-green colour, the
surface of the rocks, except where they are broken, is
a sort of chocolate-brown. One thus obtains an extraordinary combination of browns and blues, which
with the flush of the sunset and the dim purple of the
distant hill-tops forms a harmony as beautiful as any
the world knows. The flat, gravel bed of the valley is
from fifty to a hundred yards wide, and along this level
surface run numerous camel-tracks, more or less parallel with one another. Besides the inscriptions there
are other traces of ancient work: an unfinished shrine,
and a sarcophagus, abandoned owing to its having
cracked, are to be seen where the workmen of some five-
and-twenty centuries ago left them; and here and there
a group of ruined huts is to be observed.

Amidst these relics of the old world our tents were
pitched, having been removed from Bir Hammamât as
soon as breakfast had been finished; and with camera,
note-book, and sketching apparatus, the four of us dis-
persed in different directions, my own objective, of
course, being the inscriptions. The history of Wady
Fowakhîeh begins when the history of Egypt begins,
and one must look back into the dim uncertainties of
the archaic period for the first evidences of the working

of the quarries in this valley. Many beautifully made
bowls and other objects of this tuff are found in the
graves of Dynasty I, fifty-five centuries ago; and my
friends and I, scrambling over the rocks, were fortunate
to find in a little wady leading northwards from the
main valley a large rock-drawing and inscription of this
remote date. A "vase-maker" here offers a prayer to
the sacred barque of the hawk-god Horus, which is
drawn so clearly that one may see the hawk standing
upon its shrine in the boat, an upright spear set before
the door; and one may observe the bull's head, so often
found in primitive countries, affixed to the prow; while
the barque itself is shown to be standing upon a sledge
in order that it might be dragged over the ground.

In Dynasties II and IV the objects in the museums
show that the quarries were extensively worked, and in
Dynasty V one has the testimony of local inscriptions
as well. An official under King Asesa (B.C. 2675) has
left his name on the rocks on the south of the valley;
and the name of another who lived in the reign of Unas
(B.C. 2650) is to be seen there. Of the reign of Pepy I
(B.C. 2600) of Dynasty VI, there is more definite information. Scanning the rocks, one reads of chief architects, master builders, assistant artisans, scribes, treas-
urers, ship-captains, and their families stationed at the
quarries to procure stone for the ornamentation of the
pyramid buildings of the king, which are still to be seen
at Sakkâra, near Cairo; and these inscriptions mention
a certain Thethi, who was the "master pyramid-builder
of the king," and therefore was probably in charge of
the expedition.

In the reign of Aty (B.C. 2500) a ship's captain,
named Apa, came to procure stone for his master's pyra-

mid; and with him were 200 soldiers and 200 workmen.
King Imhotep (B.C. 2400) sent his son, Zaty, with 1,000
labourers, 100 quarrymen, and 1,200 soldiers, to obtain
stone; and he supplied 200 donkeys and 50 oxen daily
for its transport. But the first really interesting inscription on the rocks of the valley dates from Dynasty
XI (B.C. 2050). Here an all too brief story is told by a
great official named Henu, recording an expedition
made by him to the distant land of Pount, in the eighth
year of the reign of Menthuhotep III. The king had
ordered Henu to despatch a ship to Pount in order to
bring fresh myrrh from that land of spices, and he had
therefore collected an army of 3,000 men. He set out
from Koptos, travelled over the open desert to the little
oasis of Lagêta, and so struck the road which we had
followed. He seems to have had much consideration
for his men, for he says, "I made the road a river, and
the desert a stretch of field. I gave a leather bottle, a
carrying pole, two jars of water, and twenty loaves of
bread to each one of the men every day." When one
considers that this means 60,000 loaves of bread per
day, one's respect for the organising powers of the
ancient Egyptians must be considerable. At Wady
Fowakhîeh he seems to have organised some quarry
works for the king, and presently he pushed on towards
the Red Sea, digging wells as he went. The expedition,
which will be recorded later, is then described; and
Henu states that, on his return to Wady Fowakhîeh,
he organised the transport of some five blocks of stone
which were to be used for making statues.

In the second year of the reign of Menthuhotep IV,
(B.C. 2000)—so runs another long rock inscription—the
Vizir Amenemhet was sent to the quarries with an

expedition of 10,000 men, consisting of miners, arti-
ficers, quarrymen, artists, draughtsmen, stone-cutters,
gold-workers, and officials. His orders were to procure
"an august block of the pure costly stone which is in
this mountain, for a sarcophagus, an eternal memorial,
and for monuments in the temples." The presence of
gold-workers indicates that the gold mines near Bir
Fowakhîeh were also to be opened. Ancient workings
are still to be seen near this well, and in modern times
an attempt was made to re-open them, which, however,
was not very successful.

One must imagine this expedition as camping at
that well—Bir Hammamât—where we had camped on
the previous night, and as passing up the valley each
day to and from the quarries. This was a tedious walk,
and a nearer water supply must have been much needed.
One day there was a heavy fall of rain, which must have
lasted several hours, for when it had ceased the sandy
plain at the head of the valley was found to be a veri-
table lake of water. Rain is not at all a common occurrence in Upper Egypt. Even now, the peasants are
peculiarly alarmed at a heavy downpour; and in those
far-off days the quarrymen were ready enough to see
in the phenomenon a direct act of the great god Min,
the patron of the desert. "Rain was made," says the
inscription, "and the form of this god appeared in it;
his glory was shown to men. The highland was made
a lake, the water extending to the margin of the rocks."
The presence of the water seems to have dislodged an
accumulation of sand which had formed over an ancient
and disused well; and when the lake subsided, the
astonished labourers discovered its mouth, ten cubits
in length on its every side. "Soldiers of old and kings

who had lived aforetime went out and returned by its side; yet no eye had seen it." It was "undefiled, and had been kept pure and clean from the gazelle, and concealed from the Bedouin." If this well is, as I suppose, the Bir Fowakhîeh, it must have been a great boon to the workmen, for it is but a few minutes' walk from the quarries, and must have saved them that weary tramp down to the Bir Hammamât at the end of their hard day's work.

When the great stone for the lid of the sarcophagus had been prised out of the hillside, and had been toppled into the valley, another wonder occurred. Down the track there came running "a gazelle great with young, going towards the people before her, while her eyes looked backward, though she did not turn back." The quarrymen must have ceased their work to watch her as she ran along the hard valley, looking back with startled eyes as the shouts of the men assailed her. At last, "she arrived at this block intended for the lid of the sarcophagus, it being still in its place; and upon it she dropped her young, while the whole army of the king watched her." One can hear the quarrymen, as they clattered into the valley, shouting, "A miracle, a miracle!" and surrounded the incapacitated creature. The end of the tale is told briefly. "Then they cut her throat upon the block, and brought fire. The block descended to the Nile in safety."

Another inscription states that this sarcophagus lid was dragged down to the river by an army of 3,000 sailors from the Delta, and that sacrifices of cattle, goats, and incense were constantly made in order to lighten the labour. It must have been an enormous block to drag along; for even after it was dressed into the required shape and size by the masons in Egypt, it was some 14 feet in length, 7 feet in width, and 3½ feet in thickness. Two other blocks brought down from these quarries at about the same date are said to have been 17 feet in length, while a third was about 20 feet long.

In the reign of Amenemhet I, of Dynasty XII (B.C. 2000), an officer named Antef was sent to the quarries to procure a special kind of stone, so rare that "there was no prospector who knew the marvel of it, and none that sought it had found it." "I spent eight days," says Antef, "searching the hills for it, but I knew not the place wherein it might be. I prostrated myself before Min, before Mut, before the goddess great in magic, and before all the gods of the highlands, burning incense to them upon the fire." At last, after almost giving up the search in despair, he found the required block one morning just as the sun had topped the dark hills of the valley, and while his men were just scattering in all directions to renew the search. Although so many centuries have passed since Antef found his stone, one feels, when one reads this inscription upon the rocks, that it was but yesterday; and one may picture the sunlit scene when, as he says, "the company were in festivity and the entire army was praising, rejoicing, and doing obeisance."

Under other kings of this dynasty, one reads, as one walks up the valley, of works being carried on. A certain man quarried and carried down to the river ten blocks which were later converted into seated statues, 8½ feet high. Another official speaks of his army of 2,000 men which he had with him in this now desolate place; and a third has left an inscription, reading, "I came to these highlands with my army in safety, by the power of Min, the Lord of the Highlands."

So the work continued from generation to generation, and the quarrymen, as they sat at noon to rest themselves in the shade, could read around them the names of dead kings and forgotten officials carved upon the rocks, and could place their own names in the illustrious company. The troubled years of the Hyksos rule checked the quarrying somewhat; but in Dynasty XVIII the labours were renewed, though unfortunately no long inscriptions have been left to illuminate the darkness of the history of the valley. An inscription of the time of Akhnaton is to be seen high up on the rocks, but other figures have been cut over it by Sety I.

Various kings of Dynasties XIX and XX are mentioned on the rocks; but the only important inscription dates from the second year of the reign of Rameses IV (B.C. 1165). It seems that this king, with a degree of energy unusual in a Pharaoh of this debased period, made a personal visit to the quarries. "He led the way to the place he desired; he went around the august mountain; he cut an inscription upon this mountain, engraved with the great name of the king." This inscription is to be seen on the rocks of the valley, almost as fresh as when the scribes had written it. On his return to Egypt he organised an expedition for the purpose of quarrying the stone he had selected. A complete list of the *personnel* of the expedition is recorded, and, as it gives an idea of the usual composition of a force of this kind, I may be permitted to give it in some detail.

The head of the expedition was none other than the

High Priest of Amon, and his immediate staff consisted of the king's butlers, the deputy of the army and his secretary, the overseer of the treasury, two directors of the quarry service, the court charioteer, and the clerk of the army lists. Twenty clerks of the army, or of the War Office, as we would say, and twenty inspectors of the court stables were attached to this group. Under a military commandant there were 20 infantry officers and 5,000 men, 50 charioteers, 200 sailors, and a mixed body of 50 priests, scribes, overseers, and veterinary inspectors. Under a chief artificer and three master quarrymen there were 130 stonecutters and quarrymen; while the main work was done by 2,000 crown slaves and 800 foreign captives. Two draughtsmen and four sculptors were employed for engraving the inscriptions, etc. A civil magistrate with 50 police kept order amongst this large force, which altogether totalled 8,362 men, not including, as the inscription grimly states, the 900 souls who perished from fatigue, hunger, disease, or exposure.

The supplies for this large expedition were transported in ten carts, each drawn by six yoke of oxen; and there were many porters laden with bread, meat, and many kinds of cakes. The inscription then tells us of the sacrifices which were continuously made to the gods of the desert. "There were brought from Thebes the oblations for the satisfaction of the gods of heaven and earth. Bulls were slaughtered, calves were smitten, incense streamed to heaven, *shedeh* and wine were like a flood, beer flowed in this place. The voice of the ritual-priest presented these pure offerings to all the gods of the mountains, so that their hearts were glad."

In this remote desert, how easy it is to dream one-

self back in the olden days! The valley, pressed close
on either side by the rocks around which the whispers
for ever wander, echoes once again with the ring of the
chisels; and in the wind which almost ceaselessly rushes
over the ancient tracks, one can see the fluttering garments of the quarrymen as they pass to and from their
work. As we sat at the door of our tents, in the cool
of the afternoon, the present day seemed now as remote
as the past had seemed before; and, when the great
moment of sunset was approached, we almost felt it
fitting to burn a pan of incense to the old gods of
heaven and earth, as the officers of Rameses IV had
done.

The names of later kings, Shabaka, Taharka, Psam-
etik, Nekau, Ahmose II, and others, look down from
the rocks; and sometimes the date is precisely given,
and the names of the officials are mentioned. During
the Persian period the green tuff was in considerable
demand for the making of those life-like portrait statuettes, so many of which are to be seen in the various
museums; and the coarser tuff, which is practically
breccia, was much used for shrines and sarcophagi. It
is curious to see in this distant valley the names of the
Persian kings, Cambyses, Darius I, Xerxes I, and
Artaxerxes I, written in Egyptian hieroglyphs in the
rock inscriptions, together with the year of their reigns
in which the quarrying was undertaken. Nectanebo I
and II (B.C. 370 and B.C. 350) have left their names in
the valley; and dating from this and the subsequent
periods there are various Egyptian and Greek inscriptions.

In the reign of Ptolemy III (B.C. 240) a small temple was built near the Bir Fowakhîeh at the east end of

the valley of the quarries. Wandering over this amphitheatre amidst the hills, we came upon the remains of
the little building, which had been constructed of rough
stones augmented by well-made basalt columns. It was
dedicated to the god Min, the patron of the Eastern
Desert; but as it was only about 12 feet by 22 feet in
area, the priests of the god could not have commanded
the devotion of more than a few of the quarrymen.
Near the temple there are three or four groups of
ruined huts, nestling on the hillsides amongst the rocks;
and here the quarrymen of the Ptolemaic and Græco-
Roman ages dwelt, as the broken pottery indicates.
There are many traces of ancient gold-workings near
by, and a ruined house of modern construction stands
as a sad memorial of the unsuccessful attempt to re-
open them. In the inscriptions of Dynasties XVIII-
XX one reads of "the gold of Koptos," which must be
the gold brought into Koptos from this neighbourhood;
and at this later period the mines appear to have been
worked. A very fine pink granite began to be quarried just to the east of this well in Roman days, and one
may still see many blocks cut from the hillside which
have lain there these two thousand years awaiting
transport.

In Wady Fowakhîeh itself there are many blocks
of tuff, addressed to the Cæsars, but never despatched
to them; nor is there anything in this time-forsaken
valley which so brings the past before one as do these
blocks awaiting removal to vanished cities. There are
many Greek inscriptions to be seen, the majority being
grouped together in a recess amidst the rocks on the
south side of the valley. Here we read of persons who
worked for Tiberius, Nero, Domitian, and other em-

perors; and there are their drawings of men, animals, and boats, as fresh as when an hour at noon was whiled away in their making. From these, the last days of the quarrying, dates a causeway which passes up the hill-side on the south of the valley, and which was intended to ease the descent of blocks quarried higher up. The Romans have also left watch-towers on the hill-tops, which indicate that peace did not always reign in the desert.

The night, which closed in on us all too soon, brought with it the silence of the very grave. The wind fell, and the whisperings almost ceased. The young moon, which lit the valley, seemed to turn all things to stone under its gaze; and not a sound fell from the camel-men or the camels. The evening meal having been eaten and the pipes smoked, we quietly slipped into our beds; and when the moon had set behind the hills and absolute darkness had fallen upon the valley, we might have believed ourselves as dead and as deep in the Under-world as the kings whose names were inscribed upon the black rocks around.

On the following morning we continued our journey eastwards, towards the Red Sea, along the old trade-route. This expedition forms a subject which will be treated by itself in the next chapter, and therefore I may here pass over the week occupied by the journey, and may resume the thread of the present narrative at the date when we set out from Wady Fowakhîeh on our homeward way. The day was already hot as we trotted down the valley and past the Bir Hammamât, where, by the way, we put up another family of cream-coloured coursers. A couple of hours' trotting brought us to a cluster of sandstone rocks on the north of the now open and wide road, these having been passed in the dusk on the outward journey. Here I found one or two inscriptions in unknown letters, a few Egyptian graffiti, and a little Græco-Roman shrine, dedicated to the great god Min. On these rocks we ate our luncheon, and rested in the shade; and in the early afternoon we mounted once more, passing the second Roman station half-an-hour later. A ride of two and a half hours brought us to the Hydreuma about sunset, and here we halted to smoke a pipe and stretch our legs. Then in the moonlight we rode on once more over the open desert, which stretched in hazy uncertainty as far as the eye could see. The oasis of Lagêta was reached at about seven o'clock, and, the night having turned cold, we were glad to find the camp fires already burning and the kettle merrily boiling.

We were on the road again soon after sunrise, and riding towards Koptos, about ten or twelve miles from Lagêta, we passed another Roman enclosure, now almost entirely destroyed. Our route now lay to the north of the hills of El Gorn, the south side of which we had seen on our outward journey; and after three and a half hours' riding we came into sight of the distant Nile valley. The thin line of green trees seemed in the mirage to be swimming in water, as though the period of the inundation were upon us again. At the point where this view is first obtained there are some low hills, on the south side of the tracks, and in one of these there is a small red-ochre quarry. The sandstone is veined with ochre, and the quarry had been opened for the purpose of obtaining this material for the making of red paint; but whether the few red markings on the rocks are ancient or mediæval, I cannot say. Here we ate an early luncheon, and about noon we rode on over the sun-bathed plain down to the cultivation. Leaving the desert, our road passed between the fields towards the Nile; and by two o'clock we reached the picturesque village of Quft, which marks the site of the ancient Koptos. We spent the afternoon in wandering over the ruins of the once famous caravanserai, and in the evening we took the train back to Luxor.

Such are the quarries of Hammamât, and such is the road to them. It is a simple journey, and one able to be undertaken by any active person who will take the trouble to order a few camels from Keneh. There will come a time when tourists will travel to the quarries by automobile, for even the present road is hard-surfaced enough to permit of that form of locomotion, and with a little doctoring it will not be far from perfection. A place such as this wonderful valley, with its whispers and its echoes, seems to beckon to the curious to come, if only to be lost for awhile in the soothing solitudes and moved by the majesty of the hills. To those interested in the olden days the rocks hold out an invitation which I am always surprised to find so seldom responded to; but let any man feel for an hour the fine freedom of the desert, and see the fantasy of the hills, and that invitation will not again be lightly set aside. On camel or automobile he will make his way over the ancient tracks to the dark valley of the quarries; and there he will remain entranced, just as we, until the business of life shall call him back to the habitations of present-day men.

CHAPTER X

THE RED SEA HIGHROAD

IN the reach of the Nile, between Quft and Keneh, a few miles below Luxor, the river makes its nearest approach to the Red Sea, not more than 110 miles of desert separating the two waters at this point. From Quft, the ancient Koptos, to Kossair, the little seaport town, there runs the great highroad of ancient days, along which the Egyptians travelled who were engaged in the Eastern trade. It happened by chance that this route led through the Wady Fowak-hîeh, in which the famous quarries were situated; and in the last chapter I have recorded an expedition made to that place. From the quarries I set out with my three friends to the sea; and as the route from the Nile to Wady Fowakhîeh has already been described, it now remains to record its continuation eastwards and our journeying upon it.

The history of this highroad is of considerable interest, for it may be said to be the most ancient of the routes of which the past has left us any record; and its hard surface has been beaten down by the fall of feet almost continuously from the dawn of human things to the present day. It has been thought by some that a large element of the prehistoric inhabitants of the Nile valley came into Egypt by this road. Excavations at Quft (Koptos) have shown the city to date from Dynasty I, and the great archaic statues of Min, the god

211

of the desert, one of which is to be seen at the Ashmolean Museum, Oxford, were here found. The ancient Egyptians always believed that the home of their ancestors was in the land of Pount, the region around Suakin; and since so many archaic remains have been found at Koptos, the terminus of a route which in historical times was sometimes used by persons travelling to Pount, it seems not unlikely that there was a certain infiltration of Pountites into Egypt by way of Kossair and Quft. These people travelling in ships along the coast, Arabians sailing from the eastern shores of the Red Sea, or Bedouin journeying by land from Sinai and Suez, may have passed over this road, to trade with the inhabitants of Upper Egypt; but, on the other hand, there is no evidence to show that any extensive immigration or invasion took place. The coast of the Red Sea is utterly barren, and the wells are few in number; and one could more readily imagine the prehistoric inhabitants of Egypt pushing eastwards on hunting expeditions until they encountered the sea, and thus opening up the route, than one could picture these eastern peoples penetrating from an untenable base to a hostile country at the dawn of known days.

Upon the archaic statues of the god Min, at Koptos, there are many rude drawings scratched on the stone surface. These represent *pteroceras* shells, the saws of sawfish, a stag's head, the forepart of an elephant, a hyæna, a young bull, an ostrich, and a flying bird. It is evident that these drawings would not have been scratched upon the statue of the tribal god without some sort of meaning being attached to them, and it seems probable that one may see in them the articles of commerce which the people of Koptos imported from the Red Sea—shells, horn, ivory, feathers and skins.

The earliest written record of a journey to Kossair dates from Dynasty XI (B.C. 2020) when an official, named Henu, travelled from Koptos to Kossair, and thence to Pount. "The king sent me," says Henu, "to despatch a ship to Pount to bring for him the fresh myrrh from the chieftains of the desert, which had been offered to him by reason of the fear of him in those countries. Then I went forth from Koptos upon the road, as his majesty had commanded me. Troops cleared the way before me, overthrowing those hostile to the king; and the hunters and the children of the desert were posted as the protection of my limbs. . . . Then I reached the Red Sea, and I built this ship, and I despatched it with everything, after I had made for it a great oblation of cattle, bulls, and ibexes."

Henu, no doubt, carried the material for building the vessel across the desert, and settled down on the coast to build it, his supplies being sent to him from Koptos as often as necessary. He tells us in another part of the inscription that he dug several wells in the desert; and we can imagine his little company living quite happily beside one of these wells near the sea-shore while the vessel was hammered together on the beach below. After the lapse of four thousands of years we may still picture these scenes; the launching of the ship into the blue waters, when the savour of burnt offerings streamed up to heaven, and the shouts of the workmen rang across the sandy beach; the tedious journey along the barren coast, always the yellow hills upon the right and always the boundless sea upon the left; the landing on the strange shores of Pount, where the

precious myrrh trees abundantly grow and there was
talk of gold as of a thing of little worth; where sleek,
bearded men and amazingly fat women sat at the doors
of bee-hive huts, raised from the ground upon piles *;
and where, walking abroad, giraffes and other surprising creatures might be encountered, whose existence
would not be credited by friends at home. An Anglo-
Saxon feels that it would almost have been worth the
four thousand years of subsequent oblivion to have
seen what these adventurers saw!

During the next twenty centuries the road seems to
have been in continual use, but there are no interesting
inscriptions recording expeditions made along it, though
one may be sure that many of the trading expeditions
passed over this route to the land of Pount. The town
of Kossair seems to have been called Thaau at this
period, but in Græco-Roman days this name has developed into Tuau or Duau, a word written in hieroglyphs
simply with three stars. The trade with Arabia and
India, which flourished during the rule of the Ptolemies,
brought the road into very general use, and Kossair
became as important a trading town as any in Egypt.
The harbour, however, was so poor that a new port and
town was constructed some five miles to the north, where
a natural bay was easily able to be improved into a very
fair harbour. This new town was called Philoteras, in
honour of the sister of Ptolemy Philadelphos (B.C. 285),
while the older port was now known as Aennum by foreigners, though to the Egyptians both towns were called
Duau.

I was fortunate enough to find some blocks of a
Ptolemaic temple at the older Kossair, and on one of

* As in the sculptured scenes at Dêr el-Bahri.

them was the name Duau, followed by the hieroglyph representing a town, written twice, to indicate the existence of the two ports.

Not infrequently one finds at Koptos and elsewhere short inscriptions of this period relating to journeys made along this route to Kossair, and thence over the high seas. One example may here be quoted: "To the most high goddess Isis, for a fair voyage for the ship *Serapis,* Hermaeus dedicates this."

I must be permitted to give in full a very interesting tariff of taxes imposed on persons using the road during the Roman occupation, which was found in a ruined guardhouse, just behind Koptos, at the beginning of the highway. It reads as follows:

BY ORDER OF THE GOVERNOR OF EGYPT.—The dues which the lessees of the transport service in Koptos, subject to the Arabian command, are authorised to levy by the customary scale, are inscribed on this tablet at the instance of L. Antistius Asiaticus, Prefect of the Red Sea Slope.

For a Red Sea helmsman	drachmas	8
" a Red Sea bowsman	"	10
" an able seaman	"	5
" a shipyard hand	"	5
" a skilled artisan	"	8
" a woman for prostitution	"	108
" a woman immigrant	"	20
" a wife of a soldier	"	20
" a camel ticket	obols	1
" sealing of said ticket	"	2

For each ticket for husband, if mounted when a caravan is leaving	drachmas	1
" all his women at the rate of	"	4
" a donkey	obols	2
" a waggon with tilt	drachmas	4
" a ship's mast	"	20
" a ship's yard	"	4

The ninth year of the Emperor Cæsar Domitian Augustus Germanicus, on the 15th of the month of May.

In the above tariff it will be seen that the persons or articles on which taxes were levied were such as one might expect to have passed between the Nile and the sea; and only those items concerning women seem to call for explanation. The very large tax imposed upon prostitutes must indicate that Indian or Arabian females coming into Egypt along this route, and liable to bring with them the evils of the East, could only be admitted when they were of the richest and, consequently, best and highest class. Such women were always taxed in the Roman Empire, and in this regard a rather humorous story is told in Philostratus' *Life of Apollonius of Tyana.* That holy man was accosted by a tax-collector, when about to cross the Euphrates, and was asked his wares. He replied with the somewhat *banal* remark that he had with him *Sōphrosúnē kai Dikaiosúnē kai Ándreia*—"Temperance, Righteousness, and Courage." The official at once assessed these as *doúlas,* "female slaves," and would have taxed them as prostitutes, had not the prophet hastily corrected him by saying that they were not *doúlas,* but *despoínas,* "ladies of the house"!

The "wives of soldiers," mentioned in the tariff, shows that Mommsen was right in stating that the rule of the emperors was laxer in Egypt than elsewhere, for before the time of Severus it was not possible for legionaries to contract legal marriages while on active service; but in Egypt the marriages were so far recognised that the wives could be taxed as such, and the children could be enrolled as legionaries.

During mediæval times, this Red Sea highroad was much used by traders, but its river terminus was now removed from Koptos to Qus, a town a few miles farther up-stream, which soon became second only to Cairo in size and wealth. A pottery figure of Buddha, some mediæval Chinese vases, and a few Arabian antiquities, found in Upper Egypt, are records of the use of this route at that time. In later days the terminus again shifted to Keneh, a few miles to the north of Koptos, and to that town there still come Arabian traders from across the Red Sea, and pilgrims sometimes use it as the base of the journey to Mecca.

From Wady Fowakhîeh our party set out along this highroad at about 7 a.m. on a bracing morning in November. From Bir Fowakhîeh the road branched off to the right, along a fine valley, shut in by hills fantastic in shape and colour. Clustering on either side of the path for some distance, there were groups of ancient huts, and in the hillsides there were traces of gold mines long since abandoned. The road beneath us was hard, flat, and blue-grey in colour, as though some mighty torrent had brought down masses of gravel and had laid it level over the bottom of the valley. Gradually

it sloped upwards, and as the hills drew in on either side
we felt that the highest point of the whole road would
soon be reached. We were already half way between
the Nile and the sea, and so far there had been a continuous slope upwards, so gradual as to be almost im-
perceptible. The valley now twisted and turned nar-
rowly between the dark hills, and the gravel bed became
humped and banked up, where the early waters had
raced down some narrow gorge and had churned themselves through a natural basin into the wide bed beyond.
The cold wind beat in our faces as we trotted up the
narrowing valley, and the sun had not yet gained much
power when, after a ride of two hours, we reached the
rugged pass which forms the apex of the route.

The scenery here is superb. The pathway, such as
it is, threads its way through a cluster of great grey
boulders tumbled into the few yards' width between the
rocks of the hillside, so that on foot one may jump from
stone to stone up the whole length of the pass, and on
camel-back one has to twist and turn, rise and descend,
until the saddle-straps come near to bursting. Amidst
the rocks there is a well, known as Bir es Sid, which
may have been opened in ancient times, perhaps by the
redoubtable Henu. A few natives were encamped near
by, and not far away their goats were to be seen, in the
charge of a small girl, whose dark dress, fluttering in
the wind, caught our eye amidst the pale grey of rocks
and the cold blue of the shadows.

Riding on for another two hours, we reached an open
ridge from which an extraordinary prospect of rolling
hills and innumerable humps was obtained. On the left
of the pathway there was a hill at the top of which stood
a ruined Roman watch-tower, one of a chain of such

posts which crowned the higher peaks all along the
route. Up this hill we scrambled on foot, and climbed
the tower at the summit, burning a pipeful of tobacco
to the gods of contentment thereon. The array of hills
around us, as closely packed and yet as individual as
the heads of a vast crowd of people, were of a wonderful
hue in the morning light. Those to the north were a
dead grey, those to the east were pink and mauve, and
those to the south every shade of rich brown, while the
shadows throughout were of the deepest blue. The
wind tore past us as we sat contemplating the fair world
at our feet, and two black ravens sailed by on it, to take
stock of us. Far below, the path wound its way through
the humps; and in the distance the peaks and spires of
the darker rocks into which it penetrated bounded the
scene, and hid the sea from view.

Mounting the camels once more, we defiled down
the steep path, and for a time were lost amidst the hills.
We lunched an hour later in more open country; and
riding on afterwards for somewhat over two hours we
reached the Roman station of Abu Zerah, which lies in
the plain at the foot of a range of fine purple hills. As
is usual in these buildings, the station consists of a rectangular enclosure, the wall being still some twelve feet
high in parts. The door-posts of the main entrance are
made of sandstone, and upon one of them is an almost
obliterated Latin inscription. There are several rooms
inside the enclosure, built against the wall, a space being
left open in the middle. Just to the north there are
a few graves, around which some broken pottery of
Roman date lies scattered.

A ride of less than an hour brought us to another
Roman station, known as Hosh el Hômra, "the Red

Enclosure," where we only halted for a moment or so, in order to ascertain that there was no unique feature in this building. In the afternoon light the scene was of great beauty. Range upon range of hills surrounded us, which assumed a thousand varying colours: pink, rose, purple, blue, and olive-green in the foreground. Spires of rock shot up to a soft sky in which floated the already visible moon, and overhead seven black ravens soared past upon the wind. Soon the sun went down, and resting in the lee of a group of dark rocks, we watched the pageant of colours go by and waited for the baggage camels to come up.

The journey was resumed at an early hour next morning, and after a trot of about three-quarters of an hour, we reached the well and Roman station of Hagi Sulimân. The ancient well, lying within the enclosing wall, has been restored in modern times, and upon a tablet let into the wall is rudely written: "Briggs, Hancock, and Wood, 1832." At this point the road is joined by another from the north-west, along which we made our return journey to Bir Fowakhîeh, by way of Wady el Esh and Wady Adolla. From Bir Hagi Sulimân to Bir Fowakhîeh by this route is a trot of about six hours.

The morning was bitterly cold and the wind swinging up the valley chilled us to the bone. The tracks led now this way and now that, around sharp corners, where the wind buffeted us suddenly, across patches of sunlight, where there was some hope of warmth, and then again up shaded valleys, where we saw an occasional wagtail or sand-martin puffing its feathers out against the cold airs. A trot of two and a half hours brought us to yet another Roman ruin, called

El Litêmah. Here there is, as usual, an enclosing wall
surrounding an area in which several chambers are
built and a well is dug. The door-posts of the entrance
are made of sandstone, and some Cufic inscriptions are
written upon one of these by travellers in the middle
ages. As we entered the building, a number of sand-
grouse rose from the midst of the ruins and went off
to the north, their swift flight being visible for some
time against a background of pale limestone hills,
which told of our approach to the sea. Near here we
passed a party of Arabian traders, some riding camels
and others walking. A more evil-looking set of men
I have seldom seen, and as they eyed us and whispered
together, we felt that some mischief was afoot. It was
therefore not surprising to learn when we returned to
the Nile that a caravan had been attacked, with considerable bloodshed, at about that place and time, by
Arabians answering to this description.

An hour and a quarter later we emerged from the
hills into an open plain in which a well, known as Bir el
Inglîz, is situated. This well was dug by English
troops at the beginning of the nineteenth century, during operations against Napoleon's generals, of which
further mention will be made. A few Ababdeh natives
were here encamped, and hastened to draw water for
our thirsty camels, begging a cigarette as a reward for
the labour. In the shade of some rocks to the south-
east we partook of our luncheon.

The seat which I selected for myself proved to be
that chosen by a prehistoric hunter some sixty centuries ago, for upon the face of the rock beside it there
is a rude archaic drawing of a man holding a bow.
Two French soldiers, of 1799, have here written their

names—Forcard and Materon—which remain as memorials of a page of history little remembered at the present time.

In the afternoon we trotted over open desert and through shady valleys for about the space of an hour, at the end of which we reached the spring known as Bir Ambâgi, situated in a fine wady, with grey-green cliffs on either hand and pink limestone hills ahead. In this fair setting there grew the greenest reeds and rushes amidst pools of the bluest water. Some Ababdeh goats grazed across the valley, bleating merrily as they went; and not a few birds added their notes to the happy fluting of the wind, which blowing from over-seas, seemed to set the rushes nodding to "songs of Araby and tales of old Cashmere." Leaving this valley, we travelled down a rather dull wash-out sloping towards the sea, which at length opened sufficiently to show us a glimpse of the blue water. There is always something which penetrates to the heart in the first view of the sea after an interval of months; and now, the eyes having accustomed themselves to the barren desert, the old wonder came upon us with new weapons, and attacked the senses with fresh vigour. We might have shouted for the sheer pleasure of it; and when, presently, a group of green palms passed into view, lit by the afternoon sun, and stood between the sand and the sea, we felt to the full the power of the assault.

As the hills fell back on either side, we passed on to the wide, flat beach, and headed our camels towards the blue sea, dismounting at last a hundred yards from the rippling water. Except for the slow pulse of the waves, there was an unbroken silence over the world. Southwards the sand stretched to the foot of the hills, beyond which rose the dreamy peaks of the Turquoise Mountains; northwards the little town of Kossair lay basking in the sunlight; to the west the dark hills through which we had passed stood waiting breathlessly to surround the setting sun; and to the east the wonderful sea seemed quietly to be sleeping and sighing in its sleep. Had we stumbled against the slumbering forms of the lotus-eaters themselves, we would hardly have felt surprise; for here we might have supposed that we were in a land "where it was always afternoon," a land "where all things always seemed the same." In a little bay, or high and dry upon the sand, lay vessels of a bygone age—two-masted hulks with ponderous sterns. Beside them we could just discern two men, fast asleep; and had we awakened them, there seemed hardly a doubt they would have been found to be as mild-eyed and melancholy as the men of Tennyson's poem.

Presently, as we sat listening to the sea, the sun set, and from the minaret of a mosque in the town a boy called to the sleepy Faithful their daily summons to prayer. His voice drifting to us on the quiet air was the first human sound which had risen from the little town; but hardly had it died away before the distant sound of voices and the grunts of camels warned us of the arrival of our baggage. A few figures sauntered idly out of the town to watch us, as the tents were pitched on the beach; and thus the dream was broken, and we awoke, as it were, to the knowledge that once more a human habitation had been reached and officials had to be interviewed.

A note to the Maltese *Mudir,* or governor of the town, brought that gentleman speedily to our tents,

obviously pleased almost to tears to have the opportunity of relieving for an hour the utter boredom of his
existence. The *Mudir* was an enforced lotus-eater.
Corpulent of figure, and suffering the discomforts of a
wall-eye; having practically no duties to perform other
than those of the brief official routine; and having no
European to talk to except his wife, his little daughter,
and an Austrian mechanic, there was nothing left for
him to do but to dream of the time when a benevolent
government should transfer him to a less isolated post.
The four of us will not soon forget the ample figure of
our guest, clad in white duck, as he sat upon the edge
of our one real camp-stool in the candle-light, and told
us in disused English how little there is to tell regarding a man's life in this sleepy town. There was never
a more desolate smile than that which wreathed his
face as he spoke of the *ennui* of life, nor a braver
twinkle than that which glinted in his single eye as the
humour of his misfortunes touched him; and though
we should meet again in many a merrier situation—for
officials are not left over long at Kossair—none of us
will cease to picture this uncomplaining servant of the
government as, with unsmoked cigarette and untasted
whisky-and-soda, he told us that evening the meaning
of four years of exile.

Kossair, when he first entered upon his duties, was
a town of 1,500 inhabitants; but these persons were so
miserably poor, and found so little to do, that at their
own request the government transported about a
thousand of them to Suez and the neighbourhood where
the lotus does not grow and a man has to keep awake.
Now there were but 500 souls in the town, 300 of whom
were women and children. These people wed **very**

young, and there is much family inter-marriage; but, though they are a poor lot to look at, there is little mental degeneracy which can be traced to this cause. The *Mudir,* who was also in charge of the coastguards, was responsible for law and order in Kossair; there was a Syrian doctor in charge of the government dispensary; the above-mentioned Austrian mechanic looked after the engine for distilling the salt water; a coastguard officer and three men patrolled the coast; four or five sailors were attached to the port; and a native schoolmaster taught the children to read and write: this constituted the official element in the town. The inhabitants were all either of Arab or Ababdeh stock, Egyptians being entirely wanting. They live mainly on fish and a little imported bread; but before the population was reduced some of the poorer families were actually eating chopped straw and other food fit only for animals.

There is very little to be done here, and most of the inhabitants sleep for two-thirds of the day. A fast-diminishing trade necessitates the occasional building or mending of a boat. This trade is done with camels and goats, which are brought across from Arabia and are led over the desert to the Nile, where they are sold at Keneh or elsewhere, the money being partly expended on grain, which is then carried back to Arabia. Pilgrims on the way to and from Mecca use these vessels occasionally, but the mariners of Kossair cannot be bothered to extend the traffic.

Except for one small group of palms, there is absolutely no vegetation whatever in the neighbourhood, and even an attempt to grow a few bushes or flowers near the governor's quarters, though carefully persisted in for some time, proved an utter failure. For his supplies the *Mudir* was entirely dependent on the arrival of the government steamer every second month; and if, as had happened at the time of our visit, this steamer was late, the unfortunate gentleman became comparatively thin from sheer starvation. Except for occasional travellers or prospectors no white men ever visit Kossair; though if there is cholera at Mecca, an English doctor is sometimes sent to prevent the disease from passing into Egypt along this route. Letters and telegrams are every week conveyed across the desert by an express rider to Keneh, and an answer to a telegram might be expected in about a week.

A large sea-water distillery, set up some years ago, provides the town with pure water; but so few are the inhabitants that it is only worked twice a month. This good supply of water is largely responsible for the lack of sickness in the town. During the four years previous to our visit, only twenty persons had died, and of these ten were very young children and ten were very old people. During these years the serious illnesses had only consisted of two cases of diphtheria; there had been no cholera, enteric, dysentery or plague. Many of the inhabitants live to be centenarians, and in the town we saw several tottering old Methuselahs, who looked as though the gods of the Underworld had forgotten them utterly.

Of sports there were none for the *Mudir* to indulge in. There was no shooting; he could not bathe, even if he desired to, because of the sharks; there were no boats to sail in worthy the names; he could not leave his post to make camel trips to interesting localities, even if that amused him, which it did not; and the one pastime, the catching of crayfish on the coral reefs, bored him to distraction. The climate is so monotonously perfect that it does not form a topic even of thought; in winter it is mild and sunny, in summer it is mild and sunnier. It is never very cold nor very hot, except for the few days in summer when a hot east wind is blowing. The *Mudir* said that he neither increased nor decreased the amount of his clothing the whole year round, but always wore his underclothes, his tight white duck tunic, his loose white duck trousers, his elastic-sided boots, and his red *tarbush* or fez.

After breakfast next morning we walked along the beach to the stiff, mustard-coloured government buildings, which stand on a point of land projecting somewhat into the sea. A spick-and-span pier and quay, ornamented with three or four old French cannon and some neat piles of cannon-balls, gave us the impression that we had been transported suddenly to a small English watering-place; but passing into the building, that impression was happily removed at once. Through the sunny courtyard we went and up the stair, saluted at intervals by the coast-guardsmen, who had donned their best uniforms for the occasion, and at last we were ushered into the presence of our Maltese friend, now seated in state at his office table at the far end of a large, airy room. The windows overlooked the glorious blue sea, and the breath of an ordinary English summer drifted into the room, bringing with it the sigh of the waves. Nothing could have been more entrancing than the soft air and the sun-bathed scene, but to the *Mudir* it was anathema, and his back was resolutely turned to the windows.

After coffee and a brief conversation, we were taken

to see the water distillery, of which the town is immensely proud; and from thence we were conducted to the chief mosque of the place, a picturesque old building which has seen better days. We were readily admitted by the Reader, who, however, turned up the grass matting which covered the floor, in order, so the *Mudir* said, that our feet might not be dirtied by it, but in reality in order that the footstep of a Christian should not defile it. A few men were praying languidly at one side of the building, and in the opposite corner a man lay snoring upon his back. There was the silence of sleep upon the place, and, returning to the almost deserted lanes between the houses outside, there was hardly a sound to disturb the stillness of the morning. In the bazaar a few people were gathered around two or three shops, at which business had nigh ceased. A limp-limbed jeweller was attempting to sell a rough silver ring to a yawning youth and, if I am not mistaken, a young girl who watched the transaction with very mild interest from the opposite side of the road was to be the recipient of the jewel. Soon we passed the open door of the schoolroom, where a dozen children chanted their Arabic A B C in a melancholy minor; and presently we came to the chief sight of Kossair—the old fortress, built by the French at the end of the eighteenth century.

One enters the building through a masonry archway, closed by a heavy wooden door clamped with iron. There are still three or four cannon inside it to tell of its past life, but now the rooms and courts are whitewashed and are used as camel stables by the coastguards. I know no books which will tell me the details of the Anglo-French struggle for the possession of

Kossair, and I must therefore leave it to my readers
to correct my ignorant statements. It appears, then,
that a French force occupied the fortress during the
time of Napoleon's rule in Egypt, and that one fine
day in the year 1800, there came sailing over the sea a
squadron of English men-o'-war, which landed a
storming party so formidable that the French were
constrained to evacuate the place and to retreat across
the desert to Keneh. With the English force there was
a large body of Indian troops, and these were marched
across to the Nile in pursuit of the French; but ere
more serious operations had taken place, the capitula-
tion of Napoleon's army brought the campaign to a
close. It is said that when the Indian soldiers saw the
representation of the sacred cow of Hathor upon the
walls of the temples of Koptos and Qus, they fell upon
their knees and did obeisance as in their own temples.

The inhabitants of Kossair live to such an age and in
such stagnation, that the stirring events of these old
days are still talked of, and Englishmen are here still
endowed with the prestige of conquerors. Involunta-
rily we held our heads higher as an old Shêkh pointed
out the gate through which the French fled, and that
through which the English bluejackets entered; and
walking through the quiet streets back to the tents, we
gave a nautical hitch to our trousers, talked contemp-
tuously of "Boney," discussed the plans of Lord
Nelson, named the yawning natives whom we passed,
"lazy lubbers," murmured "Shiver my timbers," called
one another "me hearty," and, in a word, acted faith-
lessly to the *Entente Cordiale*.

In camp, the remainder of the day was spent in
that vague pottering which the presence of the sea al-

ways induces. There were some beautiful shells upon
the shore to attract us, and natives brought others for
sale, lying down to sleep in the shade of the kitchen
tent until we deigned to give them attention. There
were sketches to be made and photographs to be taken.
Amidst the houses at the south end of the town, some
fragments of a Ptolemaic temple were stumbled upon,
and the inscriptions thereon had to be copied. These
were too fragmentary to be of much importance, and
except for the above mentioned ancient name of Kossair there written, no point of particular interest requires to be noted here. We lunched and dined off
the most excellent fish, a species named *belbul* being
particularly palatable, while crayfish and a kind of
cockle were immoderately indulged in. Having arranged to try our hand at the catching of crayfish
during the night hours, we turned in early to sleep for
a short time until the fishermen should call us.

The summons having come at about 11 p.m., we
set out along the moonlit shore, two fishermen and a
boy accompanying us, carrying nets and lanterns.
Our destination was a spot at which the coral reefs,
projecting into the sea, presented so flat a surface that
the incoming tide would wash over the whole area at
a depth of not more than a few inches. In the shallow
water, we were told, the crayfish would crawl, attracted
by our lanterns, and we could then pick them up with
our fingers. These crayfish are not at first sight dis-
tinguishable from large lobsters, though a second
glance will show that the difference lies in the fact that
they have no claws, and therefore can be caught with
impunity. They are fearsome-looking creatures, nevertheless, often measuring twenty inches or so from head

to tail. In eating them it is hard to believe that one is not eating the most tasty of lobsters.

A tedious walk of over three miles somewhat damped our ardour; and as the fishermen told us that the moon was too high and the tide too low for good hunting, we were not in the best spirits when at last we turned on to the coral reef. Here, however, the scene was so weirdly picturesque that the catching of the crayfish became a matter of secondary import. The surface of the reef, though flat, was broken and jagged, and much seaweed grew upon it. In the uncertain light of the moon it was difficult to walk without stumbling; but the ghostly figures of the fishermen hovered in front of us, and silently led the way out towards the sea, which uttered continuously a kind of sobbing as it washed over the edges of the coral reef. This and the unholy wail of the curlews were the only sounds, for the fishermen had imposed silence on us, and the moonlight furthered their wishes.

As we walked over the reef we had to pick our way between several small patches of water some five or six feet in breadth, which appeared to be shallow pools, left by the last tide in the slight depressions of the rock. Presently, however, I noticed that in these pools white clouds appeared to be reflected by the sky, but quickly looking up, I saw that the heavens were cloudless. Staring closer at the water, it suddenly dawned upon me that these white clouds were in reality the sand at the bottom of the pools, and as suddenly came the discovery that that bottom lay at a depth of fifteen feet or more. Now I went on hands and knees to gaze down at these moonlit depths, and I realised that each pool was a great globular cavern, the surface area being but the small mouth of it. Calling my friends, we soon found ourselves kneeling on a projecting ridge of coral, which was deeply undermined all round; and looking down into the bowl, we were reminded of nothing so much as of an aquarium tank seen through glass. In the moonlight the cloudy bottom of the caverns could be discerned, whereon grew great anemones and the fair flowers of the sea. Sometimes an arched gallery, suffused with pale light, led from one cavern to the next, the ceiling of these passages decorated with dim plants, the floor with coloured shells. Not easily could we have been carried so completely into the realms of fairyland as we were by gazing at these depths. Presently there sailed through the still water the dim forms of fishes, and now through the galleries there moved two shining lamps, as though carried by the little men of the sea to light them amidst the anemones. Two more small lamps passed into the cavern and floated through the water, now glowing amidst the tendrils of the sea plants, now rising towards the surface, and now sinking again to the shells, the sand, and the flowers at the bottom.

It was not at once that we could bring ourselves to realise that these lights were the luminous eyes of a strange fish, the name of which I do not know; but now the fishermen, who had suddenly drawn their net across the edge of the reef and had driven a dozen leaping creatures on to the exposed rock, beckoned us to look at this curious species at close quarters. Their bodies were transparent, and from around their mouths many filmy tentacles waved. The eyes were large and brown in colour, and appeared as fantastic stone orbs set in a glass body. Many other varieties of fish were caught as the tide came in; but it appeared that the moon was too powerful for successful sport in regard to the crayfish, and the catch consisted of but four of these. The sight of the fairy caverns, however, was entertainment sufficient for one night; and it was with discontent that we turned away from these kingdoms of the sea to return in the small hours of the morning to the tents. The moonlight, the sobbing of the ocean, the deep caverns lit by unearthly lamps, left an impression of unreality upon the mind which it was not easy to dispel; and I think we all felt that a glance had been vouchsafed through the forbidden gates, and a glimpse had been obtained of scenes unthought of since the days of our childhood. Had we also tasted of the lotus, and was this but one of the dreams of dreamy Kossair?

Upon the following day I rode northwards along the coast, to visit the site of the Ptolemaic port, which lies about five miles from the modern town. An hour's ride against a hard wind brought us to the little inlet, around which the mounds and potsherds of the town are scattered. The water in the bay was of the deepest blue; a rolling plain of yellow sand lay eastwards, backed by the darker ranges of mountains; and overhead the white clouds raced by. The sea washed up in a line of white breakers on to a rising bar of sand, sparkling with a thousand varieties of shells. Behind this bar were pools of water passing inland, and here there may have been an artificial harbour. On the south side of the bay bold rocks jutted into the sea, and on the north there rose a series of mounds upon which the remains of the old town were strewn. Walking over these mounds, where the rhythmic roar of the surf falls

continuously upon the ears, my mind was filled with
thoughts of the ancient port which has so utterly fallen, and of that ancient commerce with the East which
must have been so full of adventure and romance to
the men of old. Here from these mounds the towns-
people have watched the great galleys set out over the
seas for the mysterious land of Hind, and have seen
the wealth of Pount and Arabia unloaded upon the
quay; and here, so many centuries later, the labours of
Egyptologists are beginning to make it possible to recall something of what they saw, though the spade of
the excavator has not yet touched this site.

There are two wells within reach of this spot, but
both are two or three hours' journey away, and the
water question must have been a serious one. The well
to the north is named Bir Guah, and the other, to the
west, is called Bir Mahowatât. The latter is the name
of a tribe of Bedouin living at Suez, who state that
they came originally from El Wij, in Arabia. It is
interesting to find that a well here should be named
after them, for El Wij is nearly opposite this point,
and one may realise thus what intercourse there is and
always has been between Arabia and Egypt, even as
far south as Kossair.

Returning with the wind at our backs, we soon
reached Kossair, and rode through the sleepy streets of
the town to our tents. To tea in the afternoon came
the *Mudir,* who for an hour or so entertained us with
tales of *ennui.* Kossair fell asleep when the Roman
Empire fell, awoke for a moment in the days of Napoleon, but slid into slumber once more over a century
ago. There was a time when the east coast steamers
used to call here, but now even they have left the town

to its long siesta. As we listened to the story of decaying trade and languid idleness, the vision of Tennyson's lotus-eater was ever in the mind; and our sympathy was as profound for an official stationed here as was our envy of the man who might be permitted to rest himself for awhile from his labours upon this mild, sunny shore. The *Mudir* was, at the time of our visit, anxiously awaiting the tardy arrival of the steamer which was to take him and his family to Suez for three months' leave, and his eye fixed itself upon the sea at every pause in the conversation; and when he bid us farewell at the door of the tent, it was but to return to his own doorway, where he might watch for the distant smoke until the sun should set.

Early next morning we commenced the return journey to the Nile. As we rode away over the sloping sand towards the hills in the west, we turned in our saddles to obtain a last view of the strange little dream-town which was sinking so surely to its death. The quiet sea rippled upon the sunlit shore in one long line of blue from the houses on the north to the Turquoise Mountains on the south. Not a trace of smoke nor a sound rose from the town. On the beach a group of three men lay sleeping, with their arms behind their heads, while two others crouched languidly on their haunches, watching our disappearing cavalcade. Then, in the silence of the morning, there came to us on the breeze the soft call to prayer from the minaret of the mosque. We could not hear the warbled words; but to the sleeping figures on the beach, we thought, they must surely be akin to those of the song of the lotus-eaters:—

"How sweet it were, hearing the downward stream,
With half-shut eyes ever to seem
Falling asleep in a half-dream!
To hear each other's whispered speech;
Eating the lotus day by day,
To watch the crisping ripples on the beach,
And tender curving lines of creamy spray;
To lend our hearts and spirits wholly
To the influence of mild-minded melancholy. . . ."

On the quay in the far distance we could just discern a portly white figure, gazing steadfastly out to sea, to catch the first glimpse of the steamer which had been awaited so patiently for so long.

CHAPTER XI

THE IMPERIAL PORPHYRY QUARRIES

THOSE who have travelled in Italy, and have studied in the museums and in the ruins there the sculpture and the architectural accessories of the Roman Imperial age, will be familiar with the magnificent purple stone known as Imperial Porphyry. It was one of the most highly prized of the ornamental stones employed by the artists and architects of that age of luxury; and the great distance which it had to be brought, over parched deserts and perilous seas, must have sent its price up beyond the reach of all save the rulers of the earth.

The quarries from which this porphyry was obtained are situated in the region known as Gebel Dukhân, "the Hills of Smoke," in the Eastern Egyptian Desert, some twenty-seven miles from the uninhabited and unexplored coast of the Red Sea, opposite the southern end of the Peninsula of Sinai. Two or three travellers during the last century have visited them, and the Survey Department of the Egyptian Government has published a technical report on the district; but with the exception of this and an article by the German explorer, Schweinfurth, the literature on the subject, such as it is, seems to be more or less untraceable. In 1887, a gentleman of the name of Brindley, obtained a concession there for the re-working of the quarries, but the project fell through owing to the difficulties of transporting the stone.

A few years ago, Mr. John Wells, the Director of the now defunct Department of Mines, decided to make an expedition to Gebel Dukhân to report on the possibilities of reopening the old works; and it was with considerable pleasure that I received, and found myself able to accept, his invitation to accompany him, in order to see how far the Department of Antiquities could concur in the projects of modern engineers.

We set out from Keneh, a town on the Nile some 400 miles above Cairo, in the middle of March: a time of the year when one cannot be sure of good weather in Egypt, for the winter and the summer fight together for the mastery, and the hot south winds vie with the cold north winds in ferocity. Sandstorms are frequent in the desert in this month, and these, though seldom dangerous, can be extremely disagreeable. We were, however, most fortunate in this respect; and, in spite of the fact that the winds were strong, I do not recall any particular discomfort experienced from them, though memory brings back the not rare vision of men struggling with flapping tents and flying ropes. Our caravan consisted of some fifty camels, of which about thirty-five carried the baggage and water; a dozen were ridden by ourselves, Mr. Wells' police, our native assistants, and others; and two or three belonged to the Shêkh and the guides.

The business of setting out is always trying to the patience. The camel-men attempt to load their beasts lightly in order that more may be employed; they dawdle over the packing that the day's journey may be short; the camels, unused to their burdens, perform such antics as may rid them the most quickly of the incubus; the untried ropes break as the last knot is tied, and the loads fall to the ground; the riding camels are too fresh, and, groaning loudly, revolve in small circles, as though one's whistle of encouragement were a waltz.

There are no people in the world so slovenly, so unpractical, or so asinine as the lower class inhabitants of the Eastern Desert. One has heard so often of the splendid desert tribes, of fine figures and flashing eyes, of dignity and distinction, of gracious manners and lofty words, that one has come to expect the members of a caravan to be as princely as they are picturesque. It is a shock to find them but ragged weaklings, of low intelligence and little dignity.

Is this, one asks, a son of the proud Bedouin whose ears are now being boxed by one's servant? And are these the brave men of the desert who are being kicked into shape by that smart negro policeman, the son of slaves? Look now, eight or ten of the Bedouin have quarrelled over their camels, and are feeling for their knives in preparation for a fight: shall we not see some stirring action, reminiscent of the brave days of old? No; the black policeman seizes his camel-whip and administers to as many as he can catch of the flying wretches as sound a beating as any naughty boys might receive. Lean-faced, hungry-eyed, and rather upright in carriage, they may be expected to be quick-witted and endowed with common-sense. Yet of all stupid people these unwashed miseries are the stupidest; and as one sees them at the starting of a caravan, muddling the ropes, upsetting the loads, yawning, scratching themselves, squabbling in high, thin voices, and tripping over their antiquated swords and long guns, one's dream of the Bedouin in this part of the desert fades and no more returns.

Perhaps, however, it is the point of view which is at fault. Did we live in the desert without a deed to do or a thought to think beyond those connected with the little necessities of life, and with so vague a knowledge of time and distance as such an existence requires, our notion of the practical might be different, and our idea of intelligence might be less lofty. Perhaps, too, I did not meet with the genuine types of the race; for the camel-drivers employed by an economical Shêkh, and the goatherds who wander through the valleys, may be but the riff-raff cast off from the more remote tribes. Moreover, there are a few exceptions to the general rule which may be met with even amongst the camel-men, but these are hardly sufficiently notable to record.

At last a start was made; and riding north-eastwards over the hot, sandy plain, we trotted slowly towards the distant limestone hills which rose above a shifting mirage of lake-like vapour. For some miles our road led over the hard, flat desert; but opportunely at the lunching hour we passed a spur of rock which afforded welcome shade, and here we rested for an hour or so. At this point there is a well, known as Bir Arras, rather prettily situated amidst tamarisk-bushes and desert scrub; but as it is only ten miles distant from Keneh it is not much used by travellers. Riding on in the afternoon, we verged somewhat to the left, and passed along a valley much broken up by low mounds of sand collected round the decayed roots of bushes; and here several thriving tamarisks and other small trees lent colour to the scene. Soon we

turned again to the left, and presently crossed two
projecting spurs of the low hills, upon which beacons
of stone had been erected in Roman days, on either
side of the track, to mark the road. It is interesting
to find that along the whole length of the route from
Keneh to the quarries these piles of stone have been
placed at irregular intervals in order that the traveller
should have no difficulty in finding his way.

Towards evening the tracks led us up the clearly
marked bed of a dry river, bordered by tamarisks and
other bushes; and, passing along this for a short distance, we called a halt, and pitched the tents amongst
the sand hillocks to one side. The following morning
we were on the road soon after sunrise; and, riding
along the dry river-bed, we presently reached the Roman station of El Ghaiteh, which lies, in all, some
seven and a half hour's trot from Keneh. This is the
first of the Roman posts on the road from Keneh to
Gebel Dukhân, and here the ancient express caravans
halted for the night. At the foot of a low hill there is
a fortified rectangular enclosure, in which several
rooms with vaulted roofs are built. The walls are constructed of broken stones, and still stand some twelve
feet or more in height. The entrance is flanked by
round towers, and passing through it one sees on the
left a large tank, built of burnt bricks and cement, in
which the water, brought from the well in the plain
was stored. Just to the north of the station there are
the ruins of the animal lines, where rough stone walls
have been built on a well-ordered plan, forming a courtyard in which the stalls run in parallel rows. Above
the enclosure, on the hill-top, there are some carefully

constructed buildings of sun-dried brick, which may have been the officers' quarters.

Resting in the shade of the ruins, our eyes wandered over the sun-burnt desert to the hazy hills beyond, and thence back along the winding river-bed to the bushes at the foot of the hill, where the camels lazily cropped the dry twigs, and where green dragon-flies hovered against the intensely blue sky. Then again the ruins claimed our attention, and presently we seemed to forget the things of the present time and to drift back to the days when the blocks of Imperial Porphyry were heaved and hoisted, carried and dragged along this road to the Nile and to Rome.

A ride of somewhat over three hours across wide, undulating, gravel plains brought us to the next Roman station, known as Es Sargieh, which lies between two low mounds just to the north of the main track. Here a large excavation has been made in order to obtain water, and at its edge there are the remains of troughs and tanks constructed of brick and cement. The sand and clay from the excavation have been thrown up in an embankment, so as to form a rectangular enclosure. At one end there are the ruins of a few chambers, and the animal lines near by are clearly marked. Es Sargieh marks the point where the road divides, one track leading to Gebel Dukhân, and the other to the white granite quarries of Um Etgâl; and it was thus an important watering station.

From this point for the rest of the day our road lay across a hard flat plain, bounded in the distance ahead by the dim peaks of granite mountains. As we had stopped some considerable time at the two Roman ruins, the baggage camels and men had pushed far in advance, and, with characteristic stupidity, continued to do so, though the sun went down and the stars came out. It was not till long past dinner-time that, riding furiously through the empty darkness, we managed to catch them up; and hungry, aching, and cross, we quickly devoured a cold meal and rolled into bed. During the night a gale of wind came near to overthrowing the tents, for we had bivouacked where we had overtaken the caravan, upon the vast, exposed plain. The night air felt bitterly cold as, clad in pyjamas, I pulled at ropes and hammered at pegs; and it was a surprise to find the thermometer standing at 32 degrees Fahrenheit at this time of year.

Having camped in the darkness, it was not till daybreak that we realised that we had now crossed the plain, and were already near the mouth of a valley which led into an unexplored region of dark rocks between two ranges of hills. Not long after sunrise we mounted our camels, and presently passed into this valley—the first men of our generation to do so. Jagged cliffs towered above the road, and behind them the soft brown hills rose in an array of dimly seen peaks. A ride of two hours up this valley—that is to say, altogether about five hours' trot from Es Sargieh—brought us to the Roman station of El Atrash. There is a fortified enclosure containing several regularly arranged buildings, a tank, and a deep, circular well constructed of brick. The gateway is flanked by brick towers, up which the steps can still be traced. Outside the enclosure there are the usual animal lines; and near by there lies a large block of porphyry which must have been abandoned for some reason on its way to the river. The scenery here is wild and desolate. There was a feeling, as the eye passed from range to range of menacing hills, untrodden by the foot of man, that one was travelling in the moon. The day was cold and misty, and the sharp air already told of the altitude to which we had risen—now nearly 2,000 feet.

From here the road led through valleys lying between hills of ever-increasing height. The colour of the rocks now changed from a deep brown to a kind of soft purple; while the ground over which we were moving, being composed of particles of red granite, turned to a curious rosy hue. It was as though one were looking through tinted glass; and these combinations of colour—the red valley, the purple hills, and the grey sky—gave the scene a beauty indescribable. We lunched in the shadow of the rocks, and sleeping on the ground thereafter one's dreams were in mauves and burnt siennas.

Mounting again and riding along this wonderful valley, feeling more than ever like Mr. H. G. Wells' men in the moon, early in the afternoon we reached the Roman station of Wady Gatâr, which lies in a hollow amidst lofty hills, some three and a half hours' ride from El Atrash. The station consists, as before, of an enclosure, chambers, disused well, and animal lines; but it is more ruined than the other posts which we had seen. There is a well not far from this point, to which the camels were sent to be watered; and we were thus able to spend a quiet afternoon in our camp amongst the hills.

Towards sunset I climbed to the top of a low mound of rocks which overlooked the fortress, and there the silence of the evening and the strangeness of the surrounding hues enhanced to a point almost of awe the sense of aloofness which this part of the desert imposes upon one. On the right the line of a valley drew the eyes over the dim, brown waves of gravel to the darkness of the rugged horizon. Behind, and sweeping upward, the sky was a golden red; and this presently turned to green, and the green to deep blue. On the left some reflected light tinged the eastern sky with a suggestion of purple, and against this the nearer mountains stood out darkly. In front the low hills met together, and knit themselves into shapes so strange that one might have thought them the distortions of a dream. There was not a sound to be heard, except once when an unseen flight of migratory birds passed with a soft whirr high overhead. The light was dim,—too dark to read the book which I carried. Nor was there much desire to read; for the mind was wandering, as the eyes were, in an indistinct region of unrealities, and was almost silent of thought.

Then in the warm, perfect stillness, with the whole wilderness laid prone in that listless haze which anticipates the dead sleep of night, there came—at first almost unnoticed—a small, black, moving mass, creeping over an indefinite hill-top. So silently it appeared, so slowly moved nearer, that I was inclined to think it a part of the dream, a vague sensation passing across the solemn, sleepy mind of the desert. Presently, very quietly, the mass resolved itself into a compact flock of goats. Now it was drawing nearer, and I could discern with some degree of detail the little procession—the procession of dream-ideas, it might have been, for it was difficult to face facts in the twilight. Along the valley it moved, and, fluttering in the wind, there arose a plaintive bleating and the wail of the goatherd's pipe.

He—one could see him now—was walking in advance
of his flock, and his two hands held a reed from which
he was pouring the ancient melodies of his race. From
the hill-top I could look down on the flock as it passed
below. It had become brown in colour; and as the pipe
ceased awhile the shuffle and patter of a hundred little
hoofs could be heard. It was a gentle sound, more
inclined to augment than to diminish the dreamy character of the procession. Behind the flock two figures
moved, their white garments fluttering in the wind,
changing grotesquely the form and shape of the wear-
ers. Over the gravel they went, and at a distance followed the dogs of the herd, growling as they passed.
Over the gravel and down the valley, and with them
went the gentle patter and the wandering refrain of
the reed pipe. Then a bend in the path, or may be the
fading of the dream, and the flock was seen no more.
But in the darkness which had gathered the mind was
almost too listless to feel that aught had passed beyond
its pale.

We left the Wady Gatâr the next day soon after
lunch and entered another fine valley. On the right
the granite cliffs sloped up to the misty sky in clean,
sheer faces of rock. On the left range after range of
dimly peaked hills carried one's thoughts into the
clouds. The afternoon was sunless and the air bracing
and keen. The camels, after their long drink, were
ready for work, and we were soon swinging up the
valley at a brisk trot. The road turned from side to
side, now leading in a dozen clear tracks up the wide
gravelled bed of some forgotten torrent, and now passing in a single narrow path from one valley to the next.
With every turn new groups of mountains became visi-

ble and higher peaks slid into sight. The misty air lent a softness to these groups, blending their varied colours into almost celestial harmonies of tone. Gradually the ranges mounted, until at last, as the afternoon began to draw in, the towering purple mountains of Gebel Dukhân rose from behind the dark rocks to the left of our road.

It was almost sunset before we reached the foot of this range, and the cloudy sun was passing behind the more distant hills as a halt was called. We were now in a wide, undulating valley, which was hemmed in by the superb mountains on three sides and disclosed low, open country towards the north-east. The beams of the hidden sun shone up from behind the dark hills in a sudden glare of brightness, and presently the clouded sky turned to a deep crimson. The lofty peaks of the southern mountains now caught the disappearing sunshine and sprang out of the mist in a hundred points of vivid red. For only a few minutes the conflagration lasted, but before it had fully died out the vaporous outlines in the far distance towards the north-east took form and colour, and the last gleam of sunlight revealed, some twenty miles away, the thin line of the sea, and above it the stately mountains of Sinai. A moment later the vision had passed, the sun had set, and in the gathering darkness the baggage camels, lumbering round a bend, came into sight, calling our attention to more material things.

In the semi-darkness, while our meal was being prepared, we visited a Roman station which stands in the Wady Bileh at the foot of the Gebel Dukhân mountains, about three and a quarter hours' trot from the fortress of Wady Gatâr. The porphyry quarries and the settlement lay in the valley at the other side of the range of hills at the foot of which we were now standing; and to reach them one might either climb by an ancient path over a pass in the range, or one might ride round by a tortuous valley—a journey said to be of nearly thirty miles. This station was the first night's halting-place for express caravans returning from the quarries. At one side of the wide, ancient road stands the usual small enclosure, having a doorway flanked with towers, and containing a few ruined chambers and a well. At the other side a cluster of granite rocks rising into a small mound had been surrounded by a stout wall, either in order that it should serve as a fortress, or because these rocks were for some reason sacred. There was nothing particularly noteworthy about the station, but, lying amidst such wild and magnificent scenery, it assumed in the half-light a charm which will not soon be forgotten.

At dawn next morning we set out on foot to climb over the pass to the quarries. The sun was struggling to penetrate the soft mists as we started the actual ascent, and the air was cold and invigorating. Here and there we could detect the old Roman path passing up the hillside, but it was so much broken that a climb up the dry water-course, across which it zigzagged, was preferable. At the immediate foot of the pass there is a small Roman fort containing three or four rooms, and at the highest point, which is 3,150 feet above sea-level, there is a ruined rest-house, where the tired climber, no doubt, was able to obtain at least a pot of water.

Here at the summit we had a wonderful view of the surrounding country. Behind us the mountains rose in a series of misty ranges, and before us lay the valley

of Gebel Dukhân winding between the porphyry hills,
while beyond them the northern mountains rose to a
height of some 6,000 feet in the distance. The Roman
road, descending on this side, was well preserved, and
we were able to run down the 1,200 feet or so, which
brought us breathless to the level of the valley. The
temple, town, and quarries lay about a mile down the
wady, at a point where there was a considerable
breadth of flat gravel between the hills on either side.
The town ruins—a cluster of crowded houses enclosed by a fortified wall—stand on the slope of a hill.
A fine terrace runs along the east side, and up to this
a ramp ascends. Passing through the gateway one
enters the main street, and the attention is first attracted by an imposing building on the right hand.
Here there are several chambers leading into an eight-
pillared hall, at the end of which a well-made and well-
preserved plunge-bath eloquently tells of the small
pleasures of expatriated Roman officers. A turning
from the main street brings one into an open courtyard,
where there are two ovens and some stone dishes to be
seen, besides a large quantity of pottery fragments.
Around this in every direction the little huts are huddled, narrow lanes dividing one set of chambers from
the next. The town is, of course, very ruined; but it
does not require much imagination to people it again
with that noisy crowd of Greek, Roman, and Egyptian
quarrymen. One sees them prising out the blocks of
purple porphyry from the hillside high above the valley, returning in the evening down the broad causeway
to the town, or passing up the steps to the temple which
stands on a knoll of granite rocks a couple of hundred
yards to the north-east.

The steps lead up to a platform which formed the forecourt of the temple. This court is now covered with the ruins of what was once a fine granite portico rising on the east side. Four columns supported an inscribed architrave and decorated cornice, above which was the pediment or pointed roof. Behind this portico stood the sanctuary, built of broken stones carefully mortared and plastered to the necessary smoothness. A granite doorway led from one side into the vestry. In the forecourt, amidst the ruins, stands the granite altar, in its original position; and near it lies the architrave with the proud inscription: "For the safety and the eternal victory of our Lord Cæsar Trajan Hadrian, absolute, august, and all his house; to the Sun, the great Serapis and to the co-enshrined gods, this temple, and all that is in it, is dedicated." Then follow the names of the Governor of Egypt, the Superintendent of the Mines, and other officials.

In the middle of the valley there is the well, which is now choked. A gallery, the roof of which was supported by five pillars, passes in a half-circle round one side of the well; and a shallow drain in the pavement seems to have carried a stream of water along it. Here the workmen could sit in the shade to ease the thirst which exercise on the hot hills so soon creates; and on our return journey up the pass we looked back more than once to this cool gallery and to the plunge-bath with a kind of envy of the past.

The quarries are cut here and there on the hillside without any regularity. The blocks of porphyry were prised out of the rock wherever the work could most easily be carried on, and the action of the years has so dulled the broken surfaces that they now look almost

like those of the natural mountain. The blocks were
carried down to the Nile, and in fact to Rome, in the
rough, without even a preliminary dressing; for the
work in this distant place had to be shortened as much
as possible.

Looking, in the European museums, at the fine
capitals, the polished basins, the statues, and the many
other objects cut out of Imperial Porphyry, one has
admired the work of the mason or the genius of the
artist. But here in the Hills of Smoke one thinks of
these antiquities with a feeling bordering on veneration.
If the workmanship tells of an art that is dead, how
much louder does the material cry out the praises of
an energy that is also dead? Each block of stone is
the witness of a whole history of organisation and
activity. This purple porphyry was not known to the
ancient Egyptians: a Roman prospector must have
searched the desert to find it. One would have thought
that the aloofness of the valley from which it is to be
procured would have kept its existence the secret of the
hills; for on the one side a winding pathway, thirty
miles in length, separates the spot from the little known
main road, and on the other side a barrier of steep hills
shuts it off from the Wady Bileh.

Although Gebel Dukhân is so near the Red Sea, it
was not possible for the stone to be transported by ship
to Suez. The barren coast here was harbourless, except for the port of Myos Hormos, which was too far
away to be practicable; and the stone would have had
to be unloaded at Suez, and dragged across the desert
to the neighbourhood of the modern Port Said. Every
block of porphyry had therefore to be carried across
the desert to Keneh, the old Kainepolis, on the Nile,

and thence shipped by river-barge to the sea. Here it
had to be trans-shipped to the great Mediterranean galleys, and thus conveyed across the treacherous sea to
the port of Rome.

Probably the blocks were dragged by oxen or men
upon rough waggons, for the roads are not bad, except
at certain places. To ride from Keneh to Wady Bileh,
at the quiet five-miles-an-hour trot of the camel, took
us altogether twenty-two and a half hours; that is to
say, the total distance is about 112 miles or so. The
winding path from Wady Bileh up the valley to the
quarries brings this total to about 140 miles; and the
caravans could not have covered this in less than eight
days. On the first night after leaving Keneh the camp
was probably pitched in the open. On the second night
the station of El Ghaiteh was reached, and here there
were provisions, water, and a small garrison. The
third night was spent at Es Sargieh, where water was
to be obtained. On the fourth night the houses of El
Atrash sheltered the travellers, water and provisions
being here obtainable. On the fifth night Wady Gatâr
was reached, where again there was a well. The sixth
night was passed at Wady Bileh, from whence express
messengers could pass over the hill to the quarries.
The seventh night was spent in the open, and on the following day the settlement was reached.

The long road was rendered dangerous by the incursions of the desert peoples, and many of the hills between the fortified stations are crowned with ruined
watch-towers. Roman troops must have patrolled the
road from end to end, and the upkeep of these garri-
sons must have been a considerable expense. The
numerous stone-cutters and quarrymen had to be fed

and provided for; and for this purpose an endless train
of supplies had to be brought from the Nile valley.
Oxen or donkeys for this purpose, and for the transporting of the porphyry, had to be kept constantly on
the move. Then, as now, there was always the danger
of a break-down in the water-supply; and though the
risk in this respect was not as great in those days as it
is to the modern explorer, the quarrymen must have
known that they carried their lives in their hands. At
Keneh a service of barges had to be organised, and at
the seaport the galleys had to be in readiness to brave
the seas with their heavy loads.

It is of all this—of the activity, the energy, the
bravery, the power of organisation, the persistency, the
determination—that an object executed in Imperial
Porphyry tells the story.

The quarries were worked until about the fifth century A.D., for the Byzantine Emperors derived from
their Roman predecessors an affection for this fine purple stone. There is a Greek inscription on the path
leading up to one of the workings, which reads,
"Katholeke Ekklesia," and which is perhaps the latest
example of old-world activity in the Eastern Desert.
There is no other place in the world where this
porphyry is to be found, and when the quarries at last
ceased to be worked, some time previous to the seventh
century, the use of the stone had to cease also, nor has
it ever again been procurable.

I wonder whether there will come a time when some
millionaire, fresh from the museums of Italy, will express a wish to pave his bathroom with the purple stone
of the emperors; and whether the Hills of Smoke will
again ring with the sound of the hammer and chisel,

in response to the demands of a new fashion. It may be that some day the tourist will awake to the advantages and attractions of the Eastern Desert as a motoring country, will rush through the wadys, will visit the ancient centres of activity, will see these quarries, and will desire the porphyry. With a little preparation the road from Keneh to Gebel Dukhân could be made practicable for automobiles; and when once the land ceases to be but the territory of the explorer and the prospector, one may expect its mineral products to be seen, to be talked of, and finally to be exploited.

In the late afternoon we left the valley, and climbed slowly up the Roman road to the summit of the pass, halting here to drink deeply from our water-bottles. The descent down the dry watercourse was accomplished in a long series of jumps from boulder to boulder, at imminent peril of a sprained ankle. The grey rocks were smooth and slippery, and between them there grew a yellow-flowered weed which, when trodden upon, was as orange-peel. The rapid rush down the hillside, the setting sun, and the bracing wind, caused our return to camp to take its place amongst the most delightful memories of the whole expedition. Once we halted, and borrowing the carbines of the native police, we shot a match of half a dozen rounds apiece, with a spur of stone as target. The noise echoed amongst the rocks; and a thousand feet below we saw the ant-like figures of our retainers anxiously hurrying into the open to ascertain the cause of the disturbance.

As we neared the bottom of the hill, the sun set, and once more this wonderful valley was lit with the crimson afterglow, and once more the mountains of Sinai stood out for a moment from the gathering mists above the vivid line of the Red Sea. Darkness had fallen when at last, foot-sore and weary, we reached the camp; and I was almost too tired to enjoy the sponge-down in the half basin of water which is all that can be allowed in this waterless region, and the meal of tinned food which followed. As I fell to sleep that night, my dreams were all of strenuous labours; of straining oxen and sweating men; of weary marches and unsuspected ambushes; of the sand-banks of the Nile and the tempests of the sea. But ever in the distance I seemed to be conscious of thoughtless, implacable men, dipping their bejewelled fingers into the basins of purple porphyry as they reclined in the halls of Imperial Rome.

On the following morning our party divided, Mr. Wells and the greater part of the caravan going northeast to the petroleum wells of Gebel Zeit on the seacoast, and I to Um Etgâl, the Mons Claudianus of the ancients, where the white granite, also so much admired by the Romans, was quarried from the hillside.

above the vivid line of the Red Sea. Darkness had
fallen when at last, foot-sore and weary, we reached
the camp; and I was almost too tired to enjoy the
sponge-down in the half basin of water which is all that
can be allowed in this waterless region, and the meal
that was set before me. And that night, as every
night, my dreams were all of strenuous labours; of
. . . .
of purple porphyry as they re . . . .

CHAPTER XII

THE QUARRIES OF MONS CLAUDIANUS

IN the previous chapter an account was given of a
journey made to the Imperial Porphyry quarries
of Gebel Dukhân. I returned to the Nile by way
of the white granite quarries of Um Etgâl, the ancient
Mons Claudianus, and thence past the old gold-workings of Fatîreh to Keneh.

My caravan was composed of a riding party, consisting of myself, my native assistant, my servant, and
a guide; and a baggage train of a dozen camels and
men, and a couple of guards. The guide was a picturesque, ragged old man, whose face was wizened and
wrinkled by the glare of the desert. His camel was
decked with swinging tassels of black and yellow, and
across his saddle there was slung a gun at least seven
feet long, while at his side there hung a broad-bladed
sword in an old red leather case. In his belt there were
two knives, and in his hand he carried a stout bludgeon,
something in the form of a hockey-stick. This latter is
the weapon most generally carried by the Ababdeh and
other desert peoples, and its antiquity is evidenced by
the fact that the earliest hieroglyph for "a soldier" in
the script of ancient Egypt represents a figure holding
just such a stick.

The old guide was followed by three lean, yellow
dogs, who seemed to be much bored by the journey and
dejected by the sterility around. He was a man of

some dignity, and took considerable pride in riding at the head of the little procession in order to show the way, although, except at the cross-roads, the tracks were perfectly plain, and the ancient beacons were generally to be seen. Once or twice I made an attempt to pass him so that I might have an uninterrupted view of the scenery; for the sight of a ragged, huddled back and the hindquarters of a betasselled camel is inclined to pall after a while. But these efforts ended in a short, hard race, in which I was generally the loser; nor had I the heart to order the old man to the rear thereafter.

We set out from the camp at Wady Bileh, the nearest point to Gebel Dukhân on the main road, soon after daybreak, and passed along the wonderful valley leading back to the Roman station of Wady Gatâr, which I have already described, our route branching off towards the south just before reaching that place. The road then led along a fine valley, up which a blustering north wind went whistling, and it was only by donning an overcoat and by trotting at a smart pace that I could pretend to feel comfortably warm. Soon after noon I halted near some thorn-trees, and in their shelter luncheon was presently spread. A vulture circling overhead watched our party anxiously, in the vain hope that somebody would drop dead, but on seeing us mount again to continue the journey it sailed away disgustedly over the windy hill-top.

It was still cold and stormy when, after trotting altogether for five hours from Wady Bileh, we arrived at the well of Um Disi, where the camp was pitched in order that the camels might drink and graze. The well is the merest puddle in the sand amidst the smooth boulders of a dry watercourse, hidden under the overhanging cliffs of granite. It lies in the corner of a wide amphitheatre of gravel and sand, completely shut in by the mountains. Bushes of different kinds grow in great profusion over this amphitheatre, and from the tent door, when the eye was tired of wandering upon the many-coloured hills, one might stare in a lazy dream at a very garden of vegetation, around which the grey wagtails flitted and the dragon flies slowly moved. It is an ideal place for a camp, and I but wished that more than a night could have been spent there; for I would have liked to have explored the surrounding hills and valleys, and to have stalked the gazelle which had left their footprints near the well.

The nights up here in this locality, which must be some 1,500 or more feet above the sea, were bitterly cold, in spite of the approaching summer. There is perhaps no place where one more keenly feels a low temperature than in the desert; and here at Um Disi, where the air is that of the mountains, a colder night was passed than it has ever been my lot to endure—with the exception, perhaps, of one occasion when, with another student of archæology, I spent the night upon the flint-covered hill-tops of the Western Desert. On that occasion our baggage and bedding had failed to reach us, and we were obliged to sleep in our clothes and overcoats, dividing a newspaper to act as a cover for the neck and ears. By midnight we were so cold that we were forced to dance a kind of hornpipe in order to set the circulation going again in the veins; and my friend was light-hearted enough to accompany this war dance with a breathless rendering of the hymn, "We are but little children meek," which had been dinned into his head, he told me, while staying at a mission school in another part of Egypt. Memory recalls the scene of the dark figure shuffling and swaying in the clear starlight, the biting wind whistling around the rocks in rhythmless accompaniment; and yet it does not seem that so much discomfort was then felt as was experienced in the flapping tent at Um Disi.

The journey was continued early next morning, the road leading out from the amphitheatre through a gorge on the eastern side. There was now some difficulty about the method of travelling, for only the guide knew the way, and, as he rode with us, there was danger of our losing the slowly moving baggage camels, which always followed behind, catching us up at our halts for luncheon and other refreshment; and I was quite aware that to lose one's water supply meant a very unpleasant death. I therefore took with me some bags of torn paper, and at every turning of the path, or at the cross-tracks, I threw down a few handfuls in the manner of a paper-chase; and thus, though the path here wound from one valley to another in the most perplexing manner, the caravan reached its destination almost as soon as we.

It was disappointing to find that our camel-men, born and bred in the desert, were unwilling to take the responsibility of following safely in our tracks. One would have thought that the footprints of our camels would have been as easy for them to trace on an unfrequented path as torn paper is to us. The guide, on the other hand, showed a really wonderful knowledge of the intricate paths; for it is not reasonable to suppose that he had travelled between Gebel Dukhân and Um Etgâl more than two or three times, this being off the main routes through the desert. He did not once hesitate or look round, although when questioned he declared that many years had passed since last he had been here.

In these valleys we met, for the first time for some days, one or two Bedouin. A ragged figure, carrying a battle-axe and a mediæval sword, sprang up from the rocks where he was tending a flock of goats, and hurried across to shake hands with our guide. The two entered into earnest conversation in low tones; and the old guide, after pointing with his lean finger to his bag of food, which was every day diminishing in size, and then to the hungry dogs, dismounted from his camel, tied up one of the dogs, and handed it over to his wild friend. A few hours later another ragged figure, this time a Bishari, carrying a long gun, ran forward to greet us, and to him the guide delivered over his second dog, after a similar discussion with regard to his food bag. For over a mile from this point, after the dog and his new master had diminished to mere specks on the rocks, the wind brought down to us the melancholy howls of the former and the unconcerned song of the latter to his goats.

Our way led up the wide Wady Ghrosar, which ends in a pass, from the top of which a magnificent view is obtained. This point was reached in a trot of about three and three-quarter hours from Bir Um Disi. One looks down upon a great lake of sand, amidst which the groups of dark granite hills rise like a thousand islands, while dim ranges enclose the scene on all sides. From this huge basin a hundred valleys seem to radiate, and it would be an easy matter to head for the wrong peak and to lose oneself upon the undulating sands. Descending a smooth slope, we rested for luncheon in the shade of a group of rocks; and presently mounting our camels again, we crossed the basin and entered a series of intricate valley, which became more and more narrow and enclosed as the day wore on, giving us good reason to doubt whether our baggage camels would manage to follow. At last, in the late afternoon, after a ride of rather under four hours from the top of Wady Ghrosar, a turn in the path brought the town of Mons Claudianus suddenly into view and in a moment the camels were forgotten, and the wonderfully preserved remains had carried one back to the day of the Emperors Trajan and Hadrian.

The hills of Um Etgâl supplied Rome with a fine white granite speckled with black, which was deservedly popular for building purposes during the Imperial age. The stone was not employed by the ancient Egyptians, and it was left to a Roman prospector to discover its existence and to open the quarries. The settlement which was founded here was known generally as Mons Claudianus, but in honour of the Emperor Trajan the well which supplied it with water was called Fons Trajanus, and this name was sometimes applied to the town. The stone was transported from here to the Nile on waggons drawn by oxen or men, and was placed upon barges at Keneh. It was then floated down the stream to the sea, where it was trans-shipped to the galleys which bore it across the Mediterranean to the port of Rome.

The distance from here to the Nile must be about a hundred miles; and, as will be seen, the blocks which were despatched from the quarries were of enormous size. It must have been an easier matter to transport the Imperial Porphyry from Gebel Dukhân to the river; for the objects executed in that stone were not usually of a size to require particularly large blocks. But the great pillars which were cut from the white granite were often of dimensions which one would have regarded as prohibitive to transportation. In order to reduce the weight to the minimum the columns were dressed on the spot to within an inch or so of their final surface, whereas the porphyry blocks were light enough to be sent down in the rough. This is the explanation of the fact that at Gebel Dukhân there was but a small town, whereas here at Um Etgâl the settlement was far more elaborate and extensive. Skilled masons had to live at Mons Claudianus as well as quarrymen, engineers as well as labourers; and the architects themselves may have had to visit the quarries on certain occasions. If one has admired the enterprise which is displayed in the works at Gebel Dukhân, an even greater call on one's admiration will be made at Um Etgâl; and those who would fully appreciate the power of the Roman Empire should make their slow way to these distant quarries, should realise the enormous difficulties of their working, and should think for a moment that all this activity was set in motion by the mere whim of an emperor.

The town, enclosed by a buttressed and fortified wall, stands in a valley between the rocky hills from which the white granite was quarried. A broad road leads up to the main entrance. On the left side of this stand various ruined houses, and on the right there is a large enclosure in which the transport animals were stabled. Over half this enclosure there was a roof, supported by numerous pillars; but the other half stands open, and contains line upon line of perfectly preserved stalls, at which some 300 oxen or donkeys could be stabled.

Farther up the road, on the opposite side, just before reaching the entrance to the town, there stands the bath-house. One first enters a good-sized hall, in which three small granite tanks stand. Here the bathers no doubt washed themselves before entering the baths proper. From this silent hall two doorways open. The first of these leads into a series of three small rooms, which were heated by furnaces in the manner of a Turkish bath. These chambers seem to have been heated to different degrees, for under the floor of the innermost there is a large cavity or cellar for the hot air, whereas in the other rooms there are only pottery flues, which pass down the walls behind the plaster. In one chamber there is an arched recess, which seems to have been made for ornamental purposes. The second doorway from the hall leads into a fine vaulted room, at the far end of which a plunge-bath, some nine feet long and four or five feet deep, is constructed of bricks and cement. Steps lead down into it from the floor level, and in the walls around there are ornamental niches in which statuettes or vases may have stood. In this tank the Roman officer was able to lie splashing after his hot-air bath, and there is an appearance of luxury about the place which suggests that he could here almost believe himself in his own country.

The enclosed town consists of a crowded mass of small houses, intersected by a main street from which several lanes branch to right and left. The walls are built of broken stones, and the doorways are generally constructed of granite. Some of the roofing is still intact, and is formed of thin slabs of granite supported by rough pillars. One wanders from street to street, picking a way here and there over fallen walls; now entering the dark chambers of some almost perfectly preserved house, now pausing to look through a street doorway into the open court beyond. Large quantities of broken pottery and blue glazed ware lie about, but there did not seem to be many other antiquities on the surface.

The temple lies outside the town on the hillside to the north. A flight of ruined steps, some 25 feet in breadth between the balustrades, leads up to a terrace on which stands the broken altar, inscribed as follows: "In the twelfth year of the Emperor Nerva Trajan Cæsar Augustus Germanicus Dacicus; by Sulpicius Simius, Prefect of Egypt, this altar was made." At the north end of the terrace there is a granite portico, of which the two elegant columns are now overthrown. Through this one passes into a large four-pillared hall, where there is another altar, upon which is written: "Annius Rufus; Legate of the XVth Legion 'Appolinaris,' superintending the marble works of Mons Claudianus by the favour of the Emperor Trajan." From this hall the sanctuary and other important rooms lead. The walls in the various parts of the building now only appear as orderly piles of rough stones, but when they were neatly covered with the salmon-coloured plaster, which may be seen in the bath-house and elsewhere, they must have been most imposing. Built into one of the outer walls of the temple there is a block of stone decorated with the well known Egyptian symbol of the disk and serpents; and this seems to be the only indication of Egyptian influence in the place.

THE ROMAN TOWN OF MONS CLAUDIANUS, LOOKING SOUTH
From the causeway leading to the main quarry.

MONS CLAUDIANUS
A large granite column lying to the north-east of the town.
The back wall of the town is seen behind the column, above
which the temple buildings are seen at the foot of the granite hills.

To the north-east of the town a great causeway leads up to the main quarries, and half-way along it lies a huge block of granite, abandoned for some reason before it had been dragged down to the depository below. Here at the foot of the causeway lie several huge columns already trimmed, and many smaller blocks left in the rough. Most of these are numbered or otherwise marked, and on one enormous block hewn in the form of a capital, there is written: "The property of Cæsar Nerva Trajan."

The well from which the inhabitants of Mons Claudianus drew their water lies in a valley nearly a mile from the town. It is enclosed within a courtyard, and near it stands a round tower some 25 feet in height. From this tower to a point about a quarter of a mile from the town there runs an aqueduct along which the water was evidently sent, the drop of 25 feet giving it the necessary impetus. At the town end of the aqueduct there is a building which contains a large tank and a series of rooms something in the nature of a small barrack. Here, no doubt, lived the persons who had charge of the water supply, and it was probably their duty to see that the tank was always full. Outside the building there is a trough from which the animals could drink. One imagines the quarrymen or their wives coming each day to the tank to fill their amphoræ with water, and the stablemen leading down the mules or donkeys to the trough. Here, as in the animal lines in the town, one is struck with the disciplined system shown in the arrangements, and it seems clear that the settlement was under the immediate eyes of true Romans, uninfluenced by the slovenliness of the Orient.

I first saw these ruins in the red light of sunset, and

through the streets of the town I made my way in the silence of nightfall. No words can record the strangeness of wandering thus through doorways unbarred since the days of Imperial Rome, and through houses uninhabited for so many hundreds of years. It is difficult to describe the sensations which a scene of this kind arouses. At first the mind is filled with sheer amazement, both at the freshness, the newness of the buildings, and their similarity to those in use at the present day. One cannot bring oneself to believe that so many centuries have passed since human eyes looked daily upon them or hands touched them. But presently a door seems to open in the brain, a screen slides back, and clearly one sees Time in its true relation. A thousand years, two thousand years, have the value of the merest drop of water in an ocean. One's hands may reach out and touch the hands which built these houses, fashioned these doorways, and planned these streets. This town is not a relic of an age of miracles, when the old gods walked the earth or sent their thunderbolts from an unremote heaven; but stone by stone it was constructed by men in every way identical with ourselves, whose brains have only known the sights and sounds which we know, altered in but a few details.

The fact that those far-off days are so identical with those we live in does not, however, speak to the mind of the changelessness of things, of the constancy of human customs. That is a minor thought. It tells rather of our misconception of the nature of Time; it shows how difficult it is to judge the ages by the standard of human experience. In looking at these almost unharmed relics of a life which ceased before our remotest English history had begun, one sees that their

modern appearance is not so much due to the persistence
of custom as it is to the shortness of time since the town
was built. Two thousand years is not a period which
we have the right to call long: it is but an hour in the
duration of man's existence upon earth. "A thousand
ages in Thy sight are like an evening gone," runs the
old hymn; and one feels that the ages since this town
was built must indeed be but an evening to One whose
laws of Decay and Change have not found time in
them to show more than a few signs of their working.
As I entered the temple in the twilight, and aroused
unaccustomed echoes in the silence of its halls, the
thought was that I had come rudely to awaken the
Past; and, as the son of a race that had outlived its
miracles, to bring the tidings that the gods were dead.
But when the newness, the freshness of parts of the
buildings, had opened the doors of the mind, the
thought was only that the gods were still living and
mighty who could think so lightly of twenty long
centuries.

On the following morning I busied myself in taking
notes and photographs amongst the ruins; and somewhat before noon the camp was struck. The road, now
leading westwards towards Keneh, passed for the main
part of the ride along a wide valley of great beauty;
and after trotting for about three and a half hours we
passed a small ancient quarry of fine, small-grained,
grey granite—like that of which the statue of Tutankhamen in the Cairo Museum is made—near which
a few huts were grouped. Towards sunset we crossed
the brow of a hill, and so descended into the Wady
Fatîreh, where we camped near the well of that name.
Here there is a Roman station differing very slightly

from those already described. It lies about five and a
half hours' trot from Mons Claudianus, and was thus
the first night's halting-place for express caravans on
the road from that town to Keneh.

As darkness fell, I was sitting in the fortress ques-
tioning the guide as to the road, when we were both
startled by the sound of falling stones, and looking up
we saw a large dog-like creature disappearing over the
wall. Examining the footprints afterwards, I saw
them to be the heavy marks of a hyæna; but no more
was heard of him. Hyænas are by no means rare in the
desert, though it is not usual to find them so far back
from the Nile as this. In sleeping out in the desert
travellers warn one to be careful, for a hyæna, they
say, might snap at a foot protruding from the blankets,
just as a man might take a biscuit from the sideboard;
but I do not recollect hearing of anybody who has ever
been attacked.

The ancient Egyptians used to eat hyænas, and the
scenes in the early tombs show them being fattened up
in the farms. Men are seen flinging the unfortunate
creatures on their backs, their legs being tied, while
others force goose-flesh down their throats. Probably
the archaic hunter in the desert ate hyæna-flesh for
want of other meat, and the custom took hold amongst
the sporting families of dynastic times; for with proper
feeding there is no reason to suppose that the meat
would be objectionable. The old guide told me, as we
sat in the darkness, that there are several trappers who
make their living by snaring hyænas, and there is no
part of the animal which has not a marketable value.
The skin has its obvious uses; the skull is sold as a
charm, and brings luck to any house under the threshold

of which it is buried; the fat is roasted and eaten as a great delicacy; and the flesh is also used for eating, and for medical purposes, certain parts being stewed down and swallowed by women who desire to produce a family in spite of Nature's unwillingness.

In the neighbourhood of Fatîreh we noticed several rough workings in the rocks, near which there were often a few ruined huts. These are the remains of ancient gold mines, worked by the Egyptians and the Romans. There are said to be many old mines in this neighbourhood, and an attempt has been made in recent years to re-open them, though without much success. In an inscription of Dynasty XVIII (B.C. 1580-1350) one reads of "the gold of the desert behind Koptos," which city was situated on the Nile a few miles south of Keneh; and although most of the Koptos metal was obtained from the region of Wady Fowakhîeh, of which the reader will have heard in a previous chapter, some of the gold may have been mined in the Fatîreh neighbourhood at that date, as it certainly was in Roman times. The subject is one of such interest that I may be permitted to mention here something of the methods of working the gold employed by the ancients.

A full account is given by Diodorus, who obtained his information from Agatharcides, of the mines which are situated in the Eastern Desert farther to the south; and, as the methods were no doubt similar in both districts, the information enables one to reconstruct the scenes upon which these hills of Fatîreh looked down two thousand years ago.

The persons who worked the mines were mainly criminals and prisoners of war; but with these there

were many unjustly accused, men of good breeding,
and those who had by some political action earned the
Pharaoh's or the emperor's wrath. Frequently this
class of prisoner was banished to the mines, together
with all the members of his family, and these also were
obliged to labour for the king's profit. No distinctions
were made at the mines between the classes, but all suffered together, and all were weighed down with fetters
by night and by day. There was little or no chance of
escape, for sentries were posted on every hill-top, and
the soldiers were ready to give chase through the waterless desert should a man elude the watchman. These
soldiers were all of foreign extraction, and the chances
were heavy against their understanding the speech of
the prisoners; and thus they were seldom able to be
bribed or introduced into a scheme of escape.

The work was carried on day after day without cessation, and always the labourers were under the eye of
a merciless overseer, who showered blows upon them at
the slightest provocation. In order to keep down the
expenses, no clothes were provided for the prisoners,
and often they possessed not a rag to hide their naked-
ness. Nor were they allowed to give a moment's time
to the bathing or care of their bodies. In good or in
bad health they were forced to work; and neither the
weakness of extreme age, nor the fever of sickness, nor
the infirmities of women, were regarded as proper
cause for the idleness of even an hour. All alike were
obliged to labour, and were urged thereto by many
blows. Thus the end of a man who had been banished
to these mines was always the same: fettered and unwashed, covered with bruises and disfigured by pesti-
lence, he dropped dead in his chains under the lash

of the relentless whip. The sufferings of life were such that death was hailed with joy, and it was the dying alone who possessed a single thought of happiness.

Those who have seen the old workings on the exposed face of the rocks, and have known the coldness of the winter nights and the intense heat of the summer days, will alone realise what tortures these poor wretches must have suffered. One might well think that the wind which went moaning down the valley as we rode along the path to the Nile still carried the groans of the sufferers, and that the whispering rocks still echoed the cries of utter despair. Looking at the huts where these people lived and the mines where they laboured, one could not regard the record of their woe, which Diodorus makes known to us, as a tale of long ago. Two thousand years, one may repeat, is not really a period which we should regard as long; and while walls stand upright and mines gape open, the sound of lamentation will not be hushed in these valleys.

The rock from which the gold was obtained, says Diodorus, was very hard; but the miners softened it by lighting fires under it, after which it could almost be broken with the hands. When it was thus prepared, thousands of prisoners were set to breaking it with iron tools, while the overseer directed their labours towards the veins of gold. To the strongest of the men iron picks were given, and with these, though wielded unskilfully and with great labour, they were made to attack the hillside. The galleries, following the veins, twisted and turned, so that at the depth of a few feet there was no glimmer of daylight; and for this reason the miners each carried a small lamp bound to their forehead. As the blocks of quartz were broken by the picks they were carried to the surface by children of the captives, who formed a constant procession up and down the dark galleries. These fragments were then gathered up by youths and placed in stone mortars, in which they were pounded with iron pestles until the ore was broken into pieces of the size of peas. The ore was then handed over to women and old men, who placed it in hand-mills, and thus ground it to powder. The powder was then placed upon a sloping surface, and a stream of water was poured over it, which carried away the particles of stone but left the gold in position. This process of washing was repeated several times, until all foreign matter was eliminated, and the gold dust became pure and bright. Other workmen then took the dust, and, after measuring it carefully, they poured it into an earthenware crucible; and, having added a small quantity of lead, tin, salt, and bran, they closed the vessel with a tight-fitting lid, and placed it in a furnace for the space of five days. At the end of this time the crucible was set aside to cool, and on removing the lid it was found to contain gold ready to be despatched to the Treasury.

To bear witness to the accuracy of this account one sometimes finds mortars and hand-mills lying amidst the ruins of the old mining settlements. At the mines of Um Garriât there are said to be thousands of these mills, and here at Fatîreh not a few are to be found. Sluices for washing the crushed ore have been observed in some of the old workings and of the smelting crucibles remains exist at Um Garriât and elsewhere.

Practically nothing is known of the methods em-

ployed by the Egyptians in earlier days, but they
cannot have differed very greatly from those of the
Roman period. There seems reason to suppose that
less cruelty existed in dynastic times than in the days
of the callous Romans; and in the following chapter
an account will be given of a temple, a well, and a
town built by King Sety I for the benefit of persons
who were engaged in gold-mining.

The night spent at Fatîreh was again bitterly cold,
and a violent wind necessitated a tussle with tent-ropes
and pegs: a form of exercise as annoying in the day-
time as any that exists, and in the shivering night-time
unspeakable. A couple of hours' riding next day
brought us to the end of the mountainous country and
into the open desert. For the first time for several
days the sun streamed down from a cloudless sky, but
the strong north wind continued to blow in full force;
and as we trotted over the level plains we were half-
blinded by the stinging sand. The peaked hills behind
us rose from a sea of tearing sand, and before us in
the distance rose low, undulating clay mounds, beyond
which one could catch a glimpse of the limestone cliffs
so typical of the Nile valley. In the afternoon we
crossed these mounds and descended into a very maze
of hillocks, amidst which we camped. Amongst these
mounds we met a couple of Bedouin, the purpose of
whose presence was entirely obscure. Our guide ex-
changed the usual greetings with them and then in a
low voice began to talk of the miserable dog which
trotted dejectedly behind his camel. Again he pointed
to his almost empty bag of food, and at last dismounted, fastened a rope to the creature's neck, and
handed it to the Bedouin. The usual howls floated to

us on the wind as we rode onwards, but the high spirits of the guide at his freedom from any further responsibility was a real pleasure to witness.

Early in the following morning I visited the Roman station of Greiyeh, which lies some seven hours' trot from Fatîreh, and about six hours, or rather more, from Keneh, and was thus the first night's halting-place out from the Nile, or the second from Mons Claudianus. The station is, as usual, a rectangular enclosure, in which several rooms are constructed. Particularly well preserved are the animal lines, which lie to the west of the station. They consist of a courtyard in which fourteen rows of stalls are built, while down either side there has been a shed with a roof supported by a row of pillars. Not far away is the ancient well, enclosed in a small compound.

This is the last of the Roman stations, and having passed it, the ancient world seemed to slip back out of reach. The camels were set at a hard trot over the now flat and burning sand, and by noon the distant palms of Keneh were in sight floating above the mirage. As the houses of the town grew more and more distinct in the dazzling sunlight, the practical concerns of official work came hurrying to mind; and in times and trains, baggage and bustle, the quiet desert, with its ghosts of Rome, faded away as fades some wonderful dream when the sleeper awakes.

CHAPTER XIII

THE TEMPLE OF WADY ABÂD

THE small shrine in the Eastern Desert, which I have here called the Temple of Wady Abâd, is known to Egyptologists as the Temple of Redesiyeh, although it is thirty-seven miles or more from the village on the Nile, five miles above Edfu, which bears that name. Redesiyeh seems to have been the point from which Lepsius, the German archæologist, and other early explorers set out to visit the desert shrine; and hence the name of this wholly unimportant village was given to the ruin, and nobody has bothered to find one more suitable. By the natives the building is called *El Kaneis,* "the chapel"; and since it is situated in the well-known Wady Abâd, it would seem most natural to call it the "Chapel, or Temple, of Wady Abâd." Modern prospectors and mining engineers have been puzzled to know what Redesiyeh has to do with the place; and the fact that an old German antiquarian half a century ago collected his camels at that village being wholly without significance to them, they have regarded the word Redesiyeh as a probable corruption of Rhodesia, and have spoken, to the amazement and confusion of the uninitiate, of the Temple of Rhodesia in the hills of the Upper Egyptian Desert.

The shrine was built by King Sety I (B.C. 1300), the father of Rameses the Great, for the benefit of the

275

miners passing to and from the various gold mines near the Red Sea; and the story one hears from the modern engineers, which vaguely relates that the temple was erected by King Ptolemy as a memorial to his son, who died at this spot on his return from the mines, does not require consideration. During the brilliant reign of Sety I, the gold mines were energetically worked, and the produce of those upon the road to which this shrine was built was intended especially for the upkeep and ornamentation of the king's great temple at Abydos, about 180 miles by river north of the Wady Abâd. There are so many old gold-workings between the river and the Red Sea that one cannot say definitely where Sety's miners were bound for who stopped to offer a prayer to the gods at this wayside shrine, but one may certainly say that Edfu, the old Apollinopolis Magna, and El Kab, the old Eileithyiaspolis, were the cities from which they set out. It will, perhaps, be best to state that Edfu stands on the Nile, about half-way between Aswân and Luxor—i.e., about 520 miles above Cairo—and that El Kab is situated some 10 miles down-stream from Edfu. The Wady Abâd enters the desert exactly opposite Edfu; the shrine stands about 35 miles east of that town; and the Red Sea coast is about 100 miles farther east as the crow flies.

One year, towards the end of March, when the hot south winds were driving the tourists towards the sea, and the trains from Luxor to Cairo were full to overflowing, I set out in the opposite direction, travelling southwards in an empty train as far as the little wayside station of Mahamîd, the nearest stopping place to the ruins of El Kab. The camels which were to carry

my party to Sety's temple in the desert were awaiting
us upon the platform, surrounded by an admiring
throng of native loafers. The caravan, according to
orders, which were ultimately carried out, was to consist of ten baggage and four riding camels, and an
assortment of camel-men under the leadership of a
Shêkh; but more than double that number of camels
lay grunting in the sunlight as the hot train panted
into the station. This was due to the fact that a rival
and more wealthy camel proprietor, who had not been
invited to do business on this occasion, had sent a few
camels to the rendezvous, on the chance of their being
required, and this move the chosen proprietor met by
doubling the number of his camels. The disappointed
owner was himself at the station, and eloquently
dilated upon the danger of entrusting oneself to a
Shêkh of inferior standing. In the infallible "Bædeker," one reads that for this journey it is necessary
"to secure the protection of the Shêkh of the Ababdeh
tribes"; and though the edition in which these ominous
words appear is a few years out of date, one realised
in what a dilemma a traveller who did not know the
country might have found himself. The Shêkh, it
appeared, had even telegraphed his warning to me at
the last moment; but this having been really the last
of a short series of cards which it seems that he had
played, it did not require many words to soothe matters into the normal condition of hullabaloo which
everywhere prevails in Egypt at the departure of a
caravan.

The baggage at last being despatched southwards,
we set out towards the ruins of El Kab, which could be
seen shimmering in the heat haze a few miles away. It

was our purpose to ride to Edfu, thence into the desert, and thence back to Edfu and on to Aswân. The first night was to be spent under the ruined walls of the ancient city of Eileithyiaspolis, and it did not take long to trot to the camping-ground by the river-side. Here, in explanation of the route which we followed, I must be permitted to enter into some archæological details in connection with El Kab and Edfu.

In archaic days, when the great Hawk-chieftains who glimmer, like pale stars, at the dawn of history, were consolidating their power in Upper Egypt before conquering the whole Nile valley, there stood a city on the west bank of the river, opposite El Kab, which in later times was known as Hieraconpolis, "the City of the Hawks." This was the earliest capital of Upper Egypt, and here it is probable that the great king Mena, "the Fighter," the first Pharaoh of a united Egypt, was born and bred. This king and his father conquered the whole of Egypt, and for that conquest a certain amount of wealth was necessary, even in those days when might was as good as money. For this purpose, and for the reason that the arts of civilisation were already in practice, the gold mines of the Eastern Desert began to be worked. This industry led to the establishment of a station on the east bank of the river opposite the capital, where the miners might foregather, and where the caravans and their escort of soldiers might be collected.

As larger deeds and wider actions became the order of the Pharaoh's day, so the mines were extended and the number of workmen increased; and it was not long before the station at El Kab grew into a city almost as large as the metropolis. In Dynasty XII (B.C. 2000) a wall was built around it, which stands to this day, in order to protect it from incursions from the desert. Gradually great temples were erected here, and the city, known as Nekheb, and later as Eileithyiaspolis, was one of the busiest centres in Egypt.

The ruins of the old caravanserai are of wonderful interest. One may pass through the narrow doorway of the fortified enclosure, and in the silent area where once the soldiers and miners camped, and where now a few goats graze, one feels completely shut off from the world of the present day. The dark walls rise almost to their full height, and one may still ascend and descend the sloping ramps where the sentries paced in the olden days. Here there are the ruins of the temple where the vulture-goddess was worshipped; and yonder one sees mounds of potsherds, bricks, corn-grinders, and all the debris of a forsaken town. In the side of a hill which overlooks the great ramparts there is the long row of tombs in which the princes of the district were buried; and here in the biographical inscriptions on the walls one reads of many a feat of arms and many a brave adventure.

The hills of the desert recede in a kind of bay, and walking eastwards from the town, one presently sees that there is at the back of the bay, an outlet through the range, five miles or so from the river and the enclosure. It was through this natural gateway, which the ancient Egyptians called "the Mouth of the Wilderness," that the caravans passed in early days into the great desert; and once through this doorway they were immediately shut off from the green Nile valley and all its busy life. There is a great isolated rock, which stands in the bay, and in its shadow the miners and soldiers were wont to offer their last prayers to the gods of Egypt, often inscribing their names upon the smooth surface of the stone. Here one reads of priests, scribes, caravan-conductors, soldiers, superintendents of the gold mines, and all manner of officials, who were making the desert journey, or who had come to see its starting-point.

In Dynasty XVIII, Amenhotep III (B.C. 1400) erected a graceful little temple here, to which one may walk or ride out from El Kabo over the level, gravel-covered surface of the desert, and may stand amazed at the freshness of the colouring of the paintings on its wall. Another little shrine was built, close by, a century and a half later; and in Ptolemaic times a third temple was constructed. Thus the traveller is surrounded by shrines as he sets out over the hills away from this land of shrines; it is as though the gods were loath to leave him and in solemn company came out to speed him on his way.

The road which the gold miners trod passed through the hills, and then turned off towards the south-east; and presently it met the road which started from Edfu, or rather, from Contra Apollinopolis Magna, which, as has been said, is ten miles distant from El Kab. Edfu was also a city of great antiquity, and was famous as the place where at the dawn of Egyptian history the Hawk-tribes overthrew the worshippers of Set, the god who afterwards degenerated into Satan. The great temple which now stands there, and which is the delight of thousands of visitors each winter, was built upon the ruins of earlier temples, where the hawks of Edfu had been worshipped since the beginning of things. The record of a tax levied on Edfu in the reign of Thutmose III (B.C. 1500) shows that it was mainly paid in solid gold, instead of in kind; and one thus sees that the precious metal was coming into the country at that time along the Wady Abâd route, as indeed it was along all the great routes. Edfu was the main starting-point for the mines in the days when Sety I built his temple, if we may judge from the fact that the hawk-god of that city is one of the chief deities worshipped in the shrine, while the vulture-goddess of El Kab has only a secondary place there; and in Roman times the Edfu road was perhaps the only one in general use.

This was the route which was selected for our journey; and after spending the night at El Kab, we rode next morning along the east bank of the river to a point at the mouth of the Wady Abâd, opposite the picturesque town of Edfu, where the pylons shoot up to the blue sky and dominate the cluster of brown houses and green trees. A morning swim in the river, and a trot of somewhat over two hours, was sufficient exercise for the first day; and the afternoon was spent in camp, while the camel-men collected the food for the journey and led their beasts down to the river to drink.

On the following morning, soon after daybreak, we mounted our camels and set out over the hard sand and gravel towards the sunrise. A fresh, cool wind blew from the north, and the larks were already singing their first songs, as we trotted up the wady. The brisk morning air, the willing camels, the setting out into the freedom of the desert—how shall I record the charm of it? Only those who have travelled in the desert can understand the joy of returning there; a joy which, strangely enough, has only one equal, and that, the pleasure of returning to water, to flowers, and to trees after a spell of some days or weeks in the wilderness. Here there are no cares, for there are no posts nor newspapers; here there is no fretfulness, for one is taking almost continual exercise; here there is no irritation, for society, the arch-irritant, is absent; here there is no debility and fag, for one is drinking in renewed strength from the strong conditions around. But ever enthusiasm, that splendid jewel in the ring of life, shines and glitters before one's eyes; and all one's actions assume a broader and a happier complexion. The desert is the breathing-space of the world, and therein one truly breathes and lives.

A trot of about two hours brought us to a well, known as Bir Abâd. The well is but a small, stagnant pool of brackish water, around which a few trees grow. There are six acacias, three or four small palms, a curious dead-looking tree, called *Herâz* by the natives, and a few desert shrubs. Some attempt has been made to cultivate a small area, but this has not met with success, and the native farmers have departed. The sand under the acacias offers a welcome resting-place, and here in the shade we sat for a while, listening to the quiet shuffle of the wind amongst the trees and to the singing of the sand-martins. While playing idly with the sand, an objectionable insect was uncovered, which the natives call a "ground-gazelle." It is a fat, maggot-like, beastly creature, about an inch in length, possessing a pair of nippers similar to those of an earwig. It runs fast upon its six or eight legs, but whenever possible it buries itself by wriggling backwards into the sand. A more loathesome insect could not well be imagined; and, since the species is said to be by no means uncommon, I shall not delve with my fingers so readily in the future when I chance to be lying in the shadow of desert trees.

A ride of about half-an-hour's duration along the valley and past a Shêkh's tomb, known as Abu Gehâd, brought us to the ruined Roman fortified station named after this tomb. It is much like other stations of this date, and consists of an enclosure in which a few chambers are to be seen. One enters from the west, and in the open area forming the courtyard there is a cemented tank in which a supply of water was stored for the use of travellers. The south wall of the enclosure to this day looks formidable from the outside, still standing some twelve feet in height, and being solidly built of broken stones. On this side of the station there are traces of an outbuilding, which may have been the animal lines. In the main enclosure a block of sandstone was found, bearing the cartouches of the Pharaoh Tutankhamen (B.C. 1350), and by its form it seems to have been part of a shrine which perhaps had stood at this spot. The road from El Kab here joins the Edfu route, and the Pharaoh may have marked the meeting of the ways by a little wayside temple at which the gold miners might offer a prayer to the gods of the wilderness. Some of the gold which has been found in his tomb, no doubt came along this road from the mines.

In Roman days, when this station was built, it is probable that the gold mines no longer formed the main objective of the caravans which passed along this road. Emeralds, almost unknown to the ancient Egyptians, were now deemed an ornamentation of worth and beauty; and the emerald mines of Gebel Zabâra, which are most easily approached along this route, were vigorously worked by the Romans. It was on his way to these mines that Cailliaud, in 1816, discovered the Temple of Sety I. There was also a road from Edfu to the Græco-Roman port of Berenice on the Red Sea, which was much used at this period; and stations similar to that of Abu Gehâd are to be met with at fairly regular intervals for the whole distance to the coast.

Trotting on for another two hours and a quarter, we camped under the rocks of Gebel Timsah, a well-known landmark to the Bedouin. A head of rock projects into the level valley, and upon it the people of the desert for untold generations have set up small heaps of stones, the original idea of which must have been connected with religious worship. The two tents were no sooner pitched than a gale of wind, suddenly rising, tore one of them down, and almost succeeded in overthrowing the other. A tempest of dust and sand beat in at the doorway, and covered all things with a brown layer, so that one knew not where to turn nor how to escape. Fortunately, however, like all things violent, it did not last for long, and a calm, starlit night followed.

The distance from Gebel Timsah to the temple which was our destination may be covered in about an hour and a half of trotting. We set out soon after sunrise; and presently a low ridge was crossed, the path passing between two piles or beacons of stones, set up perhaps in Roman days to mark the road; and from this point a wide, flat valley could be seen, stretchin~ between the low hills, and much overgrown with bushes and brambles. Over the plain we jogged in the cool morning air, directing the camels to a high bluff of rock

in the east, in which, the guide told us, the temple of
Sety was excavated. Soon a Roman fortress came into
sight, and later we were able to discern the portico of
the temple sheltering under the rocks. Slowly the
features became more distinct, and at last we dismounted
at the foot of the cliffs and scrambled up the slope to
explore the picturesque shrine.

It is strange that of the many Egyptologists who
have travelled in Egypt, only two—Lepsius and Golenischeff—have visited this spot. It may be that the
statement of the old Bædeker, which says that the wandering Ababdeh tribes "assume a hostile attitude" to
travellers, has confined them to the banks of the Nile;
or perhaps the reported antics of the much-maligned
camel have induced them to leave unvisited this pearl of
the past. For that matter, however, the place might be
reached upon the back of the patient ass, there being
water at Bir Abâd, and for the last few years, at the
temple itself. When one sees this building, among the
best preserved of all the Egyptian temples, one is
amazed at the lack of enterprise which has caused it to
be uncared for, unprotected, and unvisited for all these
years. A few mining engineers and prospectors alone
have seen the shrine; and, since they have disfigured its
walls with their names, one could wish that they too had
stayed at home.

The little temple consists of a rectangular hall excavated in the rock, the roof being supposed to be
supported by four square pillars, though in reality these
also are part of the living rock. At the far end there
are three shrines in which the statues of the gods are
carved. In front of this hall there is a built portico, the
roof of which rests upon four columns with lotus-bud

capitals. One enters from the north, up the slope of
fallen stones and driven sand, and so passes into the
shade of the portico. Through a hole in the roof, where
a slab of stone has fallen in, one may look up at the
towering rocks which overhang the building. Then,
through a beautifully ornamented doorway, one passes
into the dimness of the rock-cut hall, where there is a
consciousness that the whole height of the hills rests
above one's head. Both this hall and the portico are
richly decorated with coloured reliefs, and in the inner
portion of the temple the visitor will stand in wonder
at the brightness of the colours in the scenes which are
seen on all sides. It has been said that the brilliancy
of the painting in the temple of Amenhotep III, at El
Kab, is surprising; but here it is still fresher, and has
even more admirably held its own against the assaults
of time. We see the Pharaoh smiting down his negro
and Asiatic enemies in the presence of Amon-Ra and
Horus of Edfu; we watch him as he makes offerings to
the gods; and to the ceiling the eye is attracted by the
great vultures with spread wings which there hover,
depicted in radiant colours rendered more radiant by
contrast with the browns and yellows of the scenery
outside. In the niches at the end of the hall the gods
sit in serenity; and though these figures have been damaged almost beyond recognition by pious Moslems,
there still clings around them their old majesty, and
still something solemn may be found in their attitude,
so that the visitor almost pays heed to the warning inscribed on the doorway, that a man must be twice
purified before entering the little sanctuary where they
sit.

It may be asked why Sety selected this spot for his

temple, for except that it lies on the route to the mines, the reason for its location is not at once apparent. The explanation, however, is not far to seek. This great bluff of rock has a smooth cliff-like surface on its north side, and for the earliest travellers, as for those of the present day, it has cast a welcome shadow in which one might take the mid-day siesta in comfort. Here, scratched or chiselled on the rock, there are many drawings which undoubtedly date from archaic, and even prehistoric times. Numerous representations of curious boats are seen, and their character justifies one in supposing them to be the sacred arks which formed in ancient times such an essential part of Egyptian religious ceremonial. In most of these vessels there is the shrine which contained the god, and in one drawing a figure with flail raised, before which an animal is being sacrificed, is certainly the god Min himself, the patron of the desert. A few animals and figures are also drawn, and when human beings are represented in or near the arks, their arms are shown held aloft in the regular Egyptian attitude of worship.

Thus it seems that, from being a place to rest and to dream in, the rock had already in archaic times become a sacred spot, at which early man bowed himself down before the representations of the ark of Min. From this period until Dynasty XVIII, it seems, from the lack of inscriptions here, that the mines were not much used. Amenhotep III, however, sent his Viceroy of the South out here, whose name, Merimes, is written upon the rocks near the temple; and his temple at El Kab, at the beginning of the route, is further indication of his interest in the gold-workings. Just as this king had built his temple near the sacred rock at "the Mouth of the Wilderness," so Sety I, following half a century later, decided to erect his shrine at the foot of this more distant sacred rock, the half distance having already been adventured by the intermediate Pharaoh Tutankhamen. Since the place was just about a day's express ride from Edfu to El Kab, its situation was convenient; and, moreover, there was no other head of rock in the neighbourhood which offered so fine a position for a rock temple.

In the inscriptions near the mouth of the excavated portions of the shrine, Sety caused to be recorded the story of the building of the temple; and parts of this are of sufficient interest to be quoted here:—

"In the year 9 (B.C. 1304), the third month of the third season, the twentieth day.* Lo! his majesty inspected the hill-country as far as the region of the mountains, for his heart desired to see the mines from which the gold is brought. Now, when his majesty had gone out from the Nile valley, he made a halt on the road, in order to take counsel with his heart; and he said, 'How evil is the way without water! It is so for a traveller whose mouth is parched. How shall his throat be cooled, how shall he quench his thirst? For the lowland is far away, and the highland is vast. The thirsty man cries out to himself against a fatal country. Make haste! let me take counsel of their needs. I will make for them a supply for preserving them alive, so that they will thank God in my name in after years.' Now, after his majesty had spoken these words in his own heart, he coursed through the desert, seeking a place to make a water-station; and lo! the god led him

---

* This corresponded to the middle of April, when the weather is growing hot.

in order to grant the request which he desired. Then were commanded quarrymen to dig a well upon the desert, that he might sustain the fainting, and cool for him the burning heat of summer. Then this place was built in the great name of Sety, and the water flowed into it in very great plenty. Said his majesty, 'Behold, the god has granted my petition, and he has brought to me water upon the desert. Since the days of the gods the way has been dangerous, but it has been made pleasant in my glorious reign. Another good thought has come into my heart, at the command of the god, even the equipment of a town, in whose midst shall be a settlement with a temple. I will build a resting-place on this spot in the great name of my fathers, the gods. May they grant that what I have wrought shall abide, and that my memory shall prosper, circulating through the hill-country.'

"Then his majesty commanded that the leader of the king's workmen be commissioned, and with him the quarrymen, that there should be made, by excavation in the mountain, this temple. Now, after the strong-hold was completed and adorned, and its paintings executed, his majesty came to worship his fathers, all the gods; and he said, 'Praise to you, O great gods! May ye favour me for ever, may ye establish my name eternally. As I have been useful to you, as I have been watchful for the things which ye desire, may ye speak to those who are still to come, whether kings, princes, or people, that they may establish for me my work in this place, on behalf of my beautiful temple in Abydos.'"

The last words tell us for what purpose this route to the gold mines had been bettered. A second long inscription is devoted to blessings on those who keep up this shrine and the mines with which it was connected, and to curses on those who allow it to fall into neglect. A third inscription is supposed to give the speech of the travellers who have benefited by the king's thoughtfulness:—

"Never was the like of it (the temple and the well) made by any king, save by the King Sety, the good shepherd, who preserves his soldiers alive, the father and mother of all. Men say from mouth to mouth, 'O, Amon, give to him eternity, double to him everlastingness; for he has opened for us the road to march on, when it was closed before us. We proceed and are safe, we arrive and are preserved alive. The difficult way which is in our memory has become a good way. He has caused the mining of the gold to be easy. He hath dug for water in the desert far from men for the supply of every traveller who traverses the highlands.' "

Sety dedicated his temple to Amon-Ra, whom he identified with Min, the old god of the place, and to Harmachis, the sun-god, whom he seems to have identified with the hawk, Horus of Edfu. He also here worshipped Ptah, the Egyptian Vulcan, and his lion-headed consort, Sekhmet; Tum; Hathor, the Egyptian Venus; Nekheb, the vulture-goddess of El Kab; Osiris and Isis; Mut, the mother goddess; and Khonsu, the moon-god, who was the son of Amon-Ra and Mut, and with them formed the royal trinity at Thebes. All these gods one sees upon the walls of the temple, and before them Sety is shown offering incense, wine, flowers and food. Some inscriptions on the rocks near the temple, written by high officials of this period who visited the mines, make mention of two other deities:

Ra, the sun-god, and a strange goddess who rides a horse and brandishes a shield and spear.

When Sety died the temple was still not quite finished, and for some reason or other which we shall probably never know, it so remained. His temple at Abydos, too, was neglected, and the revenues ceased to be collected. Thus, in spite of the curses inscribed on the walls of the desert shrine, the king's plans for the continual working of the mines, in order to pay for the maintenance of his great masterpiece, were not carried out. At Abydos, Rameses II, in an inscription written a few years later, states that he found the temple of Sety there unfinished, and that it had not been "completed according to the regulations for it of the gold-house." He, however, finished the building, and perhaps re-established the gold-workings along the Wady Abâd route, for on one of the pillars of the hall of the desert shrine there is an inscription written by an official, which reads: "Bringing the gold for the festival in the temple of Rameses II."

Since that time until the present day the gods in the sanctuary have looked out at a long stream of travellers, soldiers, miners, and officials. Upon the rocks and on the walls of the temple there are several hieroglyphic and Greek inscriptions which tell of the coming of all manner of people. A chief of the custodians of El Kab here records his name, and a scribe of the king's troops is immortalised near by. Many of the Greek inscriptions are *ex-votos* dedicated to Pan, with whom the old Min had been identified; and as the latter was the god of desert travel, so the sprightly Pan becomes the sober patron of the roads. Miners from Syracuse and from Crete tell of their advent; and one traveller describes himself as an Indian, a voyager, perhaps, in one of the trading vessels which brought to the port of Berenice the riches of the East, to be conveyed across this great desert to the markets of Alexandria. A man named Dorion states that he had returned in safety from an elephant hunt, probably in the south. Two inscriptions are written by Jews, thanking God for their safe journeys; and it is interesting to note that one of them is called Theodotus, son of Dorion, and the other Ptolemy, son of Dionysius—all pagan names. A troop of Greek soldiers have recorded their names in the temple, and state that they kept a watch before "Pan of the Good Roads."

These travellers, besides, or instead of, writing their names, seem often to have piled a few stones at conspicuous points as a memorial of their passage. At various places in the neighbourhood, and especially at the foot of the hills opposite the temple, there are many such piles of stones; and when well built they rise from the rocks like altars, three feet or so in height, and perhaps two feet in diameter. In one or two cases there are fragments of Egyptian pottery lying beside them, and there seems no question that they are connected with religious worship. The same custom still prevails amongst the desert people, though now its significance is not remembered; and yet its meaning is not entirely forgotten, for on a hill-top near the temple we found, near such a pile of stones, three pairs of gazelle horns and a collection of Red Sea shells, pierced for stringing, a modern offering to the old gods.

In Græco-Roman times, a large fortified station was constructed near the temple, and this still stands in fairly good preservation. It is built in the plain, in front of the temple, not more than a hundred yards from the foot of the cliffs. The enclosure is somewhat larger than is usual in these stations, but the greater part of the area has never been built upon. The enclosing wall still stands to a height of ten feet or so in parts, but here and there it is almost entirely ruined. It is built in three thicknesses, so that on the inside there are two heights at which one might walk around the rampart without showing above it. One enters through a well-built masonry doorway, and on either side one may see the hole into which the beam was shot to close the wooden door at nights. On one's right there is a group of small chambers; and here an isolated house, in one wall of which a window is still intact, forms the best preserved portion of the ruin. On one's left there is a large hall, in which there was a tank, parts of which, now half choked with sand, can be seen. The next building on one's left is also a hall of considerable size— the common mess-room, probably, of the travellers. One then passes into the open courtyard, which bears off to the left, or north, and does not contain more than a trace or so of walls.

Although there are so many of these Roman stations in the Eastern Desert, their charm and interest never palls; and more than any other ancient buildings, they bring back the lost ages and recall the forgotten activities of the old world. These ruins, too, are always picturesque, and gather to themselves at dawn and at sunset the hues, the lights, and the shadows of the fairest fancy. At dawn, at noon, at sunset—all day long— this fortress in the Wady Abâd is beautiful; and for those who love the desert there is here and in its surroundings always some new thing to charm. The walls

of the enclosure, and beyond them the pillared portico
of the temple sheltering under the rugged brown cliffs,
form as delightful a picture as may be found in Egypt.
As the traveller sits in the blue shadow, he may watch
the black-and-white stone-chats fluttering from rock to
rock, and overhead there circles a vulture, as vividly
coloured as those which form the ceiling decoration of
the temple. The wide, flat plain, shut in by the distant
hills on all sides, entices him from the fortress on to its
sparkling surface, though the tumbled rocks near the
temple soon call him back to their breezy humps and
shady nooks. The hundred surrounding hill-tops vie
with one another in the advertisement of their merits,
and he attains a summit but to covet a further prospect.
Or attracted by the two or three trees and the few
bushes which grow in the plain over against the fortress,
he walks to their welcoming shade; and there he may
listen to the song of the sand-martins and to the strange,
long-drawn note of the finches.

"A book of verses underneath the bough . . ."

One knows now what the old philosopher desired to express; for the wilderness is indeed a sort of Paradise,
and here one may find the true happiness.

The day slips past in a half-dream of pleasure; and
to the student of archæology, who finds so much for his
pencil to record and his mind to consider, the hours race
by at an absurd speed. The two days which we spent
here passed like an afternoon's dream, and the memories
which remain in the mind are almost too slight to record.
Writing here in my study, I reconstruct the rugged
scene, and search for the incidents which gave gentle

colour to it. There was a flight of cranes, which sailed overhead, moving from south-east to north-west, on their way to spend the summer in Europe. Why should my memory recall so charmedly the passage of a hundred birds? There was a hyæna which, in the red dusk, stood upon a hill-top to watch us and presently disappeared. There were three vultures which rose from the bones of a dead camel, soared into the sky, and alighted again when we had passed. There came a flock of goats and sheep at noonday to the well, with much bleating and with the gentle patter of many hoofs. The shepherd in his picturesque rags eyed us curiously as his charges drank, and still watching us, passed down the wady towards the west when they had quenched their thirst. And so my memory wanders over the two days, recalling the trivialities, and passing over the more precise details of camp life and of work, until presently the tents are struck and the baggage goes bumping down the valley once more, on the backs of the grunting camels. The return journey to Edfu was soon accomplished, and the accumulated mail of five or six days which was in waiting at the end of the ride, quickly brought me back to the business of life, and relegated the Wady Abâd to the store-chamber of happy recollections.

CHAPTER XIV

THE FLOODING OF LOWER NUBIA

THE country of Lower Nubia lies between the First and Second Cataracts of the Nile. The town of Aswân, once famous as the frontier outpost of Egypt, and now renowned as a winter resort for Europeans and Americans, stands some two or three miles below the First Cataract; and two hundred miles southwards, at the foot of the Second Cataract, stands Wady Halfa. About half-way between these two points the little town of Derr nestles amidst its palms; and here the single police-station of the province is situated. Agriculturally the land is extremely barren, for the merest strip of cultivation borders the river, and in many reaches the desert comes down to the water's edge. The scenery is rugged and often magnificent. As one sails up the Nile, the rocky hills on either side group themselves into bold compositions, rising darkly above the palms and acacias reflected in the water. The villages, clustered on the hillside as though grown like mushrooms in the night, are not different in colour from the ground upon which they are built; but here and there neatly whitewashed houses of considerable size are to be observed. Now we come upon a tract of desert sand, which rolls down to the river in a golden slope; now the hills recede, leaving an open bay wherein there are patches of cultivated ground reclaimed from the wilderness; and now a dense but narrow palm-grove follows the line of the bank for a mile or more, backed by the villages at the foot of the hills.

The inhabitants are few in number. Most of the males have taken service as cooks, butlers, waiters and bottle-washers in European houses or hotels throughout Egypt; and consequently one sees more women than men pottering about the villages or working in the fields. They are a fine race, clean in their habits and cheery in their character. They can be distinguished with ease from the Egyptian *fellahîn*, for their skin has more the appearance of bronze, and their features are often more aquiline. The women do not wear the veil, and their dresses are draped over one shoulder in a manner unknown to Egypt. The method of dressing the hair, moreover, is quite distinctive: the women plait it in innumerable little strands, those along the forehead terminating in bead-like lumps of beeswax. The little children go nude for the first six or eight years of their life, though the girls sometimes wear around their waist a fringe made of thin strips of hide. The men still carry spears in some parts of the country, and a light battle-axe is not an uncommon weapon.

There is no railway between Aswân and Halfa, all traffic being conducted on the river. Almost continuously a stream of native troops and English officers passes up and down the Nile, bound for Khartûm or Cairo; and in the winter the tourists on steamers and *dahabiyehs* travel through the country in considerable numbers, to visit the many temples which were here erected in the days when the land was richer than it is now.

The three most famous ruins of Lower Nubia are those of Philæ, just above Aswân; Kalabsheh, some

forty miles to the south; and Abu Simbel, about thirty
miles below Halfa; but beside these there are many
buildings of importance and interest. The ancient remains date from all periods of Egyptian history; for
Lower Nubia played an important part in Pharaonic
affairs, both by reason of its position as a buffer state
between Egypt and the Sudan, and also because of its
gold mining industry. In old days it was divided into
several tribal states, these being governed by the Egyptian Viceroy of Ethiopia, but the country seldom re-
volted or gave trouble, and to the present day it retains
its reputation for peacefulness and orderly behaviour.

Owing to the building, and later, the heightening, of
the great Nile dam at Aswân, erected for the purpose
of regulating the flow of water by holding back in the
plenteous autumn and winter the amount necessary to
keep up the level in the dry summer months, the whole
of the valley from the First Cataract to the neighbourhood of Derr has been turned into a vast reservoir, and
a large number of temples and other ruins are flooded.
Before the dam was finished the temples on the island
of Philæ were strengthened and repaired so as to be
safe from damage by the water; and before the heightening was carried out, every other ruin whose foundations
were below the high-water level was repaired and safeguarded.

In 1906 and 1907, I went into the threatened territory, to make a full report on the condition of the monuments there; * and on my recommendation, a very large
sum of money was then voted for the work. Sir Gaston
Maspero took the matter up in the spirit which is as-

* Weigall: *A Report on the Antiquities of Lower Nubia* (Department
of Antiquities, Cairo, 1907).

sociated with his name; Monsieur Barsanti was sent
to repair and underpin the temples; French, German
and English scholars were engaged to make copies of
the endangered inscriptions and reliefs; and Dr.
Reisner, Mr. C. Firth, and others, under the nominal
direction of Captain Lyons, were entrusted with the
complete and exhaustive excavation of all the cemeteries
and remains between the dam and the southern ex-
tremity of the reservoir. As a result of this work,
practically no information of any kind was lost by the
flooding of the country.

As was to be expected, the building and heightening
of the dam caused consternation amongst the archæologically interested visitors to Egypt, and very considerably troubled the Egyptologists. Philæ, one of
the most picturesque ruins on the Nile, was to be destroyed, said the more hysterical, and numerous other
buildings were to meet with the same fate. A very great
deal of nonsense was written as to the vandalism of the
English; and the minds of certain people were so much
inflamed by the controversy, that many regrettable
words were spoken. The Department of Antiquities
was much criticised for having approved the scheme,
though it was more generally declared that the wishes
of that Department had not been consulted, which was
wholly untrue. These strictures are pronounced on
all sides at the present day, in spite of the very significant silence and imperturbation of Egyptologists, and
it may therefore be as well to put the matter plainly
before the reader, since the opinion of the person who
for several years was in charge of the ruins in question,
has, whether right or wrong, a sort of interest attached
to it.

In dealing with a question of this kind, one has to clear from the brain the fumes of unbalanced thought and to behold all things with a level head. Strong wine is one of the lesser causes of insobriety, and there is often more damage done by intemperance of thought in matters of criticism than there is by actions committed under the influence of other forms of immoderation. There is sometimes a debauchery in the reasoning faculties of the polite, which sends their opinions rollicking on their way, just as drink will send a man staggering up the highroad. Temperance and sobriety are virtues which in their relation to thought have a greater value than they possess in any other regard; and we stand in more urgent need of missionaries to preach to us sobriety of opinion, a sort of critical teetotalism, than ever a drunkard stood in want of a pledge.

This case of Philæ and the Lower Nubian temples illustrates my meaning. On the one hand, there are those who tell us that the island temple, far from being damaged by flooding, is benefited thereby; and on the other hand, there are persons who urge that the engineers concerned in the making of the reservoir should be tarred and feathered to a man. Both these views are distorted and intemperate. Let us endeavour to straighten up our opinions, to walk them soberly and decorously before us in an atmosphere of propriety.

It will be agreed by all those who know Egypt that a great dam was necessary, and it will be admitted that no reach of the Nile below Wady Halfa could be converted into a reservoir with so little detriment to *modern* interests as that of Lower Nubia. Here there were very few cultivated fields to be inundated and a very small number of people to be dislodged. There were, however, these important ruins, which would be flooded by such a reservoir, and the engineers therefore made a most serious attempt to find some other site for the building. A careful study of the Nile valley showed that the present site of the dam was the only spot at which a building of this kind could be set up without immensely increasing the cost of erection and greatly adding to the general difficulties and the possible dangers of the undertaking. The engineers had, therefore, to ask themselves whether the damage to the temple weighed against these considerations, and whether it was right or not to expend the extra sum from the taxes.

The answer was plain enough. They were of opinion that the temples would not be appreciably damaged by their flooding. They argued, very justly, that the buildings would be under water for only five months in each year, and for seven months the ruins would appear to be precisely as they always had been. It was not necessary, then, to reckon the loss of money and the added inconveniences on the one hand against the total loss of the temples on the other. It was simply needful to ask whether the temporary and apparently harmless inundation of the ruins each year was worth avoiding at the cost of several millions of precious Government money; and looking at it purely from an administrative point of view, remembering that public money had to be economised and inextravagantly dealt with, I do not see that the answer given was in any way outrageous. Philæ and the other temples were not to be harmed; they were but to be closed to the public, so to speak, for the winter months.

This view of the question is not based upon any error. In regard to the possible destruction of Philæ by the force of the water, Mr. Somers Clarke, F.S.A., whose name is known all over the world in connection with his work at St. Paul's Cathedral, and elsewhere, states definitely * that he is convinced that the temples will not be overthrown by the flood, and his opinion is shared by all those who have studied the matter carefully. Of course, it is possible that, in spite of all the works of consolidation which have been effected, some cracks may appear; but during the months when the temple is out of water each year, these may be repaired. I cannot see that there is the least danger of an extensive collapse of the buildings; but should this occur, the entire temple will have to be removed and set up elsewhere. Each summer and autumn when the water goes down and the buildings once more stand as they did in the days of the Ptolemies and Romans, we shall have ample time and opportunity to discuss the situation and to take all proper steps for the safeguarding of the temples against further damage; and even were we to be confronted by a mass of fallen ruins, scattered pell-mell over the island by the power of the water, I am convinced that every block could be replaced before the flood rose again. The temple of Mahârraka was entirely rebuilt in three or four weeks.

Now, as to the effect of the water upon the reliefs and inscriptions with which the walls of the temple at Philæ are covered. In June, 1905, I reported † that a slight disintegration of the surface of the stone was noticeable, and that the sharp lines of the hieroglyphs had become somewhat blurred. This was due to the action of the salts in the sandstone; but these salts soon

---

* Proc. Soc. Antiq., April 20th, 1898.
† *Les Annales du Service des Antiquités d'Egypte*, vii, 1, p. 74.

disappear, and the disintegration will not continue. The Report on the temples of Philæ, issued by the Ministry of Public Works, in 1908, makes this quite clear; and I may add that the proof of the statement is to be found at the many points of the Nile where there are the remains of quay walls dating from Pharaonic times. Many of these quays are constructed of inscribed blocks of a stone precisely similar in quality to that used at Philæ; and although they have been submerged for many hundreds of years, the lines of the hieroglyphs are almost as sharp now as they ever were. The action of the water appears to have little effect upon sandstone, and it may thus be safely predicted that the reliefs and inscriptions at Philæ will not suffer.

There were still some traces of colour upon certain reliefs, and these have disappeared, but archæologically the loss was insignificant, and artistically it was not much felt. With regard to the colour upon the capitals of the columns in the Hall of Isis, however, one must admit that its destruction was a loss to us. I urged very strongly that these capitals should be removed and replaced by dummies, or else most carefully copied in facsimile, but Sir Gaston Maspero did not think that the loss justified the expense, in which decision I believe him to have been gravely in error.

Such is the case of Philæ when looked at from a practical point of view. Artistically and sentimentally, of course, one deeply regrets the flooding of the temple. Philæ, with its palms, was a very charming sight, and although the island still looks very picturesque each year, both when it rises from the lake of the water and also when the flood has receded and the ground is covered with grass and vegetation, it will not again possess the rich foliage of the palms which once caused it to be known to artists as the "Pearl of Egypt." But these are considerations which are to be taken into account with very great caution, as standing against the interests of modern Egypt. If Philæ were to be destroyed, one might, very properly, desire that modern interests should not receive sole consideration; but it was not to be destroyed, or even much damaged, and consequently the lover of Philæ had but two objections to offer to the operations: firstly, that the temples would be hidden from sight during a part of each year; and secondly, that water was an incongruous and unharmonious element to introduce into the sanctuaries of the gods.

Let us consider these two objections. As to the hiding of the temple under water, we have to consider to what class of people the examination of the ruins is necessary. Archæologists, officials, residents, students, and all natives, are able to visit the place in the autumn, when the island stands high and dry, and the weather is not uncomfortably hot. Every person who desires to see Philæ in its original condition can arrange to make his journey to Lower Nubia in the autumn or early winter. It is only the ordinary winter tourist who will find the ruins lost to view beneath the brown waters; and while his wishes are certainly to be consulted to some extent, there can be no question that the fortunes of the Egyptian farmers must receive the prior attention.

And as to the incongruity of the introduction of the water into these sacred precincts, one may first remark that water stands each year in the temples of Karnak, Luxor, the Ramesseum, Shenhur, Esneh, and many

THE COLOSSI AT THEBES
  Behind them is the Theban Necropolis.

THE COLOSSI AT THEBES DURING THE INUNDATION

another, introduced by the natural rise of the Nile, thus giving us a quieting familiarity with such a condition; and one may further point out that the presence of water in a building is not (speaking archæologically) more discordant than that of the palms and acacias which clustered around the ruins previous to the building of the dam, and gave Philæ its peculiar charm. Both water and trees are out of place in a temple once swept and garnished, and it is only a habit of thought that makes the trees which grow in such ruins more congruous to the eye than water lapping around the pillars and taking the fair reflections of the stonework.

What remains, then, of the objections? Nothing, except an undefined sense of dismay that persists in spite of all arguments. There are few persons who will not feel this sorrow at the flooding of Philæ, who will not groan inwardly as the water rises each year; and yet I cannot too emphatically repeat that there is no real cause for this apprehension and distress.

A great deal of damage has been done to the prestige of the archæologist by the ill-considered outburst of those persons who have allowed this natural perturbation to have full sway in their minds. The man or woman who has protested the loudest has seldom been in a position even to offer an opinion. Thus every temperate thinker has come to feel a greater distaste for the propaganda of those persons who would have hindered the erection of the dam, than for the actual effect of its erection. We must avoid hasty and violent judgment as we would the plague. No honest man will deny that the closing of Philæ for half the year is anything but a very regrettable necessity; but it has come to this pass, that a self-respecting person will be very chary in admitting that he is not mightily well satisfied with the issue of the whole business.

A poetic effusion was published at the time, bewailing the "death" of Philæ, and because the author is famous the world over for the charm of his writing, it was read, and its lament echoed by a large number of persons. It is necessary to remind the reader, however, that because a man is a great artist, it does not follow that he has a sober judgment. A man and his art, of course, are not to be confused; and perhaps it is unfair to assess the art by the artist, but there are many persons who will understand my meaning when I suggest that it is extremely difficult to give serious attention to writers or speakers of a certain class. Philæ is *not* dead. It may safely be said that the temples will last as long as the dam itself. Let us never forget that Past and Present walk hand in hand, and as between friends, there must always be much "give and take." How many millions of pounds, I wonder, has been spent by the Government, from the revenues derived from the living Egyptians, for the excavation and preservation of the records of the past? Will the dead not make in return this sacrifice for the benefit of the striving farmers whose money has been used for the resuscitation of their history?

A great deal was said at the time regarding the destruction of the ancient inscriptions which are cut in such numbers upon the granite rocks in the region of the First Cataract, many of which are of great historical importance. Vast quantities of granite were quarried for the building of the dam, and fears were expressed that in the course of this work these graffiti would be blasted into powder. It is necessary to say, therefore, that with the exception of one inscription which was damaged when the first quarrymen set to work upon the preliminary tests for suitable stone, not a single hieroglyph was harmed. I myself numbered all the inscriptions in white paint and marked out quarrying concessions, while several watchmen were set to guard these important relics. In this work, as in all else, the Department of Antiquities received the most generous assistance from the Department concerned with the building of the dam; and I should like to take this opportunity of saying that archæologists owe a far greater debt to the officials in charge of the various works at Aswân than they do to the bulk of their own fellowworkers. The desire to save every scrap of archæological information was dominant in the minds of all concerned in the work throughout the whole undertaking.

Besides the temples of Philæ, there are several other ruins which were flooded in part by the water when the heightening of the reservoir was completed. On the island of Bigeh, over against Philæ, there is a little temple of no great historical value, which passed under water. The cemeteries on this island, and also on the mainland in this neighbourhood, were completely excavated, and yielded most important information. Farther up stream there stands the little temple of Dabôd. This was repaired and strengthened, and has not come to any harm; while all the cemeteries in the vicinity, of course, were cleared out. We next come to the fortress and quarries of Kertassi, which are partly flooded. These were put into good order, and there need be no fear of their being damaged. The temple of Tafeh, a few miles farther to the south, was also safeguarded, and all the ancient graves were excavated.

Next comes the great temple of Kalabsheh, which, when my report was made, was in a sorry state. The great hall was filled with the ruins of the fallen colonnade and its roof; the hypostyle hall was a mass of tumbled blocks over which the visitor was obliged to climb; and all the courts and chambers were heaped up with debris. Now, however, all this has been set to rights, and the temple stands once more in its glory. The water floods the lower levels of the building each year for a few months, but there is no chance of a collapse taking place, and the only damage was the loss of the colour upon the reliefs in the inner chambers, and the washing away of some later Coptic paintings in the first hall, which, however, were first copied in facsimile.

The temple is not very frequently visited, and it cannot be said that its closing for each winter is keenly felt; and since it will certainly come to no harm under the gentle Nile, I do not see that its fate need cause any consternation. Let those who are able visit this fine ruin in the early months of the winter, and they will be rewarded for their trouble by a view of a magnificent temple in what can only be described as apple-pie order. I venture to think that a building of this kind, washed by the water, is a more inspiring sight than a tumbled mass of ruins rising from amidst an encroaching jumble of native hovels, such as it was when I first reported on it.

Farther up the river stands the temple of Dendûr. This is partly inundated, though the main portion of the building stands above the highest level of the reservoir. Extensive repairs were carried out here, and every grave in the vicinity was examined. Somewhat farther to the south stands the imposing temple of Dakkeh, the lower levels of which are flooded. This temple was most extensively patched up and strengthened, and no damage of any kind has been caused by its yearly inundation. The vast cemeteries in the neighbourhood were all excavated, and the remains of the town were thoroughly examined. Finally, the temple of Mahârraka requires to be mentioned. The building in 1907 was a complete ruin, but it was carefully rebuilt, and now it is quite capable of withstanding the water. From this point to the southern end of the new reservoir there are no temples below the flood-level; and every grave and other relic along the entire banks of the river has been examined.

In 1907, the condition of the monuments of Lower Nubia was very bad. The temples already mentioned were in a most deplorable state; the cemeteries were being robbed, and there was no proper organisation for the protection of the ancient sites. There are, moreover, several temples above the level of high water, and these were also in a sad condition. Gerf Husên was both dirty and dilapidated; Wady Sabûa was deeply buried in sand; Âmada was falling to pieces; Derr was the receptacle for the refuse of the town; and even Abu Simbel itself was in a dangerous state. In my report I gave a gloomy picture indeed of the plight of the monuments. But now all this is changed. Every temple has been set in order; many new watchmen were appointed; and to-day this territory may be said to be the "show" place of the Upper Nile. Now, it must be admitted that the happy change is due solely to the attention to which the country was subjected by reason of its flooding; and it is not the less true because it is paradoxical that the proposed submersion of certain temples saved all the Lower Nubian monuments from rapid destruction at the hands of robbers, ignorant natives, and barbarous European visitors. What has been lost in Philæ has been gained a thousand-fold in the repairing and safeguarding of the temples, and in the scientific excavation of the cemeteries, farther to the south.

Here, then, is the sober fact of the matter. Are the English and Egyptian officials such vandals who have voted over a hundred thousand pounds for the safeguarding of the monuments of Lower Nubia? What country in the whole world has spent such vast sums of money on the preservation of the relics of the past as has Egypt during the years of the British occupation? The Government treated the question throughout in a fair and generous manner; and those who rail at the officials will do well to consider seriously the remarks which I have dared to make upon the subject of temperate criticism.

CHAPTER XV

THE EGYPTIAN EMPIRE

"HISTORY," says Sir J. Seeley, "lies before science as a mass of materials out of which a political doctrine can be deduced. . . . Politics are vulgar when they are not liberalised by history, and history fades into mere literature when it loses sight of its relation to practical politics. . . . Politics and history are only different aspects of the same study."

These words, spoken by a great historian, form the keynote of a book which has had an exceptionally wide popularity; and they may therefore be regarded as having some weight. Yet what historian of old Egyptian affairs concerns himself with the present welfare and future prospects of the country?—or how many statesmen in Egypt give close attention to a study of the past? To the professor, the Egypt of modern times offers no scope for his erudition, and gives him no opportunity of making those "discoveries," which often are all he cares about. To the statesman, Egyptology appears to be but a pleasant amusement, the main value of which is the finding of pretty beads and scarabs suitable for the necklaces of his lady friends. Neither the one nor the other would for a moment admit that Egyptology and Egyptian politics "are only different aspects of the same study." * And yet there can be no doubt that they are.

* *The Expansion of England.*

It will be argued that the historian of ancient Egypt deals with a period so extremely remote that it can have no bearing upon the conditions of modern times, when the inhabitants of Egypt have altered their language, religion, and customs, and the Mediterranean has ceased to be the active centre of the civilised world. But it is to be remembered that the study of Egyptology carries one down to the Mohammedan invasion without much straining of the term, and merges then into the study of the Arabic period at so many points that no real termination can be given to the science; while the fact of the remoteness of its beginnings but serves to give it a greater value, since the vista before the eyes is wider.

It is my object in this chapter to show that the ancient history of Egypt has a real bearing on certain aspects of the polemics of the country. I will take but one subject—namely, that of Egypt's foreign relations and her wars in other lands. It will be best, for this purpose, to show first of all that the ancient and modern Egyptians are one and the same people.

Professor Elliot Smith, F.R.S., has shown clearly enough, from the study of bones of all ages, that the ancient and modern inhabitants of the Nile valley are precisely the same people anthropologically; and this fact at once sets the matter upon a unique footing: for, with the possible exception of China, there is no nation in the world which can be proved thus to have retained its type for so long a period. This one fact makes any parallel with Greece or Rome impossible. The modern Greeks are not absolutely identical, anthropologically, with the ancient Greeks except in certain districts, for the blood has become rather mixed; the Italians are not altogether the same as the old Romans; the English are the result of a comparatively recent conglomeration of types. But in Egypt the subjects of the archaic Pharaohs, it seems certain, were exactly similar to those of the modern sultans, and new blood has never been introduced to an appreciable extent, not even by the Arabs. The nation has been divided for thirteen hundred years into two parts, the one Coptic or Christian and the other Moslem, and these do not inter-marry; yet they are one race, with no fundamental difference though with many dissimilar characteristics of manner and mind. Thus, if there is any importance in the bearing of history upon politics, we have in Egypt a better chance of appreciating it than we have in the case of any other country.

It is true that the language has altered, but this is not a matter of first-rate importance. A Jew is not less typical because he speaks German, French, or English: and the cracking of skulls in Ireland is introduced as easily in English as it was in Erse. The old language of the Egyptian hieroglyphs actually is not yet dead; for, in its Coptic form, it is still spoken by many Christian Egyptians, who will salute their friends in that tongue, or bid them good-morning or good-night therein. Ancient Egyptian in this form is read in the Coptic churches; and God is called upon by the same name which was given to Amon and his colleagues. Many old Egyptian words have crept into the Arabic language, and are now in common use in the country while often the old words are confused with Arabic words of similar sound.

Thus at Abydos, the archaic fortress is now called the *Shûnet es Zebîb,* which in Arabic would have the inexplicable meaning, "the store-house of raisins"; but

in the old Egyptian language its name, of similar sound,
meant, "the fortress of the Ibis-jars," several of these
sacred birds having been buried there in jars, after
the place had been disused as a military stronghold. A
large number of Egyptian towns still bear their hieroglyphic names: Aswân, (Kom) Ombo, Edfu, Esneh,
Keft, Kus, Keneh, Dendereh, for example. The real
origin of these being now forgotten, some of them have
been given false Arabic derivations, and stories have
been invented to account for the peculiar significance
of the words thus introduced. The word *Silsileh* in
Arabic means a "chain," and a place in Upper Egypt
which bears that name is now said to be so called because a certain king here stretched a chain across the
river to interrupt the shipping; but in reality the name
is derived from a mispronounced hieroglyphic word
meaning "a boundary." Similarly the town of Daman-
hûr in Lower Egypt is said to be the place at which a
great massacre took place, for in Arabic the name may
be interpreted as meaning "rivers of blood," whereas
actually in ancient Egyptian the name means simply
"the Precinct of Horus." The archæological traveller
in Egypt meets with instances of the continued use of
the language of the Pharaohs at every turn; and there
are few things that make the science of Egyptology
more alive, or remove it further from the atmosphere
of the museum, than this hearing of the old words
actually spoken by the modern inhabitants of the land.

The religion of ancient Egypt, like those of Greece
and Rome, was killed by Christianity, which largely
gave place, at a later date, to Mohammedanism; and
yet, in the hearts of the people there are still an extraordinary number of the old pagan beliefs. I will

mention a few instances, taking them at random from my memory.

In ancient days the ithiphallic god Min was the patron of the crops, who watched over the growth of the grain. In modern times a degenerate figure of this god Min, made of whitewashed wood and mud, may be seen standing, like a scarecrow, in the fields throughout Egypt. When the sailors cross the Nile they may often be heard singing *Ya Amûni, Ya Amûni*, "O Amon, O Amon," as though calling upon that forgotten god for assistance. At Aswân those who are about to travel far still go up to pray at the site of the travellers' shrine, which was dedicated to the gods of the cataracts. At Thebes the women climb a certain hill to make their supplications at the now lost sanctuary of Meretsegert, the serpent goddess of olden times. A snake, the relic of the household goddess, is often kept as a kind of pet in the houses of the peasants.

Barren women still go to the ruined temples of the forsaken gods in the hope that there is virtue in the stones; and I myself have given permission to disappointed husbands to take their childless wives to these places, where they have kissed the stones and embraced the figures of the gods. The hair of the jackal is burnt in the presence of dying people, even of the upper classes, unknowingly to avert the jackal-god Anubis, the Lord of Death. A scarab representing the god of creation is sometimes placed in the bath of a young married woman to give virtue to the water. A decoration in white paint over the doorways of certain houses in the south is a relic of the religious custom of placing a bucranium there to avert evil. Certain temple-watchmen still call upon the spirits resident in the sanc-

tuaries to depart before they will enter the building. At
Karnak a statue of the goddess Sekhmet is regarded
with holy awe; and the goddess who once was said to
háve massacred mankind is even now thought to delight
in slaughter. The golden barque of Amon-Ra, which
once floated upon the sacred lake of Karnak, is said to
be seen sometimes by the natives at the present time,
who have not yet forgotten its former existence.

In the processional festival of Abu'l Haggâg, the
patron saint of Luxor, whose mosque and tomb stand
upon the ruins of the Temple of Amon, a boat is
dragged over the ground in unwitting remembrance of
the dragging of the boat of Amon in the procession of
that god. Similarly in the *Mouled el Nêbi* procession
at Luxor, boats placed upon carts are drawn through
the streets, just as one may see them in the ancient
paintings and reliefs. The pátron gods of Kom Ombo,
Horur and Sebek, yet remain in the memories of the
peasants of the neighbourhood as the two brothers who
lived in the temple in the days of old. A robber entering a tomb will smash the eyes of the figures of the gods
and deceased persons represented therein, that they may
not observe his actions, just as did his ancestors four
thousand years ago. At Gurneh a farmer recently broke
the arms of an ancient statue which lay half-buried near
his fields, because he believed that they had damaged
his crops. In the south of Egypt a pot of water is
placed upon the graves of the dead, that their ghost, or
ka, as it would have been called in old times, may not
suffer from thirst; and the living will sometimes call
upon the name of the dead, standing at night in the
cemeteries.

The ancient magic of Egypt is still widely practised,

and many of the formulæ used in modern times are
familiar to the Egyptologist. The Egyptian, indeed,
lives in a world much influenced by magic, and thickly
populated by spirits, demons, and djins. Educated
men, holding Government appointments, and dressing
in the smartest European manner, will describe their
miraculous adventures and their meetings with djins.
An Egyptian gentleman, holding an important administrative post, told me how his cousin was wont to
change himself into a cat at night time, and to prowl
about the town. When a boy his father noticed this
peculiarity, and on one occasion chased and beat the
cat, with the result that the boy's body next morning
was found to be covered with stripes and bruises. The
uncle of my informant once spoke such strong language
(magically) over a certain wicked book that it began
to tremble violently, and finally made a dash for it out
of the window.

This same personage was once sitting beneath a
palm-tree with a certain magician (who, I fear, was also
a conjurer) when, happening to remark on the clusters
of dates twenty feet or so above his head, his friend
stretched his arms upwards and his hands were immediately filled with the fruit. At another time this
magician left his overcoat by mistake in a railway carriage, and only remembered it when the train was a
mere speck upon the horizon; but, on the utterance of
certain words, the coat immediately flew through the
air back to him, like a great flapping bat.

I mention these particular instances because they
were told to me by educated persons; but amongst the
peasants even more incredible stories are gravely accepted. An Omdeh, or headman, of the village of

Chaghb, not far from Luxor, submitted an official complaint to the police a few years ago against an *afrit* or
devil which was doing much mischief to him and his
neighbours, snatching up oil-lamps and pouring the oil
over the terrified villagers, throwing stones at passers-
by, and so forth.   Spirits of the dead in like manner
haunt the living, and often do them mischief. At Luxor,
I remember, the ghost of a well-known robber per-
secuted his widow to such an extent that she finally went
mad. A remarkable parallel to this case, dating from
Pharaonic days, may be mentioned. It is the letter of a
haunted widower to his dead wife, in which he asks her
why she persecutes him, since he was always kind to her
during her life, nursed her through illnesses, and never
grieved her heart.*

These instances might be multiplied, but those which
I have quoted will serve to show that the old gods are
still alive, and that the famous magic of the Egyptians
is not yet a thing of the past.   Let us now turn to the
affairs of everyday life.

An archæological traveller in Egypt cannot fail to
observe the similarity between old and modern customs
as he rides through the villages and across the fields.
The houses, when not built upon the European plan,
are surprisingly like those of ancient days.   The old
cornice still survives, and the rows of dried palm-stems,
from which its form was originally derived, are still to
be seen on the walls of gardens and courtyards.   The
huts or shelters of dried corn-stalks, so often erected in
the fields, are precisely the same as those used in prehistoric days; and the archaic bunches of corn-stalks
smeared with mud, which gave their form to later stone

* Maspero: *Etudes Egyptologiques,* i, 145.

columns, are set up to this day, though their stone posterity are now in ruins. Looking through the doorway of one of these ancient houses, the traveller, perhaps, sees a woman grinding corn or kneading bread in exactly the same manner as her ancestress did in the days of the Pharaohs. A native once asked to be allowed to purchase from us some of the ancient millstones lying in one of the Theban temples, in order to re-use them on his farm.

The traveller will notice in some shady corner, the village barber shaving the heads and faces of his patrons, just as he is seen in the Theban tomb-paintings of thousands of years ago; and the small boys who scamper across the road will have just the same tufts of hair left for decoration on their shaven heads as had the boys of ancient Thebes and Memphis. In another house, where a death has occurred, the mourning women, waving the same blue cloth which was the token of mourning in ancient days, will toss their arms about in gestures familiar to every student of ancient scenes. Presently the funeral will issue forth, and the men will sing that solemn yet cheery tune which never fails to call to mind the far-famed *Maneros*—that song which Herodotus describes as a plaintive funeral dirge, and which Plutarch asserts was suited at the same time to festive occasions.

In some other house a marriage will be taking place, and the singers and pipers will, in like manner, recall the scenes upon the monuments. The former have a favourite gesture, the placing of the hand behind the ear as they sing, which is frequently shown in ancient representations of such festive scenes. The dancing girls, too, are here to be seen, their eyes and cheeks heavily painted, as were those of their ancestresses; and in their hands are the same tambourines as were carried by their class in Pharaonic paintings and reliefs. The same date-wine which intoxicated the worshippers of the Egyptian Bacchus goes the round of this village company, and the same food stuff, the same small, flat loaves of bread are eaten.

Passing out into the fields, the traveller observes the ground raked into the small squares for irrigation which the prehistoric farmer made; and the plough is shaped as it always was. The *shadûf,* or water-hoist, is patiently worked as it has been for thousands of years; while the cylindrical hoist employed in Lower Egypt was invented and introduced in Ptolemaic times. Threshing and winnowing proceed in the manner represented on the monuments, and the methods of sowing and reaping have not changed. Along the embanked roads, men, cattle, and donkeys file past against the sky-line, recalling the straight rows of such figures depicted so often upon the monuments. Overhead there flies the vulture-goddess Nekheb, and the hawk Horus hovers near by. Across the road ahead slinks the jackal, Anubis; and under one's feet crawls Khepera, the scarab; and there, under the sacred tree, sleeps the horned ram of Amon. In all directions the hieroglyphs of the ancient Egyptians pass to and fro, as though some old temple inscription had come to life. The letter *m,* the owl, goes hooting past. The letter *a,* the eagle, circles overhead; the sign *ur,* the wagtail, flits at the roadside, chirping at the sign *rekh,* the peewit. Along the road comes the sign *ab,* the frolicking calf; and near it is *ka,* the bull; while behind them walks the sign *fa,* a man carrying a basket on his head. In all directions

GERF-HUSEN
    A typical Nubian Village.

INSCRIBED GRANITE ROCKS NEAR THE FIRST CATARACT

are the figures from which the ancients made their hieroglyphic script; and thus that wonderful old writing at
once ceases to be mysterious, a thing of long ago, and
one realises how natural a product of the country it was.

In a word, ancient and modern Egyptians are
fundamentally similar. Nor is there any great difference to be observed between the country's relations with
foreign powers in ancient days and those of the last hundred years. For three or four thousand years Egypt
has been occupied by foreign powers or ruled by foreign
dynasties, just as at the present day; and a foreign army
was retained in the country during most of the later
periods of ancient history. There were always numerous foreigners settled in Egypt, and in Ptolemaic and
Roman times Alexandria and Memphis swarmed with
them. The great powers of the civilised world were
always watching Egypt as they do now, not always in
a friendly attitude to that one of themselves which occupied the country; and the chief power with which
Egypt was concerned in the time of the Ramesside
Pharaohs inhabited Asia Minor, and perhaps Turkey,
just as in the Middle Ages and the last century. Then,
as in modern times, Egypt had much of her attention
held by the Sudan, and constant expeditions had to be
made into the regions above the cataracts. Thus it
cannot be argued that ancient history offers no precedent for modern affairs because all things have now
changed. Things have changed extremely little, broadly
speaking; and general lines of conduct have the same
significance at the present time as they had in the past.

I wish now to give an outline of Egypt's relationship to her most important neighbour, Syria, in order
that the bearing of history upon modern political mat-

ters may be demonstrated; for it would seem that the records of the past make clear a tendency which is now somewhat overlooked.

From the earliest historical times the Egyptians have endeavoured to hold Syria and Palestine as a vassal state. One of the first Pharaohs with whom we meet in Egyptian history, King Zeser of Dynasty III, is known to have sent a fleet to the Lebanon in order to procure cedar-wood, and there is some evidence to show that he held sway over the country. For how many centuries previous to his reign the Pharaohs had overrun Syria we cannot now say, but there is reason to suppose that Zeser initiated the aggressive policy of Egypt in Asia. Sahura, a Pharaoh of Dynasty V, attacked the Phœnician coast with his fleet, and returned to the Nile valley with a number of Syrian captives. Pepi I, of the succeeding dynasty, also attacked the coast cities, and Pepi II had considerable intercourse with Asia. Amenemhet I, of Dynasty XII, fought in Syria, and appears to have brought it once more under Egyptian sway. Senusert I seems to have controlled the country to some extent, for Egyptians lived there in some numbers. Senusert III won a great victory over the Asiatics in Syria; and a stela and statue belonging to Egyptian officials have been found at Gezer, between Jerusalem and the sea. After each of the above-mentioned wars it is to be presumed that the Egyptians held Syria for some years, though little is now known of the events of these far-off times.

During the Hyksos dynasties in Egypt there lived a Pharaoh named Khyan, who was of Semitic extraction; and there is some reason to suppose that he ruled from Baghdad to the Sudan, he and his fathers having created a great Egyptian Empire by the aid of foreign troops. Egypt's connection with Asia during the Hyksos rule is not clearly defined, but the very fact that these foreign kings were anxious to call themselves "Pharaohs" shows that Egypt dominated in the east end of the Mediterranean. The Hyksos kings of Egypt very probably held Syria in fee, being possessed of both countries, but preferring to hold their court in Egypt.

We now come to the great Dynasty XVIII, and we learn more fully of the Egyptian invasions of Syria. Ahmose I drove the Hyksos out of the Delta and pursued them through Judah. His successor, Amenhotep I, appears to have seized all the country as far as the Euphrates; and Thutmose I, his son, was able to boast that he ruled even unto that river. Thutmose III, Egypt's greatest Pharaoh, led invasion after invasion into Syria, so that his name for generations was a terror to the inhabitants. From the Euphrates to the Fourth Cataract of the Nile the countries acknowledged him king and the mighty Egyptian fleet patrolled the seas. This Pharaoh fought no less than seventeen campaigns in Asia, and he left to his son the most powerful throne in the world. Amenhotep II maintained this empire and quelled the revolts of the Asiatics with a strong hand. Thutmose IV, his son, conducted two expeditions into Syria; and the next king, Amenhotep III, was acknowledged throughout the country.

That extraordinary dreamer, Akhnaton, the succeeding Pharaoh, allowed the empire to pass from him owing to his religious objections to war; but, after his death, Tutankhamen once more led the Egyptian armies into Asia. Horemheb also made a bid for Syria;

and Sety I recovered Palestine. Rameses II, his son, penetrated to North Syria; but, having come into contact with the new power of the Hittites, he was unable to hold the country. The new Pharaoh, Merenptah, seized Canaan and laid waste the land of Israel. A few years later, Rameses III led his fleet and army to the Syrian coast and defeated the Asiatics in a great sea-battle. He failed to hold the country, however, and after his death Egypt remained impotent for two centuries. Then, under Sheshonk I of Dynasty XXII, a new attempt was made, and Jerusalem was captured. Takeloth II, of the same dynasty, sent thither an Egyptian army to help in the overthrow of Shalmaneser II.

From this time onwards, the power of Egypt had so much declined that the invasions into Syria of necessity become more rare. Shabaka, of Dynasty XXV, concerned himself deeply with Asiatic politics, and attempted to bring about a state of affairs which would have given him the opportunity of seizing the country. Pharaoh Necho, of the succeeding dynasty, invaded Palestine and advanced towards the Euphrates. He recovered for Egypt her Syrian province, but it was speedily lost again. Apries, a few years later, captured the Phœnician coast and invaded Palestine; but the country did not remain for long under Egyptian rule. It is not necessary to record all the Syrian wars of the Dynasty of the Ptolemies. Egypt and Asia were now closely connected, and at several periods during this phase of Egyptian history the Asiatic province came under the control of the Pharaohs. The wars of Ptolemy I in Syria were conducted on a large scale. In the reign of Ptolemy III there were three campaigns, and I cannot refrain from quoting a contemporary record of the king's power, if only for the splendour of its wording:—

"The great King Ptolemy . . . having inherited from his father the royalty of Egypt and Libya and Syria and Phœnicia and Cyprus and Lycia and Caria and the Cyclades, set out on a campaign into Asia with infantry and cavalry forces, and a naval armament and elephants, both Troglodyte (Bedouin) and Ethiopic. . . . But having become master of all the country within the Euphrates, and of Cilicia and Pamphylia and Ionia and the Hellespont and Thrace, and of all the military forces and elephants in these countries, and having made the monarchs in all these places his subjects, he crossed the Euphrates, and having brought under him Mesopotamia and Babylonia and Susiana and Persia and Media, and all the rest as far as Bactriana . . . he sent forces through the canals . . ." (here the text breaks off).

Later in this dynasty Ptolemy VII was crowned King of Syria, but the kingdom did not remain long in his power. Cleopatra and Antony were rulers of a vast empire whose destinies were directed from Egypt. Then came the Romans, and for many years Syria and Egypt were sister provinces of one empire.

There is no necessity to record the close connection between the two countries in Arabic times. For a large part of that era Egypt and Syria formed part of the same empire; and we constantly find Egyptians fighting in Asia. Now under Es Zâhir Bêbars, of the Baharide Mameluke Dynasty, we see them helping to subject Syria and Armenia; now under El-Mansûr Kalaun, Damascus is captured; and now En Nâsir Mohammed is found reigning from Tunis to Baghdad. In the Circassian Mameluke Dynasty we see El Muayyad crushing a revolt in Syria, and El Ashraf Bursbey capturing King John of Cyprus and keeping his hand on Syria. And so the tale continues, until, as a final picture, we see Ibrahîm Pasha leading the Egyptians into Asia and crushing the Turks at Iconium.

Such is the long list of wars waged by Egypt in Syria. Are we to suppose that these continuous incursions into Asia have suddenly come to an end? Are we to imagine that because there has been a respite for a hundred years the precedent of six thousand years has now to be disregarded? By the re-conquest of the Sudan it has been shown that the old political necessities still exist for Egypt in the south, impelling her to be mistress of the upper reaches of the Nile, whence, in ancient times, she levied the great armies of splendid black fighting-men by whose aid she waged her wars. Is there now no longer any chance of her expanding in other directions should her hands become free?

The reader may answer with the argument that in early days England made invasion after invasion into France, yet ceased after a while to do so. But this is no parallel. England was impelled to war with France because the English monarchs believed themselves to be, by inheritance, kings of a large part of France; and when they ceased to believe this they ceased to make war. The Pharaohs of Egypt never considered themselves to be kings of Syria, and never used any title suggesting an inherited sovereignty. They merely held Syria as a buffer state, and claimed no more than an overlordship there. Now Syria is still a buffer state, and

the root of the trouble, therefore, still exists. I am quite
sure that it is no meaningless phrase to say that England, so long as she has a controlling voice in the councils of Egypt, will most carefully hold this tendency in
check and prevent an incursion into Syria; but when that
control is relaxed, it would require more than human
strength to eradicate an Egyptian tendency—nay, a
habit, of six thousand years' standing. Try as she may,
Egypt, as far as an historian can see, will not be able
to prevent herself and her armies from the Sudan passing ultimately into Syria again. How or when this will
take place, an Egyptologist cannot see, for he is accustomed to deal in long periods of time, and to consider
the centuries as others might the decades. It may not
come for a hundred years or more, for France and England at present have Syria and Palestine in their hands,
and the Sudan is well held; but a readjustment of
power might bring it about at any time.

In 1907, there was a brief moment when Egypt
appeared to be, quite unknowingly, on the verge of an
attempted re-conquest of her lost province. There was
a misunderstanding with Turkey regarding the delinea-
tion of the Syrio-Sinaitic frontier; and, immediately,
the Egyptian Government took strong action and insisted that the question should be settled. Had there
been bloodshed, the seat of hostilities would have been
Syria; and supposing that Egypt had been victorious,
she would have pushed the opposing forces over the
North Syrian frontier, in Asia Minor, and when peace
was declared she would have found herself dictating
terms from a point of vantage three hundred miles
north of Jerusalem. Can it be supposed that she would
then have desired to abandon the re-conquered terri-

tory? In the late war, the British and Arab forces fought the Turks in Palestine, Egypt being the base of these operations; and it was a mere chance that the Egyptian army did not participate. The phrase "England in Egypt" has been given such prominence of late, that a far more important phrase, "Egypt in Asia," has been overlooked. Yet, whereas the former is a catchword of only forty years' standing, the latter has been familiar at the east end of the Mediterranean for forty momentous centuries, at the lowest computation, and rings in the ears of the Egyptologist all through the ages. I need thus no justification for recalling it in these pages.

Now let us glance at Egypt's north-western frontier. Behind the deserts which spread to the west of the Delta lies the oasis of Siwa; and from here there is a continuous line of communication with Tripoli and Tunis. Thus, in 1911, the outbreak of cholera at Tripoli necessitated the despatch of quarantine officials to the oasis, in order to prevent the spread of the disease into Egypt, and in the late war that region had to be patrolled constantly. Now, of late years we have heard much talk regarding the Senussi fraternity, a Mohammedan sect which is often said to be preparing to descend upon Egypt. In 1909, the Egyptian Mamûr of Siwa was murdered, and I remember it was freely stated that this act of violence was the beginning of the trouble. I have no idea as to the future danger, nor do I know whether this bogie of the west, which causes occasional anxiety in Egypt, is but a creation of the imagination; but it will be interesting to notice the frequent occurrence of hostilities in this direction.

When the curtain first rises upon archaic times, we

find those far-off Pharaohs struggling with the Libyans, who penetrated into the Delta from Tripoli and elsewhere. In early dynastic history they are the chief enemies of the Egyptians, and great armies have to be levied to drive them back through Siwa to their homes. Again, in Dynasty XII, Amenemhet I had to despatch his son to drive these people out of Egypt; and at the beginning of Dynasty XVIII, Amenhotep I was obliged once more to give them battle. Sety I, of Dynasty XIX, made war upon them, and repulsed their invasion into Egypt. Rameses II had to face an alliance of Libyans, Lycians, and others, in the western Delta. His son, Merenptah, waged a desperate war with them, in order to defend Egypt against their incursions, a war which has been described as the most perilous in Egyptian history; and it was only after a battle in which nine thousand of the enemy were slain that the war came to an end. Rameses III, however, was again confronted with these persistent invaders, and only succeeded in checking them temporarily. Presently the tables were turned, and Dynasty XXII, which reigned so gloriously in Egypt, was Libyan in origin. No attempt was made thenceforth for many years to check the peaceful entrance of Libyans into Egypt, and soon that nation held a large part of the Delta. Occasional mention is made of troubles upon the north-west frontier, but little more is heard of any serious invasions. In Arabic times disturbances are not infrequent, and certain sovereigns, as for example, El-Mansûr Kalaun, were obliged to invade the enemy's country, thus extending Egypt's power as far as Tunis.

There is one lesson which may be learnt from the above facts—namely, that this frontier is somewhat exposed, and that incursions from North Africa, by way of Siwa, are historic possibilities. If the Senussi invasion of Egypt is ever attempted, it will not, at any rate, be without precedent.

When England entered Egypt in 1882, she found a nation without external interests, a country too impoverished and weak to think of aught else but its own sad condition. The reviving of this much-bled, anæmic people, and the reorganisation of the Government, occupied the whole attention of the Anglo-Egyptian officials, and placed Egypt before their eyes in only this one aspect. Egypt appeared to be but the Nile valley and the Delta, and, in truth, that was, and still is, quite as much as the hard-worked officials could well administer. The one task of the regeneration of Egypt was all absorbing, and the country came to be regarded as a little land wherein a concise, clearly-defined, and compact problem could be worked out.

Now, while this was most certainly the correct manner in which to face the question, and while Egypt has benefited enormously by this singleness of purpose in her officials, it was, historically, a false attitude. Egypt is not a little country: Egypt is a crippled empire. Throughout her history she has been the powerful rival of the people of Asia Minor. At one time she was mistress of the Sudan, Somaliland, Palestine, Syria, Libya, and Cyprus; and the Sicilians, Sardinians, Cretans, and even Greeks, stood in fear of the Pharaoh. In Arabic times she held Tunis and Tripoli, and even in the last century she was the foremost power at the east end of the Mediterranean. Napoleon, when he came to Egypt, realised this very thoroughly, and openly aimed to make her once more a mighty empire. But in 1882 such fine dreams were not to be considered; there was too much work to be done in the Nile valley itself. The Egyptian Empire was forgotten, and Egypt was regarded as permanently a little country. The conditions which were found there were taken to be permanent conditions. They were not. England arrived when the country was in a most unnatural state as regards its foreign relations; and she was obliged to regard that state as chronic. This, though wise, was absolutely incorrect. Egypt in the past never has been for more than a short period a single country; and all history goes to show that she will not always be single in the future.

With the temporary loss of the Syrian province Egypt's need for a navy ceased to exist; and the fact that she is really a naval power has now passed from men's memory. Yet it was not much more than a century ago that Mohammed Ali fought a great naval battle with the Turks, and utterly defeated them. In ancient history the Egyptian navy was the terror of the Mediterranean, and her ships policed the east coast of Africa. In prehistoric times the Nile boats were built, it would seem, upon a seafaring plan; a fact that has led some scholars to suppose that the land was entered and colonised from across the waters. One talks of Englishmen as being born to the sea, as having a natural and inherited tendency towards "business upon great waters"; and yet the English navy dates only from the days of Queen Elizabeth. It is true that the Plantagenet wars with France checked what was perhaps already a nautical bias, and that had it not been for the Norman conquest, England, perchance, would have become a sea power at an earlier date. But at best, the tendency is only a thousand years old. In Egypt it is six or seven thousand years old. It makes one smile to think of Egypt as a naval power. It is the business of the historian to refrain from smiling, and to remark only that absurd as it may sound, Egypt's future is largely upon the water, as her past has been. It must be remembered that she was fighting great battles in huge warships three or four hundred feet in length at a time when Britons were paddling about in canoes.

One of the ships built by the Pharaoh Ptolemy Philopator is said to have been four hundred and twenty feet long and to have had several banks of oars. It was rowed by four thousand sailors, while four hundred others managed the sails. Three thousand soldiers were also carried upon its decks. The royal *dahabiyeh,* which this Pharaoh used upon the Nile, was three hundred and thirty feet long, and was fitted with state rooms and private rooms of considerable size. Another vessel contained, besides the ordinary cabins, large bath-rooms, a library, and an astronomical observatory. It had eight towers, in which there were machines capable of hurling stones weighing three hundred pounds or more, and arrows eighteen feet in length. These huge vessels were built some two centuries before Cæsar landed in Britain.*

In conclusion, then, it must be repeated that the present Nile-centred policy in Egypt, though infinitely best for the country at this juncture, is an artificial one, unnatural to the nation except as a passing phase; and what may be called the Imperial policy is absolutely certain to take its place in time. History tells us over and over again that Syria is the natural dependant of Egypt, fought for or bargained for with the neighbour-

* Athenæus v, 8.

ing countries to the north; that the Sudan is likewise a natural vassal which from time to time revolts and has to be re-conquered; and that Egypt's most exposed frontier lies to the north-west. In conquering the Sudan at the end of the nineteenth century, the Egyptians were but fulfilling their destiny: it was a mere accident that their arms were aided by England and were directed against a Mahdi. In discussing seriously the situation in the western cases, they are working upon the precise rules laid down by history. And if their attention is not turned after a few years of independence to Syria, they will be defying rules even more precise, and, in the opinion of those who have the whole course of Egyptian history spread before them, will but be kicking against the pricks. Here, surely, we have an example of the value of the study of a nation's history, which is not more or less than a study of its political tendencies.

Speaking of the relationship of history to politics, Sir J. Seeley wrote: "I tell you that when you study English history, you study not the past of England only, but her future. It is the welfare of your country, it is your whole interest as citizens, that is in question when you study history." These words hold good when we deal with Egyptian history, and it should be the statesman's business to learn the political lessons which the Egyptologist can teach him, as well as to listen to his dissertations upon scarabs and blue glaze. Like the astronomers of old, the Egyptologist studies, as it were, the stars, and reads the future in them; but it is not the fashion for kings to wait upon his pronouncements any more! Indeed, he reckons in such very long periods of time, and makes startling statements about events which probably will not occur for

very many years to come, that the statesman, intent
upon his task, has some reason to declare that the study
of past ages does not assist him to deal with urgent
affairs. Nevertheless, in all seriousness, the Egyptologist's study is to be considered as but another aspect
of statecraft, and he fails in his labours if he does not
make this his point of view.

In his arrogant manner the stay-at-home Egyptologist will remark that modern politics are of too fleeting
a nature to interest him. In answer, I would tell him
that if he sits studying his papyri and his mummies
without regard for the fact that he is dealing with a
nation still alive, still contributing its strength to spin
the wheel of the world around, then are his labours
worthless and his brains misused. I would tell him that
if his work is paid for, then he is a robber if he gives no
return in information which will be of practical service
to Egypt in some way or another. The Egyptian Government spends enormous sums each year upon the
preservation of the magnificent relics of bygone ages—
relics for which, I regret to say, many Egyptians care
very little. Is this money spent, then, to amuse the
tourist in the land, or simply to fulfil obligations to
ethical susceptibilities? No; there is another justification for this very necessary expenditure of public money
—namely, that these relics are regarded, so to speak,
as the school-books of the nation, which range over a
series of subjects from pottery-making to politics, from
stone-cutting to statecraft. The future of Egypt may
be read upon the walls of her ancient temples and
tombs. Let the Egyptologist never forget, in the
interest and excitement of his discoveries, that his
knowledge has a living application.

CHAPTER XVI

THE GATEWAY OF THE EAST

WHEN Egypt first came under the care of Britain, in 1882, the country was in a state of most abject misery. The fields were largely untilled, the towns were falling into ruin, the cruelly taxed inhabitants were dying like flies, the native government was bankrupt and neither able nor willing to give any help, and on the Upper Nile, in the words of Sir Samuel Baker, "there was hardly a dog left to howl for a lost master."

When, therefore, the small company of British officers and civilians began the work of restoration, Egypt, as has been said in the last chapter, was regarded by them simply as a sad little country wherein a clearly defined problem had to be worked out. The reorganisation of the Government, the re-establishment of the country's credit, the revival of the half-dead people, were tasks which seemed to be the sole object of their mission; and in the urgency of the work of relief that lay to hand, there was little time for dreaming of the days when Egypt had been the centre of a mighty empire, or of the days when once again she should become a power in the world. The land of the Pharaohs thus presented itself to the British eyes as a little corner of Africa, aloof from the high affairs of the nations; a country which, at best, could be converted into a small model state, a kind of side-show in the great exhibition of mankind's activities.

To-day, however, this aspect of the matter is obsolete. Egypt is again a self-supporting and wealthy country, conscious of its great history, and stirred by enthusiastic hopes for the future. The inhabitants are prosperous and happy, the population is rapidly increasing, the Government is rich and progressive, trade flourishes, and the splendid old spirit of the people is fast reviving. Their energy and animation are coming back to them, the anæmia and despair of many generations are passing from them, and they are once more about to take their place as a nation which has to be reckoned with in the business of the world. Nowadays we must no longer think of Egypt as a limited tract of land in which a concise piece of work has to be accomplished. We must think of her as a great kingdom which has passed through a serious illness and is now convalescent. We must not remember her as she was when England found her, emaciated and sick unto death; but we must try to recall the fine figure she cut in the past, when, with head erect, she towered above the surrounding nations and bent the knee to no man. For there is every reason to hope that she will once more resume something of her ancient glory.

From the earliest times the geographical position of Egypt has given her a peculiar importance, and to-day that importance has been enormously increased. Tunis, Algiers, Morocco, are backed by the barren desert; but Egypt is the natural northern outlet of the trade of all Africa. Behind her lies the vast Sudan, which extends, with unbroken highways, into the lands about the equator; and behind these again is South

Africa. The old trade-routes are re-opening, and one day the Egyptian sea-coast will be in direct railway communication with the Cape. Alexander the Great founded the city of Alexandria to serve as the port from which the produce of Africa might be shipped to Europe; but extensive as was the commerce which ensued during the days of Græco-Roman control, the future trade along this route will be infinitely greater. Moreover, Egypt stands astride the highway from Europe to the East.

Already in the fourteenth century before Christ, a canal was cut across the Isthmus of Suez, linking the Nile and Mediterranean with the Red Sea, and opening up this road to the Orient; and, when this waterway fell into disuse, the Greeks and Romans established a great commercial route from the Nile valley across to the Red Sea coast, and thence over the sea to India. Julius Cæsar at one time seems to have contemplated making Egypt the base of a great expedition to the East *; and in 1672, Leibnitz explained to Louis XIV of France that he might best hope to subjugate the Dutch, not by the invasion of Holland, but by an attack on Egypt, for, said he, "there you will find their great Indian commercial route."

In 1798, Napoleon led an expedition to Egypt, in order, as he wrote in his Memoirs, "to supply our commerce with all the products of Africa, Arabia, and Syria, and to lead an army to the Indies." A hundred years ago, travellers to India often took ship to Egypt, journeyed by caravan across the desert to the port of Suez, and thence sailed over the Indian Ocean; and since the opening of the Suez Canal, in 1869, Egypt

* Weigall: *Life and Times of Cleopatra.*

has become the all-important point on the route to the Orient. Again, the Nile valley has always been a meeting place of the continents, for her commercial connection with Syria can be traced back into prehistoric times; and now that Cairo and Jerusalem are linked by railway, the importance of this connection is increased a hundredfold. In ancient times, Alexandria was thought to be one of the main points of rendezvous for all nations; and, owing to its geographical position, Julius Cæsar seriously considered the advisability of making it the capital of the Roman Empire.

But, apart from its situation, Egypt was in olden days notorious for its wealth. It was called "the granary of the world"; and during the rule of the Cæsars, vast quantities of corn were shipped to Italy. The gold mines in the Eastern Desert and in the Sudan were also very productive; and in the fifteenth century B.C. we read of foreign kings who wrote to the Pharaohs asking for supplies of the precious metal, for, they said, in Egypt gold is "as plentiful as dust." All manner of industries thrived in the country, and the inhabitants seem always to have been hard-working and thrifty, as indeed they are at the present day. It was due to this wealth, rather than to any other cause, that the Egyptians managed to obtain so great an ascendency over their neighbours; for they themselves have never been a warlike people, but they have been able to levy and pay for great armies from the Sudan, and many regiments of mercenaries. Indeed, Professor Erman, of Berlin, calls attention in true German manner to the "unfortunate" fact that the Egyptians "had no heroes of battle whom they could celebrate in song, their heroes being merely wise kings and princes; and they never experienced the invigorating influence of a great national war." They were ever a thoughtful, industrious, law-abiding people; and as such they are gradually coming back into the world's ken, now that something of their old prosperity and wealth has been restored to them.

In Pharaonic times, the Egyptians were generally masters of Syria, and in the reign of Thutmose III (B.C. 1500) they ruled over all the country from the Euphrates to the Fourth Cataract of the Nile, as indeed they had done some centuries earlier under their alien Pharaoh Khyan. In the third century B.C., Ptolemy III could boast that he ruled over Egypt, Libya, Syria, Phœnicia, Cyprus, Lycia, Caria, Cilicia, Pamphylia, Ionia, the Hellespont, Thrace, Mesopotamia, Babylonia, Susiana, Persia and Media. In the Middle Ages the Caliphs of Egypt reigned over vast territories, sometimes extending from Tunis to Baghdad; and as late as 1839, Mohammed Ali, the founder of the present ruling house of Egypt, made himself master of Syria and the Levant. These conquests were usually effected by means of foreign aid; but the Egyptians, though not of martial breed, generally put up a good enough fight. Certainly at the battle of Nezib, in 1839, they gave the Turks a sound beating, and their excellent behaviour at Omdurman is within memory.

The fact that Egypt has been regarded as a little country, and not as the centre of an empire, which history shows us was her usual rôle in the past, has led us, perhaps, somewhat to under-value the possibilities of her future; and moreover, the country has so recently been released from the incubus of Turkish suzerainty, that we have not yet begun to think what heights she may attain to now that the burden is lifted. But if we recall to mind the extraordinary history of the Nile valley, and if we recollect that the Egyptians are, as is now definitely established, the same people to-day that they were in Pharaonic times, we shall realise that a great destiny may well await them.

In the first place, we must remember that they have been civilised, and subject to law and order, for a greater length of time than any other nation, so far as is known. Nearly four thousand years before Christ their cities were flourishing, their commerce was extensive, their arts and crafts were highly developed; and already thirty centuries B.C. they were capable of building the great pyramids—monuments which to this day are unrivalled in bulk and almost unrivalled in mathematical exactitude and clean workmanship. At that time their literature was already prolific; and we can read the biographies of the great men of those distant ages, study their mentality, be stirred by their poetry, and laugh at their jokes. Twenty centuries B.C., under the great Pharaohs of the Twelfth Dynasty, Egyptian civilisation reached an amazing height, and we may still read, with a kind of awe, the moral discourses of the philosophers of the time, still appreciate the justice of the laws, and still be charmed by the works of the artists and craftsmen.

In the famous Eighteenth Dynasty, which was founded B.C. 1580, we find a civilisation the equal, in its way, of that of Greece or Rome. Now we see the great Queen Hatshepsut building her superb temples and sending her ships to the ends of the known world; now it is Thutmose III who passes into view, marching to the banks of the Euphrates; now we fall under the spell of the luxury and exquisite art of the reign of Amenhotep III; and now we watch with wonder the exalted and beautiful life of Akhnaton who has been called "the world's first idealist." Then, thirteen centuries B.C. comes Rameses the Great, in whose prosperous reign were built some of the huge temples which we so much admire.

And so the wonderful story continues; and though the power of Egypt rose and fell, the people are seen to have been ever the same: hard-working, contented, capable, artistic and law-abiding. Three hundred years B.C., the Greek dynasty of the Ptolemies was established: and now Egypt became a very centre both of culture and of commerce, until the days of Cleopatra, when the wealth of Alexandria enticed the greatest men of Rome to the Egyptian shores. Under the Roman emperors the prosperity of the country continued for some centuries, only declining when the power of Rome declined.

In the Middle Ages, Cairo was for many years the seat of the Caliphs of Islâm, and the greatness of Egypt in these days rivalled that of the times of the Pharaohs. A picture of the magnificence of the Egyptian court has been left us by the ambassadors of Venice, who visited Sultan Kansuh some four hundred years ago. They describe how, on reaching the entrance of the royal palace, they dismounted from their horses and ascended a splendid staircase of about fifty steps, at the top of which was the great portal, where three hundred chieftains, dressed in white, black, and green, were ranged, so silent and so respectful that they looked like monks. They then passed through eleven other doorways, between rows of eunuchs, all seated with a marvellous air of pride and dignity. When they reached the twelfth door, they were so tired that they had to sit down; but when they were rested, they passed on into a courtyard, which they judged to be six times the size of St. Mark's Square. On either side were 6,000 men, and facing them was a silken tent with a raised platform, covered with a rich carpet, on which was seated the Sultan, dressed in gorgeous robes, a naked scimitar by his side.

This description will give some idea of the glory of Egypt in mediæval times; but suddenly the picture changes. In 1517, like a blight, the Turks descended upon the country, and Selîm I, of Turkey, was declared Sultan of Egypt. At that time, Mutawakkîl, a descendant of the Prophet's uncle, resided at Cairo as Caliph of Islâm; but Selîm, though a foreigner and not of the sacred line, seized the Caliphate from him, and stripped Egypt of its religious dominion, taking the Prophet's banner and other holy relics back with him to Constantinople, where to this day the Ottoman Sultans hold the supreme religious office, which Selîm had usurped. Robbed and fleeced, Egypt soon deteriorated into a mere province of the Turkish Empire; and it was in miserable condition when Napoleon invaded the country. The French army in Egypt surrendered to the British in 1801, who themselves evacuated the country two years later. Shortly after this, Mohammed Ali, "the Lion of the Levant," made himself ruler of Egypt, and in 1831 he declared war against the Turks, whom he and his son Ibrahîm decisively defeated at Konia, in 1833, and at Nezib, in 1839. It is an interesting fact that at the latter battle the Egyptian forces were led by French officers, while those of the Turks were led by Germans.

The grandson of Mohammed Ali was the famous Ismail Pasha, whose extravagance was so prodigal that in 1875 his personal debts amounted to £75,000,000. Under his rule the Egyptian peasants were mercilessly treated, and so high was the taxation imposed upon them that many once rich farmers preferred to wander about the country as beggars than till their fields; and when at last Ismail was deposed by the Sultan of Turkey, against whom he had more than once prepared to go to war, Egypt was left in a state of penury and misery which no words can describe. During the reign of Ismail's successor, Tewfik, an anti-foreign revolution was led by Arabi Pasha; and the various European powers left Great Britain to restore order in the country. Arabi was defeated by Sir Garnet Wolseley at Tel-el-Kebîr, in 1882, and a year later Lord Cromer, or Sir Evelyn Baring, as he then was, assumed control of Egyptian affairs, backed by a British army of occupation, and assisted by a band of British officers and civilians, by whose energy and self-sacrifice the country was gradually restored to its prosperity.

When we look back upon this long and proud history, we cannot but be impressed by the spirit which has carried the Egyptians so nobly through the ages; and we must surely realise that a great future awaits them now that they have cast off the Turkish yoke. "Remember," said the late Sultan of Egypt, "we have three great assets—the Nile, the Egyptian sun, and, above all, the peasants who till our fruitful soil. You will not find a race of men more accessible to progress, better tempered, or harder working." This is indeed the fact, and it is upon these foundations that the high hopes of the country's future are mainly based; these, and its geographical situation. In his first interview with the Governor of St. Helena, Napoleon said emphatically, "Egypt is the most important country in the world"; and if these words had any truth a hundred years ago, when the fair land of the Pharaohs was ground down by the heel of the Turk, how much more are they true to-day, when the nation is prosperous,. and the country is linked with Syria and the vast Sudan by railway, and, by reason of the Suez Canal, has become the very gate of the East!

In Egypt itself there are all manner of industries, for which it was once famous, awaiting to be developed. For example, one may mention the making of wine. Athenæus states that the vine was cultivated in the Nile valley at a date earlier than that at which it was grown by any other people; and Strabo and other writers speak of the wines of Egypt as being particularly good, and various kinds emanating from different localities are mentioned. Strict Mohammedans, of course, would not participate in this industry, and there is some reason to think that Prohibition may be introduced by the new native Parliament; but a little wine maketh glad the heart, and the Copts and foreigners are sufficiently numerous to follow the Biblical hint without causing offence. Then, again, there are the gold mines in the Eastern Desert, which were once worked with energy, but have never been properly tackled in modern times. There is much reason to suppose that these Egyptian mines are the famous Ophir of King Solomon's day, and throughout history they were extensively worked. And also in the Eastern Desert there are all manner of ornamental stones waiting to be quarried out of the hillsides, as was done on so large a scale in ancient times.

The beautiful Imperial Porphyry, so often used in
Rome, is to be found only in this region; as also is the
black and white speckled granite, known as Granito del
Foro, which was so popular in the Eternal City.
Breccia, serpentine, black basalt, diorite, and many
other fine stones were here worked in Pharaonic and
Roman times; and the alabaster quarries were used
throughout the Middle Ages. As soon as the not difficult problems of transport are solved by the making of
roads or railways, this desert will once more be alive
with quarrymen, as it was in early days. Again, the
Egyptians were always famous in the past for their arts
and crafts, and to this day almost any peasant can turn
his hand to this kind of work. The manufacture of pottery and ornamental tiles only awaits revival, and now
that the new railways have opened the markets, much
may be expected from these industries. Agriculturally, too, Egypt is capable of enormous developments.
The cotton crops will soon be greatly increased, the fine
Egyptian dates will be grown more abundantly, and
there should be large surplus stocks of grain to be sent
oversea. In all directions the commerce of the country
should now advance triumphantly, until, as the late
Sultan predicted, "Egypt will become a centre of
intensive cultivation."

It may be asked in what way the dismissal of the
Turk will benefit the country. In the first place, Egypt
is no longer obliged to pay a large yearly tribute to the
Porte, and therefore it will have more money in hand
for the development of its resources. Then again, as a
Turkish province, it was not really allowed to establish
diplomatic or commercial agencies in foreign countries,
for, as Lord Cromer emphatically stated, "There could

be no such thing as an Egyptian state or an Egyptian nationality separate from Turkey." Moreover, the Capitulations—that is to say, the rights granted by the Porte to foreigners in regard to Egypt—were a constant check upon the development of the nation; for practically no progressive measure could be undertaken without the individual consent of almost every country in Europe. It must always be remembered that, until the Protectorate was established, Egypt was, in spite of British control, an integral part of the Turkish Empire. The ruling house reigned by permission of the Ottoman Sultan; taxes were collected in the Sultan's name; the Turkish flag was flown; the coinage bore the Sultan's signature; and no treaties with foreign powers were allowed to be made except through the Porte. And, most serious of all, the devastating and deadly influence of the Turkish administration was always felt in many a subtle way, poisoning the mind and taking the heart out of the worker. Good man though he was, the Turk was not a good master, and his rule was the menacing black cloud that ever darkened the Egyptian sky; and no matter in what direction one moved, there hung the forbidding shadow of lethargic inaction and opposition to progress.

Now, however, Egypt, itself active and virile, is under the influence of an energetic race, and the skies are clear. But not only is the menace gone from the Nile; it has also been swept from the neighbouring countries; and this, in view of Egypt's geographical position, is of equal importance. Some years ago the Turk was turned out of Tripoli, and that country, now being friendly, may one day be linked by railway with the Egyptian Delta. Syria, Palestine, and Mesopotamia are now free to develop their trade with Egypt; and Arabia is at last in touch with the Nile valley.

Thus, on all sides, Egypt is faced by friendly countries, in most of which the spirit of progress is evident; and already it is hard to recall the picture of the land as she was when Great Britain found her, bankrupt and starving, and surrounded by hostile and impoverished peoples, a pathetic little tract of territory, eloquent in its misery of Turkish misrule. But it is every year becoming more easy to remember her as she was in the past, before the Turks had created their ill-omened Empire, for the same spirit now animates the resuscitated people, as when Rameses sat upon the throne of the Pharaohs or the Sultan Kansuh received the ambassadors of Venice. And truly one may paint a prophetic picture of the Egypt of the future in colours which shall surpass in brilliance those wherewith all her earlier scenes were painted; for never before has she so truly been the Portal of Africa and the Gateway of the East.

CHAPTER XVII

THE MEANING OF CIVILISATION

DURING the late war we constantly heard it said that Civilisation itself hung in the balance, and the spokesmen of our cause often employed the word "Civilisation" to describe the condition of society which, they declared, we were endeavouring to maintain against the barbarous attacks of our enemies. On the other hand, the German propagandists, with equal insistence, told their readers that the war was being waged between their own "Civilisation" and the unruly forces of a lower plane of intelligence. American writers frequently declared that their people had joined with ours on behalf of "Civilisation"; and at the same time the German accused them of allying themselves with those who would overthrow "Civilisation."

One became very tired of the word, and it was apparent that it required to be defined; for in actual fact, Civilisation was not endangered, and neither the one side nor the other was fighting for its maintenance. Civilisation was a basic condition common to all the belligerents; but we were fighting for the maintenance of certain ideals which are not an intrinsic part of Civilisation at all. Civilisation is simply an organised condition of human society which constitutes the soil wherein the higher idealism or the lower materialism of man may be cultivated. It is the ground on which goodly crops or noxious weeds may be grown; and the allies in the war were but endeavouring to protect the wheat from the tares. The ground itself, however, that is to say, Civilisation, was not menaced. Throughout the known history of the world civilisation in general has never been overthrown, for when its banner has been dropped by one nation, it has been picked up and borne aloft by another. Persia, for instance, rose to the height of its intellectual glory during the Dark Ages in Europe; and Greek learning was maintained and expounded in Arabic literature when Greece itself had collapsed. No catastrophe that history has ever recorded has been sufficiently widespread to damage more than a corner of civilisation; and if all Europe or America were now to be reduced to chaos, some other civilisation would take up its burden.

What, then, is the meaning of Civilisation? It has nothing to do with humane conditions, or the cessation of human suffering. Ancient Assyria was highly civilised; and yet the Assyrians flayed their captured enemies alive, and empaled them, and so left them to die in torment by the thousand on the battlefield. Ancient Rome was a centre of civilisation; and yet the populace witnessed with excited interest the horrible excesses of the arena. The people of China of fifty years ago were highly civilised, as their arts and their philosophy testify; and yet the most ghastly forms of torture were commonly practised amongst them.

Civilisation has nothing to do with the democratic rights of the individual. Europe and America are civilised, yet they make use of trained and disciplined hordes and masses in their armies or their trade unions, accomplishing the purposes of the few by the blind obedience of the many, and like the Zulu chieftains and their *impis,* attempting to attain their objects by mere force of numbers.

Civilisation has nothing to do with honour or integrity; for bribery and corruption have been rife in the most civilised communities. It has nothing to do with sexual decency. Immorality and vice apparently have thrived best in the atmosphere of civilisation. It has nothing to do with freedom of opinion or mutual tolerance. The Pilgrim Fathers shook off from their shoes the dust of a civilised country. It has nothing to do with the development of spirituality or tenderness. The highly civilised men of Palestine crucified Him, who said, "Suffer little children to come unto Me."

An antiquarian who excavates the ancient cities of Africa or Mexico tells you that he has discovered the relics of a forgotten civilisation. He means that he has found traces of fine architecture, advanced sculpture or painting, written documents or monumental records, and other indications of an organised and intelligent state of society. He will have found, perhaps, a code of laws, a number of pots and pans, and some signs of a central government. Nothing more than this has come to light; and yet he is perfectly justified in speaking of this newly-discovered phase of man's activities as a civilisation. He means simply a prosperous communal condition, in which arts and crafts flourished, some code of laws was obeyed, and some sort of justice administered. That is Civilisation.

When we speak of modern civilisation, we add somewhat to this definition. We mean a far more complicated code of laws, a far stricter administration of justice. We mean the wearing of trousers and collars and hats; the use of railway trains, electric light and telephones; refined feeding; good systems of drainage; medical and surgical skill; fine broad streets and open parks; theatres; and so forth. The war endangered none of these things. Civilisation did not hang in the balance.

We were fighting for a condition of human mentality far transcending mere Civilisation, or mere culture. Our object was to preserve not merely the Tables of the Commandments, but an unwritten law; not merely the vista of fair streets and fine buildings, but an indefinable point of view; not merely telephones and electric light, but an inner voice and an inner illumination which cannot be clearly formulated in words. We were fighting for what may be termed the heart of the world, and Civilisation is not to be confounded with that heart any more than the coat is with the man. Nor is that heart to be confused with Culture, or Kultur, as the Germans term it.

Primarily, Kultur is the condition of mental and emotional training in which the Arts are appreciated, but the Arts have not necessarily anything to do with that aspect of human affairs on behalf of which we were fighting. A man can be an artist and a brute at the same time. High art and low moral conditions have often gone hand in hand. Kultur is also a condition of intellectuality and brain-cultivation, wherein philosophy, metaphysics, and natural sciences, are studied and analysed. But the ranks of the world's criminals have contained many a man of great intellectual attainments, and intellect has never been, nor ever will be, the passport of the Millennium.

One often hears the question asked how it is that the Germans could have behaved in warfare with such ungoverned ferocity and cruelty, when their country had always been regarded as the home of quiet learning, music, the modern schools of painting, and all the arts, crafts, and sciences of Civilisation. The answer is simple: Civilisation is not a state which precludes a low moral attitude. Intellectuality, culture or refinement of artistic tastes, are conditions which are quite distinct from high-mindedness. The Germans are probably the most highly-civilised people in the world; and yet, at the same time, their methods of warfare sickened mankind. Their submarines, their liquid-fire, their gas, were the products of Civilisation—not of barbarism.

We were not fighting for the preservation of Civilisation any more than for the preservation of scientific inventions. We were fighting for a moral ideal, for high principles, for the tender things of life which are derived from our own application of the benefits of Civilisation. Civilisation itself does not bring with it that universal peace and goodwill for which we all hope. We have to formulate all manner of qualities which do not intrinsically belong to Civilisation, before we can define the ideal condition of society which we would like to see established; and to say, as we then did, that we were struggling simply for "Civilisation," was to lower our standpoint to that of the Germans. Civilised institutions are desirable, and indeed essential, but they are not in any way demonstrative of the finality of our ideals. They constitute no more than the foundations of the great edifice which we would build. The practice of arts, crafts, and sciences, the utilisation of intellect and organised effort, the cultivation and control of the emotions, the administration of the law, were conditions as dear to the Germans as to ourselves.

It was absurd to say that the German method of submarine warfare, for example, was uncivilised. Civilisation is not distinguished by a tender regard for individual existence. The more coldly intellectual we are, the more we accept death merely as the polite solution of the quandary of life; and this wonderful steel vehicle which is propelled by complicated machinery underneath the waves of the sea, and which deals death by the highly-skilled employment of a marvellous invention, is the quintessence of Civilisation. Submarine warfare, as practised by the Germans, was hideous to us, and altogether reprehensible, not because it was uncivilised, but because it was a cold, calculated application of the forces of Civilisation, which offended in us a sensibility that had a far deeper origin. To us this kind of warfare was not in accord with the dictates of humanity, but the whole range of history shows that the dictates of humanity are not an essential part of Civilisation.

The explanation of this seeming paradox is simple; but to understand it we must divest our minds of a certain habit of thought in which we have grown up.

Hundreds of thousands of years ago, when ape-like man began to assert his superiority over the other creatures of the earth, his mastery of the animal world was secured by means of his intellect. He began to think consecutive thoughts, capable of being turned into actions; he outwitted the other creatures; and every desire or habit or instinct which could be resolved into a concrete thought was rapidly turned by him to utilitarian account in the bitter struggle for existence which was then proceeding.

As the centuries rolled on and man became lord of

the earth, this power of definite communicable thought led him to formulate rules of conduct, and to order his life in accordance with a concise principle of self-preservation. And at length, during the last ten or twenty thousand years, when human society began to organise itself into groups of intelligent entities, whose internal warfare was largely curtailed, the power of concrete thought, the power of intellect, came to be the criterion of a man's value. In his own domestic human affairs, as in his struggle with the animals, brute strength either gave ground before, or was used by, the power of intellect; and a man's usefulness as a unit in society was reckoned either by his own intellect, or his willingness to obey the behests of some other person's.

But the mind of man contains many more sensibilities, dormant or active, than can be concentrated into definite thought. He has still a thousand mental feelings which he shares in common with the animals, and which have persistently failed to be expressed in those brain-motions by which his ascendency over the animal kingdom has been secured; and he has an untold quantity of undefinable intuitions which remain quite separate from those thoughts capable of being formulated or expressed. Man, in fact, is a creature having definite thoughts, which are able to be expressed by language and put into execution by action, and also having intuitive feelings incapable of direct transmission into words or deeds, and only able to be expressed indirectly in the general lines of his conduct.

These intuitions which he cannot collect into concise thought or clearly express, constitute a large portion of his mentality, and have the acutest bearing on his point of view and his individuality; but, being inexpressible,

they have not contributed to the building up of that
Civilisation which is the natural outcome of the development of his precise intellect. The civilisation of the
human race is simply the outcome of the definite reasoning abilities of mankind: it is a method of existence
which has grown up by means of mental adroitness, and
not by means of those undefined qualities which lie hidden within him. Civilisation is the product of pure
intellect; a development of the exercise of that cunning
which first raised men above the level of the other animals. It is nothing more exalted than that.

I can differentiate best between definite thought
upon which Civilisation is founded, and indefinite and
intuitive feeling, by naming two or three instances of
the manifestation of each.

If we consider the subject of Justice, on the one
hand we find that "An eye for an eye and a tooth for
a tooth," is a maxim which is purely an intellectual
proposition, a method of conduct based solely on the
reasoned need of the suppression of violence for the
sake of the preservation of the race; but, on the other
hand, we can at once see that an intrinsic sense of justice, as, for example, when a person refuses to condemn
a woman for a sexual irregularity which he would con-
done in a man, is based, not on a concrete thought or a
rule of Civilisation, but on an indefinite feeling of fair
play. Again, to be kind to one's friend is an intellectual
consideration which can be attributed to a clear process
of reasoning; but to wish to treat one's enemy kindly is
a desire that comes largely from an intuition which cannot be analysed or ascribed to any process of definite
reasoning. Or again, the *fear* of God is an obvious
result of intelligent reasoning, possibly of an erroneous

character; but the *love* of God is derived not from a definite thought but from an unreasoned sense or state of mind. The three spiritual qualities so exalted by Christian doctrine, namely, Faith, Hope, and Charity, are all examples of this undefined condition of mind, and have no direct connection with concrete thought or definite reasoning.

I think that the reader who has had an ordinary religious education will best comprehend my meaning if I divide man's mental activities into two simple groups: those springing from the dictates of intellect, and those derived from the dictates of what is called the heart.

Civilisation is the final outcome of the exercise of simple intellect; but in its development the other and intangible resources of the mind have not been tapped to any considerable degree.

The ordinary civilised man is considered to be one who obeys the laws which have been formulated for the preservation of society, and whose method of life conforms to a certain standard of refinement. Whatever sort of villain he may be at heart, he is a civilised creature if his outward conduct is regulated in accordance with the common law. Add to this an appreciation of the refinements of life; senses and emotions so trained and controlled that they respond to the stimulus of the Arts; a certain inquisitiveness of mind, which stretches out beyond religion to a study of metaphysics and natural sciences; and we have a cultured man, a devotee of Kultur. This is the ultimate elaboration of the brain of the ape-man; and Civilisation and Kultur, with all their wonders, all their excellence, and all their advantages, are in essence nothing more than the manifestation of intellect, defined thought, and trained emotions, and are altogether distinct from that high-mindedness upon which the peace of the world is to be based.

The civilisation of the material conditions amongst which we live is desirable; but the really important matter is the civilisation of our souls. What we are accustomed to call "Civilisation" is not a condition in which we have banished our primitive squabbles, our fighting instincts, our greed, based on self-preservation, our tantrums, and our instinctive love of smashing things; and we would do well to remember that, in spite of our civilised organisation, we are, by nature, very close to the cave-man.

In our twentieth-century arrogance we are in the habit of regarding the savage ages of the human race as being entirely separated from us by the barriers of Time; and, thinking in years instead of in generations—if, indeed, we think at all—we forget how close we are in blood and breed and disposition to those wild men of long ago.

Most western pedigrees show an average of about three generations to the century, but often there are no more than five generations to two hundred years. Thus, in the direct line of descent, seven or eight persons will bring us back to the murderous days of Bloody Mary; that is to say, all our direct ancestors back to that time could be put into an ordinary automobile, or accommodated around the drawing-room fire on a sofa and three or four chairs. The great-grandfather of our great-grandfather's great-grandfather was born, very likely, in the reign of Richard the Third of England; and it is not improbable that *his* great-grandfather fought in

the wars of the Black Prince. About thirty-six individuals in a single genealogical line—as many as would
fill a street-car—would bridge the distance from the
present day to the time when the Romans left Britain.

In Oriental countries there are sometimes even
fewer generations to the century on the male line; for
the men often marry young wives in their old age.
Thus there must be some modern Egyptians who are
removed by no more than about a hundred individuals
from the savage dawn of Egypt's history, six thousand
years ago; and a Jew's forefathers, back to the days of
Tutankhamen and the Exodus might number no more
than fifty—a little company such as is often collected
in a drawing-room on some festal occasion.

We know that the earliest Egyptians differed in no
physical respect from the men of that nation to-day.
For example, the statue of the Pharaoh who built the
Third Pyramid is an exact likeness of a modern Egyptian; and if six thousand years is, thus, not long enough
to make any change whatever in type, can we suppose
that we are much different from our own prehistoric
ancestors whom we are accustomed to regard as some
extinct species? If you have a long nose or a large
mouth, you may be quite sure that your prehistoric,
cave-dwelling ancestor had it too; and he probably had
that hearty laugh, or that obstinate temper of yours,
which you thought you inherited merely from your
grandfather.

Civilisation, as the war proved, has not altered our
animal natures; and it never will alter them until we set
about the civilisation of our souls as well as that of our
bodies. Civilisation, I repeat, is simply an organised
social state, based on the law of race-preservation; and,

as we know it to-day, it shows no great ethical advance
on the civilisation of the ancient world.

Such thoughts as these came very forcibly into my
mind during the work which was being conducted at
the tomb of Tutankhamen. The civilisation revealed
by the Egyptian monuments of that period, and by the
objects discovered in the royal sepulchre, was of a very
high order; and I asked myself whether we who live
nearly thirty-three centuries later have improved upon
it in any but superficial matters. Are we *at heart* more
refined, more spiritualised? I think not. The passage
of the years has left civilised men more or less as they
were. Their intellect has increased, their knowledge
has widened, their inventions have become more ingenious; but their hearts show little improvement, because
Civilisation itself is based on the hard, concrete thoughts
of the brain, and not on our intangible sensibilities.

Let us give Civilisation its true value: do not let us
make of it a sort of fetish. It does not imply the acting
upon the dictates of humanity; it does not mean that its
exponents are men of a tolerant habit of mind, sympa-
thetic, generous, merciful, just, high-principled, spiritual, idealistic, or freedom-loving. All these qualities
in their higher manifestations are derived from an inner
consciousness, disconnected with the gymnastics of intellect and emotion. They are seated, so to speak, at
the back of the mind; and they can be developed only
by a certain method of education and mental environ-
ment. In Germany, the young are trained in the use
of their intellect: formulated knowledge is pumped into
their brains, in the belief that that alone counts. In
England and America we pay far less attention to
learning; we strive to inculcate our children with the

principles of freedom, fair-play, individual volition, and such-like qualities. It is true that we do this blindly, and without much conscious method; nevertheless, our education, in its blundering way, gives considerable opportunity for the development of the higher sensibilities, whereas the German system gives very little.

Until it dawns upon us all that mere intellectuality, mere culture, mere Civilisation, is not the end but the beginning of human development, not the harvest, but the soil, there will be no great forward progress of mankind. But when at length we realise that what may be termed the soul of man is the thing that counts, then, and not till then, shall we suddenly leap forward, so that the days of Tutankhamen, and the more remote but still proximate age of the cave-man will be left far behind, and the salvation of the world will be in sight.

INDEX

INDEX

A

C

D

E

F

G

H